The Isms: Modern Doctrines and Movements

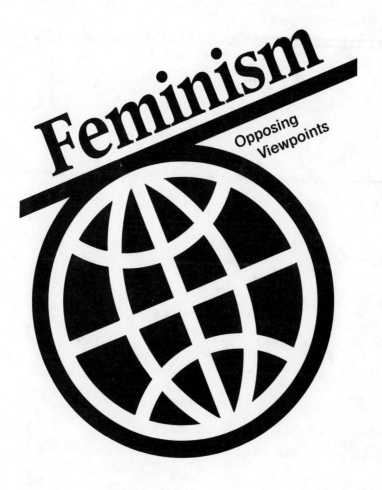

Feminism

Opposing
Viewpoints

Andrea Hinding

Greenhaven Press
577 Shoreview Park Road
St. Paul, Minnesota 55126

Other Volumes Available in the *ISMS SERIES:*

Capitalism
Communism
Internationalism
Nationalism
Racism
Socialism

The Isms: Modern Doctrines and Movements

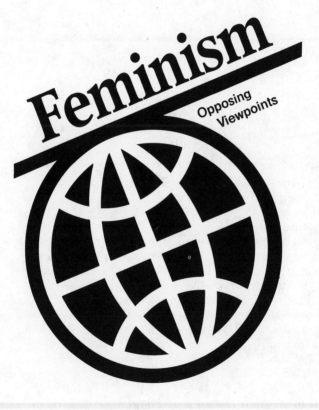

Feminism

Opposing
Viewpoints

Library of Congress Cataloging-in-Publication Data

Feminism : opposing viewpoints.

(The Isms: modern doctrines and movements)
Bibliography: p.
Includes index.
Summary: An anthology tracing the development of feminist issues from the mid-nineteenth century to the present and including debates on such topics as women and the vote, the differences between men and women, and the future of feminism.
1. Feminism. 2. Feminism—United States. 3. Women—Suffrage. 4. Women—Suffrage—United States. 5. Women—Employment. 6. Women—Employment—United States. [1. Feminism. 2. Women—Suffrage. 3. Women—Employment] I. Hinding, Andrea. II. Series: Isms.
HQ1154.F444   1986   305.4   86-3096
ISBN 0-89908-388-9 (lib. bdg.)
ISBN 0-89908-363-3 (pbk.)

"Congress shall make no law...
abridging the freedom of speech,
or of the press."

first amendment to the U.S. Constitution

The basic foundation of our democracy is the first amendment guarantee of freedom of expression. The Opposing Viewpoints books are dedicated to the concept of this basic freedom and the idea that it is more important to practice it than to enshrine it.

Contents

                                                            Page
Why Consider Opposing Viewpoints?   9
Preface   13
Chapter 1: An Early Feminist Debate:
          Should Women Vote?
  Introduction   16
  1. Biological Characteristics Prove Women Should
     Not Vote   18
       Francis Parkman
  2. Voting Should Not Be Tied to Sex Differences   26
       Elizabeth Cady Stanton
  3. The Vote Will Achieve Economic Equality
     for Women   34
       Robert L. Owen
  4. The Vote Will Not Achieve Economic Equality
     for Women   40
       Lyman Abbott
  5. Women's Suffrage Would Aid Governmental Reform   45
       Jane Addams
  6. Women's Suffrage Would Harm
     Governmental Reform   51
       Margaret C. Robinson
  A Critical Thinking Skill: Recognizing Stereotypes   59
  Bibliography   61

Chapter 2: Should Women Work
          Outside the Home?
  Introduction   63
  1. Women's Work Is the Home   65
       Flora McDonald Thompson
  2. Women's Work Should Not Be Restricted
     to the Home   71
       Vernon Lee
  3. Being a Housewife and Mother Is Woman's
     Greatest Work   78
       Agnes E. Meyer
  4. Housewives Are Slaves   86
       Edith M. Stern

5. Working Women Should Be Like Men   93
   Robert E. Gould

6. Working Women Should Be Themselves   100
   Mary Kay Blakely

A Critical Thinking Skill: Distinguishing Between
   Fact and Opinion   107

Bibliography   109

Chapter 3: Does Marriage Fulfill Women?

Introduction   111

1. Women Should Devote Themselves to Marriage   113
   Anna A. Rogers

2. Women Should Not Marry   119
   Emma Goldman

3. Marriage Can Make Women Secure   123
   Phyllis Schlafly

4. Marriage Cannot Make Women Secure   128
   Germaine Greer

5. Marriage Fulfills a Woman's Life   134
   Midge Decter

6. Marriage Enslaves Women   142
   Sheila Cronan

A Critical Thinking Skill: Recognizing Statements
   That Are Provable   149

Bibliography   151

Chapter 4: What Are the Roots of Male/Female Differences?

Introduction   153

1. Male/Female Differences Are Innate   155
   Erik H. Erikson

2. Male/Female Differences Are Culturally Imposed   162
   Kate Millet

3. Male/Female Differences Are Obvious   168
   Michael Levin

4. Proof of Male/Female Differences Is Dubious   176
   Ruth Bleier

5. Male/Female Differences Serve Society   182
   Sarah Bonnett Stein

6. Over-Emphasis on Male/Female Differences
   Damages Society   188
   Letty Cottin Pogrebin

7. Men and Women Should Be Judged as Individuals 195
   Dorothy L. Sayers

A Critical Thinking Skill: Distinguishing
   Bias from Reason 201

Bibliography 203

Chapter 5: How Does Feminism Affect Society?

Introduction 205

1. Feminism Rescues Women from Oppression 207
   Sally Kempton

2. Feminism Destroys Men 214
   Stephen Koch

3. Feminism Isolates Women 221
   Mona Charen

4. Feminism Enriches Women 229
   Amanda Spake

5. Feminists Can Now Work Toward Broader Goals 236
   Betty Friedan

6. Feminists Must Continue to Work
   for Women's Rights 242
   Ellen Willis

7. Feminism Ignores Race and Class Oppression 248
   Bell Hooks

A Critical Thinking Skill: Evaluating Sources
   of Information 254

Bibliography 256

General Bibliography 257
Index 258

Why Consider Opposing Viewpoints?

"It is better to debate a question without settling it than to settle a question without debating it."

Joseph Joubert (1754-1824)

The Importance of Examining Opposing Viewpoints

The purpose of the Opposing Viewpoints books, and this book in particular, is to present balanced, and often difficult to find, opposing points of view on complex and sensitive issues.

Probably the best way to become informed is to analyze the positions of those who are regarded as experts and well studied on issues. It is important to consider every variety of opinion in an attempt to determine the truth. Opinions from the mainstream of society should be examined. But also important are opinions that are considered radical, reactionary, or minority as well as those stigmatized by some other uncomplimentary label. An important lesson of history is the eventual acceptance of many unpopular and even despised opinions. The ideas of Socrates, Jesus, and Galileo are good examples of this.

Readers will approach this book with their own opinions on the issues debated within it. However, to have a good grasp of one's own viewpoint, it is necessary to understand the arguments of those with whom one disagrees. It can be said that those who do not completely understand their adversary's point of view do not fully understand their own.

A persuasive case for considering opposing viewpoints has been presented by John Stuart Mill in his work *On Liberty*. When examining controversial issues it may be helpful to reflect on this suggestion:

> The only way in which a human being can make some approach to knowing the whole of a subject, is by hearing what can be said about it by persons of every variety of opinion, and studying all modes in which it can be looked at by every character of mind. No wise man ever acquired his wisdom in any mode but this.

Analyzing Sources of Information

The Opposing Viewpoints books include diverse materials taken from magazines, journals, books, and newspapers, as well as statements and position papers from a wide range of individuals, organizations and governments. This broad spectrum of sources helps to develop patterns of thinking which are open to the consideration of a variety of opinions.

Pitfalls to Avoid

A pitfall to avoid in considering opposing points of view is that of regarding one's own opinion as being common sense and the most rational stance and the point of view of others as being only opinion and naturally wrong. It may be that another's opinion is correct and one's own is in error.

Another pitfall to avoid is that of closing one's mind to the opinions of those with whom one disagrees. The best way to approach a dialogue is to make one's primary purpose that of understanding the mind and arguments of the other person and not that of enlightening him or her with one's own solutions. More can be learned by listening than speaking.

It is my hope that after reading this book the reader will have a deeper understanding of the issues debated and will appreciate the complexity of even seemingly simple issues on which good and honest people disagree. This awareness is particularly important in a democratic society such as ours where people enter into public debate to determine the common good. Those with whom one disagrees should not necessarily be regarded as enemies, but perhaps simply as people who suggest different paths to a common goal.

Developing Basic Reading and Thinking Skills

In this book carefully edited opposing viewpoints are purposely placed back to back to create a running debate; each viewpoint is preceded by a short quotation that best expresses the author's main argument. This format instantly plunges the reader into the midst of a controversial issue and greatly aids that reader in mastering the basic skill of recognizing an author's point of view.

A number of basic skills for critical thinking are practiced in the activities that appear throughout the books in the series. Some of the skills are:

Evaluating Sources of Information The ability to choose from among alternative sources the most reliable and accurate source in relation to a given subject.

Separating Fact from Opinion The ability to make the basic distinction between factual statements (those that can be demonstrated or verified empirically) and statements of opinion (those that are beliefs or attitudes that cannot be proved).

Identifying Stereotypes The ability to identify oversimplified, exaggerated descriptions (favorable or unfavorable) about people and insulting statements about racial, religious or national groups, based upon misinformation or lack of information.

Recognizing Ethnocentrism The ability to recognize attitudes or opinions that express the view that one's own race, culture, or group is inherently superior, or those attitudes that judge another culture or group in terms of one's own.

It is important to consider opposing viewpoints and equally important to be able to critically analyze those viewpoints. The activities in this book are designed to help the reader master these thinking skills. Statements are taken from the book's viewpoints and the reader is asked to analyze them. This technique aids the reader in developing skills that not only can be applied to the viewpoints in this book, but also to situations where opinionated spokespersons comment on controversial issues. Although the activities are helpful to the solitary reader, they are most useful when the reader can benefit from the interaction of group discussion.

Using this book and others in the series should help readers develop basic reading and thinking skills. These skills should improve the readers' ability to understand what they read. Readers should be better able to separate fact from opinion, substance from rhetoric and become better consumers of information in our media-centered culture.

This volume of the Opposing Viewpoints books does not advocate a particular point of view. Quite the contrary! The very nature of the book leaves it to the reader to formulate the opinions he or she finds most suitable. My purpose as publisher is to see that this is made possible by offering a wide range of viewpoints which are fairly presented.

David L. Bender
Publisher

Preface

"Are women human?" Dorothy Sayers, a distinguished theologian and novelist, once asked. Ms. Sayers' question gently ridiculed the tendency of society to treat men as the norm for human beings, and to define women as a separate class. While it is obvious that women differ from men in their ability to bear and nurse children, does this mean that their lives should be subjugated to this biological function? Does it mean that they are, indeed, a separate class from men, an inevitably inferior class?

From the nineteenth century to the present, feminists have organized to end what they perceive as the historic misconception that men are superior to women. Feminists have endeavored to prove that social inequality is not ordained by the laws of God or nature but results from societal conditions that can and should be changed. Feminists seek legal, political, educational, and other reforms that will allow women to choose lives that are compatible with their own interests and talents rather than accept those imposed on them by family, church, or stereotype.

Not all feminists pursue identical goals: For example, some want the right to devote themselves wholeheartedly to home and family and still be considered as valuable to society as any corporate executive, while others want the right to use their skills to fullest advantage in the business or academic worlds. Additionally, race, social class, sexual preference, and personal values divide feminists. They often disagree strenuously about priorities for the women's movement and whether to use radical or more moderate tactics to achieve their ends. Ultimately, however, they all seek the goal of equality for all women.

Those who oppose feminism likewise share a common belief— that, as Sigmund Freud wrote, "Anatomy is destiny." Anti-feminists have resisted the changes urged by feminists because they believe that such changes will destroy traditional male and female roles and this in turn will threaten the stability of society itself. Women's biological function of bearing children is too important, they assert, to be diluted by quests for other forms of personal fulfillment.

They believe women should devote their energy and talent to the private world of home and family and should, as a consequence, expect men to continue their dominance of the public world of work, politics, and culture.

Like feminists, opponents of feminism disagree on some issues, among them what political and legal rights women should have and how much education or access to employment they need. But most anti-feminists are united in a belief that the traditional pattern of male-female relations is the product of thousands of years of biological evolution. To change this pattern, they believe, will threaten the future of the human race.

The enduring importance of feminism can be seen in the growth of women's movements around the world, perhaps especially in underdeveloped nations where women have related feminism to the struggles for subsistence and modernization. But whether the issues are important basic rights such as participation in government and equal opportunity in education and employment, or more personal issues such as family roles and individual fulfillment, women—and men—continue to struggle with questions about the differences between women and men and what these differences mean.

Feminism's most important aspect is its most obvious: we are all either women or the fathers, sons, brothers, husbands, or friends of women; feminist issues touch our lives each day. Daily, each of us faces more or less troubling questions of who will raise the children, support the family, sacrifice a career for a spouse's, clean the house, make the coffee at work, and pay for a date. Each of us has to wonder if it is possible for anyone, male or female, to have a family, a career, leisure, and autonomy and if not, how men and women should compromise on such issues.

The chapters in *Feminism: Opposing Viewpoints* focus on five questions which are or have been central to feminism: Should Women Vote? reflects the 19th and early 20th century debates leading up to the 1920 constitutional amendment guaranteeing women suffrage. Should Women Work Outside the Home? and Does Marriage Fulfill Women? each contain an array of views from the early part of this century to the present. Mirroring the changing attitudes in a dramatically changing century, these viewpoints offer some surprising answers to questions which, to some readers, may not at first appear to be issues requiring debate. The fourth chapter debates a question basic to feminism: What Are the Roots of Male/Female Differences? It considers how significant gender differences are and what causes the differences—biology or society. Finally, How Does Feminism Affect Society? debates the impact feminism has had and is having on society and on individuals. The viewpoints are presented independent of editorial comment. The reader is left to draw his or her own conclusions.

An Early Feminist Debate: Should Women Vote?

Feminism

Introduction

When the 19th Amendment to the United States Constitution was ratified in 1920, it ended decades of struggle to enable women to vote. The amendment was formally proposed in 1878 by A.A. Sargent, a senator from California. His resolution declared:

> The rights of citizens of the United States to vote shall not be denied or abridged by the United States or by any state on account of sex.

The simplicity of the Amendment's language gives little indication of the enormous investment of money, energy, and talent made by generations of women and men who participated in a national debate that was to last for more than seventy years.

The campaign for the ballot began informally in 1848 when Elizabeth Cady Stanton, Lucretia Mott, and others held the first women's rights convention at Seneca Falls, New York. The women who met there wrote what amounted to a women's declaration of independence. One of the rights demanded was women's right to vote.

In the 72 years from Seneca Falls to passage of the 19th Amendment, proponents made nearly 500 separate campaigns before state legislatures and before 19 successive United States Congresses. Suffrage proponents finally won their first victories at the state level. Wyoming granted women limited suffrage when it became a territory in 1869 and retained suffrage for them when it became a state in 1890. Colorado passed suffrage legislation in 1893 and was followed in 1896 by both Utah and Idaho. Fourteen years passed, however, before another state, Washington, granted suffrage, and not until 1913 did a state east of the Mississippi, Illinois, extend the right to vote to women.

Both supporters and opponents of woman suffrage formed a large number of organizations at the city, state, and national level. The most prominent suffrage organization, the National American Woman Suffrage Association (NAWSA) was formed in 1890 by the merger of the radical National Woman Suffrage Association, led by Elizabeth Cady Stanton and Susan B. Anthony, and the more conservative American Woman Suffrage Association, which was led by Lucy Stone and other New Englanders. By 1917, when the total population of the United States was slightly more than 100 million, NAWSA had an astounding membership of more than two million. Anti-suffrage associations, which included large numbers of women, proliferated as well, most notably among them the Massachusetts and New York State Associations Opposed to the Extension of Suffrage to Women. In 1916 the Massachusetts organization had an impressive 60,000 members.

Prominent members of these organizations not only appeared before state legislatures and the Congress, but also wrote hundreds of books, articles, and pamphlets and held thousands of public meetings to debate the merits of suffrage. Presidents, major religious leaders, scholars, and other important public figures joined what became for half a century the single most important and extended debate in the United States.

Why did the 19th Amendment, which consisted of one seemingly innocuous sentence, become so important? Society in the 19th century was built on the assumption that men and women occupied separate spheres. Men occupied a public sphere of business and politics while women managed the private sphere of home and family, an arrangement most people then believed was sanctioned by religion, history, and the natural law. When feminists argued that women should vote, they were striking at the core of the established social order. Once women's right to vote was acknowledged, feminists were convinced, women would inevitably become full partners in all human enterprises. Opponents of woman suffrage believed it posed an irrevocable threat to home, family, and society and saw a moral obligation to fight against it.

"It has been claimed as a right that women should vote. It is no right, but a wrong."

Biological Characteristics Prove Women Should Not Vote

Francis Parkman

A descendant of an old New England family, Francis Parkman (1823-1893) was educated at Harvard University and practiced law before beginning his study of American history. His extensive work made him a leading historian and an important public figure in 19th century America. *The Oregon Trail* is his best known work. In the following viewpoint, Mr. Parkman argues that because of their biological characteristics—both physical and mental—women should not be allowed to vote.

As you read, consider the following questions:

1. What does the author believe are the essential roles of men and women?
2. What reasons does Mr. Parkman give to support his thesis that women are ill-equipped for voting?
3. If women achieved the vote, according to the author, what would happen to civilization?

Francis Parkman, "The Woman Question," *North American Review.* October 1879.

It has been claimed as a right that women should vote. It is no right, but a wrong, that a small number of women should impose on all the rest political duties which there is no call for their assuming, which they do not want to assume, and which, if duly discharged, would be a cruel and intolerable burden. This pretense of the female suffragists was reduced to an absurdity when some of them gravely affirmed that, if a single woman wanted to vote, all the others ought to be required to do so.

Government by doctrines of abstract right, of which the French Revolution set the example and bore the fruits, involves enormous danger and injustice. No political right is absolute and of universal application. Each has its conditions, qualifications, and limitations. If these are disregarded, one right collides with another, or with many others. Even a man's right to liberty is subject to the condition that he does not use it to infringe the rights of his neighbors. It is in the concrete, and not in the abstract, that rights prevail in every sound and wholesome society. They are applied where they are applicable. A government of glittering generalities quickly destroys itself. The object of government is the accomplishment of a certain result, the greatest good of the governed; and the ways of reaching it vary in different countries and different social conditions. Neither liberty nor the suffrage are the end; they are nothing but means to reach it; and each should be used to the extent in which it is best adapted to its purpose. If the voting of women conduces to the greatest good of the community, then they ought to vote, and otherwise they ought not. The question of female suffrage thus becomes a practical question, and not one of declamation.

Suffrage Erodes Civilization

High civilization, ancient or modern, has hitherto rested on the family. The family, and not the individual, has been the political unit, and the head of the family, *in esse* or *in posse*, actual or prospective, has been the political representative of the rest. To give the suffrage to women would be to reject the principle that has thus far formed the basis of civilized government.

It is said, and incessantly repeated, that the influence of women has kept even pace with the growth of civilization. As respects direct political influence, this is certainly untrue. In former times, and under low social conditions, women have occasionally had a degree of power in public affairs unknown in the foremost nations of the modern world. The most savage tribe on this continent listened, in solemn assembly, to the counsels of its matrons, with a deference that has no parallel among its civilized successors. The people of ancient Lycia, at a time when they were semi-barbarians, gave such power to their women that they were reported to live under a gynecocracy, or female government. The

19

word gynecocracy, by the way, belongs to antiquity. It has no application in modern life; and, in the past, its applications were found, not in the higher developments of ancient society, but in the lower. In the splendid civilization of Athens, women held a very subordinate place. In the France of two centuries and more ago, they had a share of political power greater than at any time since, though France had not then mounted to her full height.

A certain benign influence, indefinite and almost mystical in character, has been ascribed to "woman," which, it is proclaimed, will purify our politics. That, in some relations of life, the instincts of women are preeminently delicate and true; that in them the moral nature and the better emotions are more apt to rule than in the other sex; that their conscience is more sensitive, and their religious susceptibilities quicker and more controlling—is, happily, not to be denied; but they are no whit less human than men. Like them, they have "the defects of their qualities," and the very delicacy and impressibility of their mental and moral structure give efficacy to these defects. There are circumstances under which they rarely appear to advantage, or avail much for good....

Women Prone to Rash Decisions

One of the chief dangers of popular government is that of inconsiderate and rash legislation. In impatience to be rid of one evil, ulterior consequences are apt to be forgotten. In the haste to redress one wrong, a door may be opened to many. This danger would be increased immeasurably if the most impulsive and ex-

Politics   **Home-Rule**

Courtesy of the Social Welfare History Archives, University of Minnesota, Minneapolis, Minnesota.

citable half of humanity had an equal voice in the making of laws. And, in the administration of them, abstract right would then be made to prevail after a fashion somewhat startling. A lady of intelligence and admirable intentions, an ardent partisan on principles of pure humanitarianism, confessed that, in the last Presidential election, Florida had given a majority for the Democrats; but insisted that it was right to count it for Hayes, because other States had been counted wrongfully for Tilden. It was impossible to make her comprehend that government conducted on such principles would end in anarchy. In politics, the virtues of women would sometimes be as dangerous as their faults....

Limiting the Vote Impossible

It may be said that the advocates of female suffrage do not look to political women for the purifying of politics, but to the votes of the sex at large. The two, however, can not be separated. It should be remembered that the question is not of a limited and select female suffrage, but of a universal one. To limit would be impossible. It would seek the broadest areas and the lowest depths, and spread itself through the marshes and malarious pools of society. Those instincts that dart to their goal while the reason of man gropes and wanders; that love of the good and the beautiful which is to soothe the raging waters, and guide their currents in ways of peace and right—these belong to the chosen of their sex alone; and, even in them, it may be doubted whether they would find profitable exercise in American politics. Faith is indispensable to all achievement; but it must not quarrel with common sense, nor walk with eyes shut. If it does, it will lead not to success, but to disaster. Now, the most ardent faith, if joined with common sense and the faintest knowledge of human nature, will fail to discern in the great mass of the female sex any promise of purer and wiser government. Women, as a whole, have less sense of political responsibility than men. For this there are various reasons, but one will suffice. They have shared very imperfectly in the traditions, and not at all in the practice of self-government. The men of free countries have been trained to a sense of political responsibility by long striving for political rights, the memory of which has acted as a continual education, special to one sex because the other has had neither the will nor the opportunity to share it. By slow progress in the acquisition of these rights, they have acquired a consciousness of their value, some knowledge of the conditions on which they rest, and the skill to use them. In the freest countries, and our own among the rest, there are large numbers of men who have not received this training, have never learned the art of self-government, and can not share in it without injury and danger to the state. Women as a whole may be said to be in the

21

condition of persons devoid of this training, and of the sense of political responsibility that grows out of it, excepting a minority composed of the more thoughtful, who have acquired it by education, conscientiousness, and association with the better sort of men. But the vast majority have little or none of it; and hence, if they are to be admitted at all to a share in public affairs, they should be admitted very gradually. We say nothing here of those differences of nature that have hitherto in all ages, countries, and races, made men the governing half of the race. What we urge is, that now and for generations to come, women as a whole must of necessity come into politics far less prepared for them than men as a whole. Large masses now vote who are unprepared to vote.

Women's Vote a Regression

One may well look with grave anxiety at what is really *a revolution of* the natural order, utterly unable to conjecture what the results may be when women shall have become, not only *votresses,* but legisla*tresses,* mayor*esses,* and alder*women.* It is the favorite habit of women arguing this cause to deal with it as though woman's suffrage were an *evolution.* But it cannot fairly be considered as, in any way, a progress along the line of that steady advance in the power and position of women, which has been wrought out by Christian civilization. It would not be progress, it would be retrogression.

William Croswell Doane, *North American Review,* September 1895.

The unprepared women are incomparably more numerous, and in many of them the women are incomparably more numerous, and in many of them the want of preparations is complete and absolute. This is the condition of nearly all those in the lower strata of society. We shall of course be told that they must go into the water before they can learn to swim; but what is proposed is not to teach them to swim: it is to throw them all at once into a fathomless ocean, where they will drown themselves, and pull down those who were swimming there, or trying to swim before them.

Mobs of Women

A French statesman once said that, against a mob of women, the Government is entirely helpless. There are no means of repression. Bullets, bayonets, sabers, and grapeshot are out of the question. And yet, in the French Revolution, female mobs were fiercer and more destructive than those of men. To give women the suffrage is to expose the most excitable part of the human race to the influence of political passions with no means of defense against possible consequences. A body of legislators coerced by a female mob would be in a position as pitiable as ridiculous. There are those who think that the suffrage would act as a safety-valve to political passions; but it has not so acted in the case of men. Dissatisfied masses, foiled of their purpose at the polls, are more apt to resort to force than if they had not already tried lawful means without success. The bloody riots of 1877 were the work of men in full enjoyment of the suffrage. It is to the dread of lead and steel that the friends of order must look in the last resort; and, when this does not exist, political frenzy will have its way.

If the better class of women flatter themselves that they can control the others, they are doomed to disappointment. They will be outvoted in their own kitchens, without reckoning the agglomerations of poverty, ineptitude, and vice that form a startling proportion of our city populations. It is here that the male vote alone threatens our system with its darkest perils. The female vote would enormously increase the evil, for it is often more numerous, always more impulsive, and less subject to reason; and, through causes which we gave above, almost devoid of the sense of responsibility. Here the bad politician would find his richest resources. He could not reach the better class of female voters, but the rest would be ready to his hand. Many women will sell themselves; many more would sell their votes. Three fourths of them, when not urged by some pressing need or contagious passion, would be moved, not by principles, but by personal predilections. These, even with the best of their sex, do not always lean to the soundest and most stable wisdom, either for public or private life. We deprecate any interpretation of disrespect. We have known a gracious and noble example of cultured womanhood who could by no means be persuaded that one of the worst of our politicians, reputed also one of the most agreeable, was not all that he appeared; and who would infallibly have given him her vote, if she had had one to give. The female cohorts of crowded cities would espouse the cause of their favorites with a vehemence unknown to men; but it would be fatuity to believe that they would choose them in the interest of good government. We say nothing of the outcasts of society; though they, too, would have their watchword and their chief.

Evils of Universal Suffrage

The evils of universal female, as of universal male suffrage, would be greatest in dense industrial populations. In the country, they would be less felt, and least of all in the rough and simple life of the thinly-settled borders, or the far West. Like other political evils, they would reach their climax in great cities. The government of these is difficult enough already. To make it impossible would be madness.

If it is urged that tax-paying women ought to vote in virtue of their tax-paying, it should be remembered that men have no such right. With us, the beggar and the millionaire vote alike. No political power is granted to the rich that is not granted to the poor; or, in other words, property is not acknowledged as a basis for representation. It is taxed, not because it confers a franchise, but because the Government protects or is presumed to protect it. The same measure of protection is given to the property of a woman as to that of a man. If female tax-payers were allowed to vote, one of two things would happen: a principle of government which was repudiated in the interest of democracy would be restored in the interest of wealth; or else all women, rich or poor, would receive the franchise together. The first alternative is hardly possible; under the second, the female property-holder would have her own vote to defend her property along with several needy female votes to imperil it; for the poor women outnumber the rich.

The Question of a Woman's Vote

The restlessness and discontent to which I have referred is most strongly manifested in a movement which has for a long time been on foot for securing to women the right to vote and otherwise participate in public affairs....

At a very recent meeting of these radicals a high priestess of the faith declared: "No matter how bad the crime a woman commits, if she can't vote, and is classed with idiots and criminals and lunatics, she should not be punished by the same laws as those who vote obey." This was said when advocating united action on the part of the assembled body to prevent the execution of a woman proved guilty of the deliberate and aggravated murder of her husband. The speaker is reported to have further announced as apparently the keynote of her address: "If we could vote we'd be willing to be hanged." It is a thousand pities that all the wives found in such company cannot sufficiently open their minds to see the complete fitness of the homely definition which describes a good wife as "a woman who loves her husband and her country with no desire to run either"; and what a blessed thing it would be if every mother, and every woman, whether mother, wife, spinster or maid, who either violently demands or wildly desires for women a greater share in the direction of public affairs, could realize the everlasting truth that "the hand that rocks the cradle is the hand that rules the world."

Grover Cleveland, *The Ladies' Home Journal*, May 1905.

Those who wish the Roman Catholic Church to subvert our school system, control legislation, and become a mighty political force, can not do better than labor day and night for female suffrage. This, it is true, is opposed to every principle and tradition of that great Church, which, nevertheless, would reap from it immense benefits. The priests have little influence over a considerable part of their male flock; but their power is great over the women, who would repair to the polls at the word of command with edifying docility and zeal.

Voting and Fighting Linked

The right of voting and the duty of fighting should never be divorced. Women, though non-combatant, are abundantly combative when excited. It is conceivable that they might discover a *casus belli* when the men could not see it; and, with or without the help of sympathizing male zealots, might vote in majority that the men should fight. This they would probably refuse to do against their wishes and convictions, and the women, with law clearly on their side, could not help themselves. Law with no power to enforce it is futile and sometimes ridiculous. The above contingency is not likely to occur; but that it is simply possible shows the false position of a government subject to female suffrage.

Neither Congress, nor the States, nor the united voice of the whole people could permanently change the essential relations of the sexes. Universal female suffrage, even if decreed, would undo itself in time; but the attempt to establish it would work deplorable mischief. The question is, whether the persistency of a few agitators shall plunge us blindfold into the most reckless of all experiments; whether we shall adopt this supreme device for developing the defects of women, and demolish their real power to build an ugly mockery instead. For the sake of womanhood, let us hope not. In spite of the effect on the popular mind of the incessant repetition of a few trite fallacies, and in spite of the squeamishness that prevents the vast majority averse to the movement from uttering a word against it, let us trust that the good sense of the American people will vindicate itself against this most unnatural and pestilent revolution. In the full and normal development of womanhood lie the best interests of the world. Let us labor earnestly for it, and, that we may not labor in vain, let us save women from the barren perturbations of American politics. Let us respect them, and, that we may do so, let us pray for deliverance from female suffrage.

25

"A difference in sex has no more to do
with the civil and political rights of a
citizen than a difference in race."

Voting Should Not
Be Tied to Sex Differences

Elizabeth Cady Stanton

Elizabeth Cady Stanton was a brilliant orator and an able journalist who strove for women's legal, political and industrial rights.
Most influential in the late nineteenth century, her writings and
ideas are still an inspiration for women today. In 1848 Ms. Stanton helped convene the first women's rights convention, which
was held at Seneca Falls, New York. As president of the National
Woman Suffrage Association from 1869 to 1890, she led the campaign for woman suffrage and for more radical changes in the
economic and social status of women. In the following viewpoint,
written as a rebuttal to the previous viewpoint by Francis
Parkman, Ms. Stanton argues that while men and women may
be different in some ways, the right to vote belongs to all citizens
regardless of sex.

As you read, consider the following questions:

1. Does the author believe that differences between men and
   women are significant?
2. What does Ms. Stanton want the "best men" of America to
   do for women?

Elizabeth Cady Stanton, "The Other Side of the Woman Question," *North American
Review*, November 1879.

Mr. Francis Parkman's essay is devoted to a consideration of the differences of sex, in which he asserts—1. That the advocates of woman's rights deny that sex is based on differences rather than resemblances; 2. That these differences set well-defined limitations to woman's activities, and make her inferior to man.

1. The advocates of woman's rights do not deny a difference in sex, but, on the contrary, base their strongest arguments for equal rights on this very principle, because of its mutually protecting, elevating, invigorating power over the sexes. But sex does not necessarily compel so broad a difference in the capacities and employments of men and women as some of Mr. Parkman's positions would indicate, for the resemblances of sex are as great as their differences.

Darwin says that, in every female, all the secondary male characteristics, and, in every male, all the secondary female characteristics, exist in a latent form, ready to be evolved under certain conditions. Galton and Ribot, in their works on heredity, show that daughters more frequently inherit the characteristics of the father, and sons the characteristics of the mother. Since, then, physiological and psychological forces move in continuous circles, men and women can not be so absolutely different in their feelings and capacities as to require entirely separate spheres of action....

Women's and Men's Duties Alike

Why not, then, avail ourselves of these natural forces for the best development of men and women by closer association in the higher departments of thought and action? The old idea of different spheres should now give place to the higher idea of different responsibilities in the same sphere. Wherever duty summons man, woman has a corresponding duty in the same place. If to war, man fights the battles, woman does good service in the hospitals. If to the home, the mother guides the household, the father supplements his home duties with some profitable occupation outside. When he is inefficient, disabled, or dead, the mother fills both offices, as housekeeper and provider, and the facts of life show that this is no uncommon experience. And Mr. Parkman himself admits that, "between the life for which women alone are fit and that for which men alone are fit, there lies a region where both may prosper." As physicians, lawyers, pastors, teachers, laborers in many forms of industry, they now occupy the same positions as men, and as legislators there is no reason why they might not do equally good work for the state.

No Natural Limitations

As women have ably filled all offices in life, "Nature's limitations" are yet to be discovered, unless we accept Mr. Parkman's physical encounters in "lonely places" with the lowest orders of

"Well, boys, we saved the home."

Rollin Kirby's famous cartoon in the *New York World*, November 3, 1915.

manhood. And even here a right public sentiment would do much to insure woman's safety everywhere. You can not go so low down in the scale of being as to find a class of men who would desecrate our churches, profane the altars, and toss about the symbols of the sacrament, because they have been taught from their earliest infancy a holy reverence for the priesthood and their temples. But where are taught lessons of respect for woman? And yet, as mother of the race, she is more than churches, altars, symbols, priests, and, in her highest development, will do more to draw man from the hells to heaven than all other powers combined. I hold men in high places responsible for the outrages of the lower orders.

The contemptuous phrases and unjust statutes for women learned in our law schools; the allegory of the creation of woman, the curse, the injunctions for her subjection studied in our theological schools; and the general tone of literature and the daily press, all tend to degrade woman in the mind of the masses. If all these influences were turned in the direction of justice, equality, and honor for woman, the moral atmosphere would soon be purified. The compass is not a surer guide for the mariner amid darkness and danger than the opinions of leading minds for the multitude. If our best men with pen and word would do for woman now what with their swords brave knights did in the age of chivalry, our daughters would soon be safe everywhere, alike in "lonely places" and the crowded marts of trade....No rude jest from an ignorant ruffian could so stir a proud woman's blood as a well-written travesty on her sex from the pen of a man of learning and position.

General Inferiority a Sham

2. Mr. Parkman clearly makes a difference of sex involve a general inferiority for woman. In the whole range of government, the most exalted of all sciences, he considers her incapable. When we contemplate the wide field thus covered—all our political, religious, educational, commercial, and social interests; the sanitary condition and the discipline of our cities, schools, asylums, jails, prisons, and homes—the question arises, Where is woman capable and where is her sphere of action, if she is to have no voice in the legislation on all these vital subjects? By quoting the opinions of two cultivated women on a given point where right is as clear as the sunlight, from their obtuseness Mr. Parkman argues a general deficiency in woman's moral perceptive faculties.

Again, though Mr. Parkman asserts that "women and not men are of necessity the guardians of the integrity of the family and the truth of succession," yet, even here, he makes "the family unit" man, who is to vote on all questions concerning the home. True, in his analysis of woman, Mr. Parkman refers to some "high and priceless qualities," but seems to take more delight in casting slurs at the ideal enfranchised woman. She is governed by "emotion" rather than by "reason," he informs us; that she is "impetuous," her will is "intractable," she is "impulsive," "excitable," full of "artfulness, effrontery, insensibility"; endowed with "a pushing self-assertion, and a glib tongue"; moved by "motives of love, predilection; jealousy, or schemes of alliance"; she would possess "the cowardly courage of the virago," a "tongue more terrible than the sword," and would give vent to "shrill-tongued discussions," etc.

If this is the idea that the sons of the Pilgrims have of us, no wonder they are afraid to take the word "male" out of the Constitution and admit us to the political arena. But Mr. Parkman tells us that "a man's tongue is strong only as the organ of reason and eloquence." I would his pen were always strong in the same direction! But, had man's tongue through the ages been his only weapon of defense, it might also have come to be "more terrible than the sword." The honest testimony from one hundred families as to the self-control, sound reason, and lofty eloquence with which men use their tongues in domestic life—especially when asked for money—would afford some interesting statistics by which to estimate the comparative merits of the sexes in their general tone of conversation.

Out in the Cold

For forty-five years the workers in the suffrage cause have been going up and down working, and even shouting as they have been accused of doing, in season and out of season, as some have thought, asking for the application of the fundamental principle of our government. Forty-five years, half a decade longer than the children of Israel wandered in the wilderness....

Now we are tired of it, friends! I am tired of having every stripling of twenty-one, half drunk or half nothing, think that he is superior to me and knows more than any woman living. I am tired of being out in the cold.

Report of the Annual Meeting of the Brooklyn Woman Suffrage Association, *The Woman's Journal*, December 2, 1893.

It may be confidently asserted, however, that woman has proved herself man's equal in all the great struggles of humanity. Always at a disadvantage on account of artificial burdens and restraints, she has, nevertheless, shown herself possessed of the same courage, intelligence, and moral elevation in all the varied trials she has been called upon to suffer. Brute force should be thrown out of this question, especially as among men our scholars, heroes, statesmen, and orators are so frequently small, delicately organized, and of the same sensitive, nervous temperament as the majority of women. The organism of woman is as complete as that of man. Because a man-of-war could sink one of our magnificent ocean-steamers, does not prove the former superior except for the one purpose of destruction. In the every-day uses of life the steamer has the advantage. The experiment of co-education has proved girls equal to boys in every department of learning....

Civil and Political Rights a Necessity

A difference in sex has no more to do with the civil and political rights of a citizen than a difference in race; and this brings us to the second part of Mr. Parkman's essay, in which he discusses woman suffrage *per se*. His objections may be summed up as follows: 1. Women do not want to vote; the best would not, the worst would. 2. Women would debase politics rather than elevate it. 3. Woman suffrage would destroy the unity of the family. 4. If women vote, they must do military duty. 5. Woman suffrage would strengthen the Roman Catholic Church. 6. Woman suffrage based on taxation is opposed to the genius of our Government. 7. Suffrage is not a natural right.

Examples from Other States

The first three points are answered by the fact, that though women are voting in England and Canada on municipal questions, in Wyoming Territory on the same conditions as men, in some of our States on school affairs...the testimony of able and distinguished gentlemen as to the real results are, in all cases, favorable. These facts should outweigh Mr. Parkman's speculations. In Wyoming, where women have voted for nine years, the evidence shows that the best women do go to the polls, the worst do not; that the women are governed by the highest moral considerations in discharging the great responsibilities of citizenship; that family life has not been disturbed; that the women have not become "nervous," "excitable," or "impulsive," but more calm, dignified, and sedate in assuming their new duties. On all these points the printed opinion of three successive Governors of the Territory, a Judge who sat on the Wyoming bench four years, the leading editors of the Territory, and prominent citizens of both sexes and of both parties, agree. The Hon. John W. Kingman, late Judge of the Wyoming Supreme Court, testified as follows before the Joint Special Committee of the Massachusetts Legislature on woman suffrage in 1876: "At our last election a larger proportion of women voted than of men. We have had no trouble from the presence of bad women at the polls. It has been said that the delicate and cultured women would shrink away, and the bold and indelicate come to the front in public affairs. This we feared; but certainly nothing of the kind has happened. The women manifest a great deal of independence in their preference of candidates, and have frequently defeated bad nominations. They are becoming every year more and more interested in public affairs; they are less under the influence of private interest, friendship, and party feeling, and are less subject to the temptations which bias the political action of men. As jurors women have done excellent service. They are less subject to the distracting influences which sometimes sway the action of men in the jury-box. With a stronger tension on the conscience, they seem more anxious to do right. On petit juries the women held the men up to a higher tone of morality and stricter sense of honesty than they would have exercised if left to themselves."

As regards the number of women who vote in England, the London "Examiner" says: "In sixty-six municipal elections, out of every 1,000 women who enjoy equal rights with men on the register, 516 went to the poll, which is but forty-eight less than the proportionate number of men. And out of 27,949 women registered, where a contest occurred, 14,416 voted. Of men there were 166,781 on the register, and 90,080 at the poll."

Women Are Men's Peers

The day will come when men will recognize woman as his peer, not only at the fireside, but in the councils of the nation. Then, and not until then, will there be the perfect comradeship, the ideal union between the sexes that shall result in the highest development of the race.

Susan B. Anthony, *The Arena May*, 1897.

3. To say that it would destroy the unity of the family to educate our daughters like our sons with a knowledge of the principles of political economy and constitutional law, and give them an equal right to express their opinions at the ballot-box, is a very serious reflection on the men of our households, and justifies John Stuart Mill's remark that "the generality of the male sex can not yet tolerate the idea of living with an equal." "The family unit" assumption is opposed to our republican idea of individual rights, to our Protestant tenet of private judgment and conscience. We might as well say that the family is a religious unit, as to assert that it is a political unit, and claim that the head must do the family repenting, praying, and confessing, and represent the family in the courts of heaven as well as at the polling-booth. The doctrine that the head of the family is alone destined for the joys of heaven and the woes of hell would relieve the minds of women and children from many gloomy forebodings. Fortunately for the honor of manhood the experiment in Wyoming proves that woman suffrage does not destroy the peace of home. The editor of the Laramie (Wyoming) "Sentinel," in the number for December 16, 1878, says: "While women in this Territory frequently vote contrary to their husbands, we have never heard of a case where the family ties or domestic relations were disturbed by it; and we believe that among the pioneers of the West there is more honor and manhood than to abuse a wife because she does not think as we do about politics or religion."

4. As none of our constitutions make military capacity a qualification for suffrage, this point has no significance. The weakness of this trite objection can be easily shown by a glance at the large class of men who vote but never fight. All the office-

holders under Government—and their name is legion—are exempt from military duty. So are the clergy, paupers, the Quakers, the lame, the halt and the blind; but each and all have the right to vote.

5. We are warned against the women of the Romish Church, so absolutely under the power of the priests, as a dangerous element in our free institutions if permitted to vote. The same fear is sometimes expressed in regard to Protestant women: they would destroy the secular nature of our Government if given the ballot. If women were enfranchised, they would not be priest-ridden. Too much of their activity is now confined to the churches. Throw politics open to woman, and you weaken the hold of the Church upon her.

6. If suffrage based on taxation is opposed to the genius of our Government, is not taxation without representation equally opposed to it?

7. Suffrage *is* a natural right. The right of self-government, of self-protection, the right to defend one's person and property, to secure life, liberty, and happiness, not a natural right? It is the key-stone of the arch on which rests our temple of liberty. In a warm debate on the Fourteenth Amendment in the Senate a member said, "Suffrage is a political right, that the few may give or withhold at their pleasure." "Let that idea," replied Sumner, "crystallize in the minds of our people and we have rung the death-knell of American liberties." To deny this principle takes all significance from the grand debates of the century on human rights that culminated in our civil war! In the most celebrated document which has been put forth on this side of the Atlantic, our ancestors declare that "governments derive their just powers from the consent of the governed." This principle, ofttimes repeated by distinguished statesmen and eminent jurists, in varied forms and language, as far back as Blackstone, should find a ready response in the mind of every American citizen.

"*[The ballot] is necessary to enable [women] to receive equal pay for equal work.*"

The Vote Will Achieve Economic Equality for Women

Robert L. Owen

Robert L. Owen, an attorney who was part Cherokee Indian, practiced law and promoted Indian rights in Indian Territory which became the state of Oklahoma in 1907. A member of the US Senate from 1907 until 1925, Mr. Owen strongly believed that women should have the right to vote. In the following viewpoint, he argues that the vote is essential if women are to achieve wages that are equivalent to men's.

As you read, consider the following questions:

1. What economic change in America life does the author believe makes woman suffrage necessary?
2. Does the author believe woman suffrage will improve moral standards in American life?
3. Who will gain from woman suffrage, according to the author?

Robert L. Owen, "Introductory Remarks of the Presiding Officer on 'Significance of the Woman Suffrage Movement,' " *Annals of the American Academy of Political and Social Science,* May 1910.

Women compose one-half of the human race. In the last forty years, women in gradually increasing numbers have been compelled to leave the home and enter the factory and work-shop. Over seven million women are so employed and the remainder of the sex are employed largely in domestic services. A full half of the work of the world is done by women. A careful study of the matter has demonstrated the vital fact that these working women receive a smaller wage for equal work than men do and that the smaller wage and harder conditions imposed on the woman worker are due to the lack of the ballot.

Many women have a very hard time and if the ballot would help them, even a little, I should like to see them have it. Carroll D. Wright, National Commissioner of Labor, in an address at Smith College on February 22, 1902, said: "The lack of direct political influence constitutes a powerful reason why women's wages have been kept at a minimum." This evidence is thoroughly established by the rise in women's wages for a given amount of work in those countries which have established the equal suffrage, as, New Zealand, South Australia, West Australia, Tasmania, Victoria, Colorado, Wyoming, Utah and Idaho.

Denied a Decent Living

I do not understand how a self-respecting man, after being satisfied of the truth of this statement, can deny to woman, as a human being, this opportunity to make her living decently, at a fair wage for a given amount of work. I know the ancient hostility and prejudice against women having equal rights. Under the old system of government where the wages of men were abundant to take care of the home, and where the wife was mistress of a home, industriously engaged by the occupations of home, and supplied by a loving husband with materials for home use, it was a beautiful system and required no exercise of the suffrage. That system is almost entirely gone in many localities. It is absolutely gone with regard to millions of women, who work for their living with their own hands. More than seven million women are now supporting themselves outside the home and many millions of women in addition, are supporting themselves in the houses of those who are well off, by performing domestic service. Women whose husbands are well to do, do not appreciate the importance of equal pay for an equal amount of labor, desired by the poor woman who works in factory, or work-shop and perhaps is required to stand on her feet from ten to sixteen hours a day in order to earn a bare living. The rich woman does not see the neglected girl in the sweat-shop where her hopeless poverty is often preyed upon by the vice of men. I intend to do what I can to give women and working women, a fair opportunity to receive equal pay for equal work. I shall not mock their necessity by calling them queens of the homes, and then denying them the ballot, which

Why Women Want to Vote

WOMEN ARE CITIZENS

AND WISH TO DO THEIR CIVIC DUTY

WORKING WOMEN need the ballot to regulate conditions under which they work.
Do working **MEN** think they can protect themselves without the right to vote?

HOUSEKEEPERS need the ballot to regulate the sanitary conditions under which they and their families must live.
Do **MEN** think they can get what is needed for their district unless they can vote for the men that will get it for them?

MOTHERS need the ballot to regulate the moral conditions under which their children must be brought up.
Do **MEN** think they can fight against vicious conditions that are threatening their children unless they can vote for the men that run the district?

TEACHERS need the ballot to secure just wages and to influence the management of the public schools.
Do **MEN** think they could secure better school conditions without a vote to elect the Mayor who nominates the Board of Education?

BUSINESS WOMEN need the ballot to secure for themselves a fair opportunity in their business.
Do business **MEN** think they could protect themselves against adverse legislation without the right to vote?

TAX PAYING WOMEN need the ballot to protect their property.
Do not **MEN** know that "Taxation without representation" is tyranny?

ALL WOMEN need the ballot because they are concerned equally with men in good and bad government; and equally responsible for civic righteousness.

ALL MEN need women's help to build a better and juster government, and

WOMEN need **MEN** to help them secure their right to fulfil their civic duties.

NATIONAL WOMAN SUFFRAGE PUBLISHING COMPANY, INC.
PUBLISHERS FOR THE
NATIONAL AMERICAN WOMAN SUFFRAGE ASSOCIATION
505 Fifth Avenue   **New York City**

Courtesy of the Social Welfare History Archives, University of Minnesota, Minneapolis, Minnesota.

is necessary to enable them to receive equal pay for equal work.

Equal pay for equal work is the first great reason justifying this change of governmental policy. There are other reasons which are persuasive: First, women, take it all in all, are the equals of men in intelligence, and no man has the hardihood to assert the contrary. To do so, subjects him to an instant intellectual and spirtual peril, which justifies the argument that such an assertion can not be maintained. The intelligence of women is devoted to objects in which they take a peculiar interest, and the same is true with men.

The man is usually better informed with regard to State government, but women are better informed about house government, and she can learn State government with as much facility as he can learn how to instruct children, properly feed and clothe the household, care for the sick, play on the piano, or make a house beautiful. It avails nothing to say that women are not familiar with State laws. They know pretty nearly as much as the average man, and if they had the right to participate, would soon know quite as much as the average man, and this would be a distinct gain in government for the whole community.

The woman ballot will not revolutionize the world. Its results in Colorado, for example, might have been anticipated. First, it did give women better wages for equal work; second, it led immediately to a number of laws the women wanted, and the first laws they demanded were laws for the protection of the children of the State, making it a misdemeanor to contribute to the delinquency of a child; laws for the improved care of defective children; also, the Juvenile Court for the conservation of wayward boys and girls; the better care of the insane, the deaf, the dumb, the blind; the curfew bell to keep children off the streets at night; raising the age of consent for girls; improving the reformatories and prisons of the State; improving the hospital service of the State; improving the sanitary laws, affecting the health of the homes of the State. Their interest in the public health is a matter of great importance. Above all, there resulted laws for improving the school system.

Several important results followed; both political parties were induced to put up cleaner, better men, for the women would not stand a notoriously corrupt or unclean candidate. The headquarters of political parties became more decent and the polling places became respectable. The bad women, enslaved by mercenary vice, do not vote and good women do vote in as great proportion as men. Every evil prophecy against granting the suffrage has failed. The public men of Colorado, Wyoming, Utah and Idaho give it a cordial support.

Woman Suffrage Has Not Revolutionized Society

The testimony is universal:

First, it has not made women mannish; they still love their homes and children just the same as ever, and are better able to protect themselves and their children because of the ballot.

Second, they have not become office-seekers, nor pothouse politicians. They have not become swaggerers and insolent on the streets. They still teach good manners to men, as they always have done. It has made women broader and greatly increased the understanding of the community at large of the problems of good government; of proper sanitation, of pure food, of clean water, and all such matters in which intelligent women would naturally take an interest.

It has not absolutely regenerated society, but it has improved it. It has raised the educational qualification of the suffrage, and has elevated the moral standard of the suffrage, because there are more criminal men than criminal women. In Colorado and Utah only two per cent of the prisoners in the penitentiary are women, and in Wyoming and Idaho there are no women prisoners.

The venerable Mrs. Eva Moore, of Guthrie, Oklahoma, put the argument in a nut-shell, when she said, in giving her reasons for wanting the ballot: "I am a human being, an individual, seventy-three years old, making my own living and my opportunity to do so is controlled by the law. My property rights are subject to the law.

"If I commit a crime, they may deprive me of my liberty, or of my life. Is there any righteous reason that I should not have a voice in the election of worthy, honorable men to make just laws and administer them?"

Suffrage and Economic Independence

Woman suffrage will come as a result of the increasing economic independence of women, which will in turn sharpen her intellect, force upon her an interest in the social and economic conditions which are determining her own destiny in so great a measure, and finally give her that self-respect and self-sufficiency which prevent her from being content with the alternate adoration and contempt of the opposite sex.

Charles A. Beard, *Eminent Opinions on Woman Suffrage*, pamphlet published by the National American Woman Suffrage Association, c. 1912.

The great doctrine of the American Republic that *"all governments derive their just powers from the consent of the governed,"* justifies the plea of one-half of the people, the women, to exercise the suffrage. The doctrine of the American Revolutionary War that taxation without representation is unendurable, justifies women in exercising the suffrage. One great advantage, however, of the suffrage is in raising women to a position of greater honor and dignity so that the children of the land shall show and feel greater reverence and honor for their mothers, and that the mothers may teach the elementary principles of good government while they are teaching them good manners, morality and religion.

No nation can rise higher than its women, and for this reason it is of prime importance to give the women of the land the suffrage, so as to elevate their status, and this, not alone for their sake, but for the sake of the whole community.

It is not alone that women need the ballot to protect their rights to a livelihood and to protect their children from vice, and to afford their children every means of instruction and guidance a civilized law should afford, but the country needs the female influence, because this influence will be especially exerted to improve the State charities, State sanitation, the protection of children and the beautifying of cities, and no possible harm can come from, according to the women of the land, this new respect and dignity. Are we afraid to trust our own wives, our own mothers, our own daughters! We can trust them with our lives and be assured of their fidelity and loyalty, and I, for one, intend to give them in public the confidence and trust I entertain in my private life.

"I have looked in vain in the publications of the woman suffragists for any facts to show even remotely that political suffrage involves economic gain."

The Vote Will Not Achieve Economic Equality for Women

Lyman Abbott

A leading member of the Congregational clergy, Lyman Abbott (1835-1922), was also an attorney, author, and editor of the progressive Christian journal, *The Outlook*. The following viewpoint, excerpted from remarks made at a meeting of the American Academy of Political and Social Science in New York, reflects his fifty years of study of and opposition to the woman suffrage movement.

As you read, consider the following questions:

1. What are the five main arguments for woman suffrage and how does the author refute them?
2. What does Mr. Abbot say the study of history contributes to the debate on woman suffrage?
3. How does the author use the image of St. George and the dragon to prove his point?

Lyman Abbott, "Answer to the Arguments in Support of Woman Suffrage," *Annals of the American Academy of Political and Social Science, Supplement,* May 1910.

In my study of the suffrage movement, and it has been a subject of study with me for fifty years past, I have discovered but five arguments in support of this revolutionary demand.

It is claimed that the suffrage is a natural right...and that we must do justice though the heavens fall. The notion that suffrage is a natural right is a relic of the French Revolution which has not survived in political philosophy the doctrinaires who gave birth to it. The rights of person are absolute and unconditioned. Whatever his age and condition, the child has a right to his life—killing the unborn infant is murder; his right to his property is absolute and unconditioned—if he is not old enough to administer it himself, a guardian is appointed, or his natural guardian is intrusted with its keeping and its care.

The right of suffrage is always determined by the community which grants it; it depends upon an age artificially determined on, upon a residence artificially defined. The would-be voter must have resided in the Nation a certain number of years, in the State a certain number of months, in the District a certain number of days. In some States he must have an educational qualification, in others a property qualification, and in others he must have paid taxes. But the payment of taxes does not give him a right to vote. He may pay taxes in every State in the Union, and in every county of the State, but he can vote only in one county of one State. Suffrage is a prerogative conferred by the community and conditioned when it is conferred. A man has no more natural right to vote in a political campaign than he has to vote in a State Legislature.

It is claimed that women must be given the suffrage to protect themselves from the injuries inflicted on them by men. I confess that this claim arouses my indignation. To set class against class is bad, to set race against race is worse, to set religion against religion is even more perilous; but to set sex against sex is a degradation so deep that political polemics can no further go. That a hundred years ago women suffered under legal limitations which worked injustice is undoubtedly true. Some of them were framed for women's protection; others of them were a relic of an earlier barbarism. Both have disappeared with advancing civilization....

Woman Suffrage Unnecessary

That the suffrage is not necessary to protect women against the oppressions of man is strikingly illustrated by a recent decision of the Supreme Court of the United States in which it was decided that a law limiting the hours of woman's labor in the factory is constitutional and that she has a special right to protection by the law because of her special disadvantages, a right which the man working at her side does not possess.

This decision, rendered by a masculine court, upon briefs presented by masculine lawyers, serves to furnish at least an illus-

trative reply to those who contend that woman's suffrage is necessary to benefit the condition of woman wage-earners. Whatever
legislation can accomplish for women wage-earners, this decision
makes clear, can be accomplished under present conditions. What
cannot be accomplished by legislation cannot be accomplished by
suffrage. I have looked in vain in the publications of the woman
suffragists for any facts to show even remotely that political
suffrage involves economic gain. It is true that the farm laborers
of England obtained the suffrage and afterwards obtained increase
of wages.... In our own country it is certain that the industrial con
dition of the negro under limited suffrage is far better than it was
in the reconstruction period under unlimited suffrage, but it would
be illogical to claim that the limitation of the suffrage has promoted
economic welfare.

As to Woman's Wages

The ballot could not help the working girl in the way the suffragists
claim, since legislation affects the business of the country only in
a general way, helping or hurting all the workers alike in any special
industry. The question of wages is one of supply and demand simply! So the general wages of women will always depend greatly on
the amount of skill acquired by the mass of them. What especially
affects woman's wages is the temporary character of her work! The
ranks are constantly being filled up with raw, untrained girls, while
those who have attained to some degree of skill are constantly drop-
ping out. The natural expectation of every normal girl should be
that sooner or later she will marry and leave her work; therefore,
there is not that incentive that men have to become highly skillful.

The problem, therefore, resolves itself into this—how to regulate
justly the distribution of wages between a sex which works
throughout life and a sex which works with only temporary expectations, looking toward withdrawal in a few years from the labor
market, and withdrawing to take with it its acquired skill, leaving
only inexperience in its stead. The wiser of the suffragists
acknowledge that the suffrage will not of itself solve the problem
of wages, dependent as it is on other than political considerations.

Issued by *The Massachusetts Association Opposed to The Further Extension of Suffrage
to Women*, c. 1912.

It is also claimed, with what adequacy of evidence I do not know,
that wage-earning women desire the ballot, not merely...because
it will increase their wage, but because, as a symbol of equality,
it would secure for them a greater respect in business dealings with
men. The fact that twenty per cent of women are wage-earners and
that only five per cent of the women in industrial Massachusetts
voted that they wished the suffrage, does not confirm this claim.

But were it true, what then? Over two-thirds of the wage-earning women in the United States cease to be wage-earners at thirty-five; over half cease to be wage-earners at twenty-five; that is, wage-earning largely ceases at the marrying age. It would be interesting to know how many of the wage-earning women who want the ballot as a symbol of equality before marriage desire its responsibilities after marriage. Certainly it is clear that those responsibilities should not be imposed on eighty per cent of the women of the United States on a vague suspicion that an unknown proportion of twenty per cent of temporarily employed wage-earners think it might add to their business standing during the temporary engagement in business.

Women as Dragon Fighters

Finally, we are asked to impose the ballot upon women as a means of securing moral reforms which the men are either unwilling or incompetent to accomplish. Perhaps the argument which has been most effective to counterbalance the objection of women to assume the responsibilities of the suffrage has been the argument that they could vote for the abolition of the saloon. In the ancient legend, St. George rescues the maiden from the dragon. I confess that I have small sympathy with the spirit which calls on the maiden to fight the dragon and leaves St. George on the other side of the wall looking on to see how the conflict will terminate. The women who are affected by this argument, and perhaps the women who use it, forget that Hebrew history had a Jezebel as well as a Queen Esther, and a European history a Lucretia Borgia and a Catherine de Medici as well as a Queen Victoria. Vice, ignorance, and superstition are not confined to either sex. Advocates of woman's suffrage aver improvement of conditions in woman suffrage States; opponents of woman's suffrage aver deteriorated conditions in woman suffrage States. Into the contention between these two classes of observers, each of whom probably see what they wish to see, I decline to enter. I accept instead the testimony of such impartial observers as the President of the United States, who has said: "I am unable to see that there has been any special improvement in the position of women in those States in the West that have adopted woman suffrage as compared with those States adjoining them that have not adopted it. I do not think that giving the women suffrage will produce any marked improvement in the condition of women."

I accept the testimony of Mr. James Bryce, as disinterested, impartial, and sympathetic an observer of American conditions as America has ever known: "No evidence has come in my way tending to show that politics either in Wyoming or in Washington are in any way purer than in the adjoining States and Territories. The most that seems to be alleged is that they are no worse; or, as the Americans express it, 'Things are very much what they were before, only more so.'" This was published in 1888. It is safe to say that nothing has occurred within the last twenty years materially to change this judgment.

No Freer Human Being

The slavery of American women exists only in the warped imaginations and heated rhetoric of a few people, who have screamed themselves hoarse upon platforms or written themselves into a rage in newspapers. There is no freer human being on earth to-day, thank God, than the American woman. She has freedom of person, of property, and of profession, absolute and entire. She has all liberty that is not license.

William Croswell Doane, *North American Review*, September 1895.

President Roosevelt, in his address before the Mothers' Meeting in Washington in 1905, said: "The primary duty of the husband is to be the home-maker, the breadwinner for his wife and children (and, may I add, to be her protector from violence); the primary duty of the woman is to be the helpmeet, the housewife and mother." In these words Mr. Roosevelt has gone to the heart of the woman question. The call to woman to leave her duty to take up man's duties is an impossible call. The call on man to impose on woman his duty, in addition to hers, is an unjust call. Fathers, husbands, brothers, speaking for the silent woman, I claim for them the right to be exempt in the future from the burden from which they have been exempt in the past. Mothers, wives, sisters, I urge you not to allow yourselves to be enticed into assuming functions for which you have no inclination, by appeals to your spirit of self-sacrifice. Woman's instinct is the star that guides her to her divinely appointed life, and it guides to the manger where an infant is laid.

"If...permitted to bear an elector's part....[woman] would bear her share of civic responsibility, not because she clamors for her rights, but because she is essential to the normal development of the city."

Women's Suffrage Would Aid Governmental Reform

Jane Addams

Jane Addams founded Chicago's Hull House, a community center for neighborhood poor that later served as a center for social reform activities and became one of the nation's most important settlement houses. Ms. Addams crusaded for woman suffrage, pacifism, and social and political reforms. The author of a number of books on these issues, she was a recipient of the 1931 Nobel Peace Prize. In the following viewpoint, Ms. Addams bases her case for woman's suffrage on the idea that women would be an asset to governmental reform. With the vote, women could become important advocates for improving social welfare programs.

As you read, consider the following questions:

1. What special talents do women bring to governmental reforms, according to the author?
2. How does the author believe that society will benefit from women's political participation in civil life?
3. How does Ms. Addams believe women will benefit from their participation in civic life?

Jane Addams, "The Modern City and the Municipal Franchise for Women," in *Woman Suffrage: Arguments and Results, 1910.*

It has been well said that the modern city is a stronghold of industrialism, quite as the feudal city was a stronghold of militarism; but modern cities fear no enemies and rivals from without, and their problems of government are solely internal. Affairs, for the most part, are going badly in these great new centers, in which the quickly-congregated population has not yet learned to arrange its affairs satisfactorily. Unsanitary housing, poisonous sewage, contaminated water, infant mortality, the spread of contagion, adulterated food, impure milk, smoke-laden air, ill-ventilated factories, dangerous occupations, juvenile crime, unwholesome crowding, prostitution and drunkenness, are the enemies which the modern cities must face and overcome, would they survive. Logically, their electorate should be made up of those who can bear a valiant part in this arduous contest, those who in the past have at least attempted to care for children, to clean houses, to prepare foods, to isolate the family from moral dangers; those who have traditionally taken care of that side of life which inevitably becomes the subject of municipal consideration and control as soon as the population is congested. To test the elector's fitness to deal with this situation by his ability to bear arms is absurd. These problems must be solved, if they are solved at all, not from the military point of view, not even from the industrial point of view, but from a third, which is rapidly developing in all the great cities of the world— the human-welfare point of view.

There are many evidences that we are emerging from a period of industrialism into a period of humanitarianism, and that personal welfare is now being considered a legitimate object of government. The most noticeable manifestation of this civic humanitarianism is to be found in those cities where the greatest abuses of industrialism and materialism exist, where a thousand conflicts arise between the individual interest and the social interests. It is in these cities that selfishness is first curbed and the higher social feelings developed, and in them men learn to submit to a minute regulation of their affairs which they would find intolerable anywhere else.

Because the delicate matters of human growth and welfare cannot be nurtured by mere brute strength, a new history of municipal government begins with a serious attempt to make life possible and human in large cities which have been devoted so exclusively to industrial affairs that...they are unspeakably ugly, and unnecessarily devoid of green and growing things.

Housekeeping for a City

A city is in many respects a great business corporation, but in other respects it is enlarged housekeeping. If American cities have failed in the first, partly because office-holders have carried with them the predatory instinct learned in competitive business, and cannot help "working a good thing" when they have an opportu-

WOMEN IN THE HOME

We are forever being told that the place for women is in the HOME. Well, so be it. But what do we expect of her in the home? Merely to stay in the home is not enough. She is a failure unless she attends to the health and welfare, moral as well as physical, of her family, and especially of her children. She, more than anyone else, is held responsible for what they become.

SHE is responsible for the cleanliness of her house.
SHE is responsible for the wholesomeness of the food.
SHE is responsible for the children's health.
SHE, above all, is responsible for their morals.

How Far Can the Mother Control These Things?

She can clean her own rooms, BUT if the neighbors are allowed to live in filth, she cannot keep her rooms from being filled with bad air and smells, or from being infested with vermin.

She can cook her food well, BUT if dealers are permitted to sell poor food, unclean milk or stale eggs, she cannot make the food wholesome for her children.

She can care for her own plumbing and refuse, BUT if the plumbing in the rest of the house is unsanitary, if garbage accumulates and the halls and stairs are left dirty, she cannot protect her children from the sickness and infection resulting.

She can take every care to avoid fire, BUT if the house has been badly built, if the fire-escapes are inadequate, she cannot guard her children from the horrors of being maimed or killed by fire.

She can open her windows to give her children the air that we are told is so necessary, **BUT** if the air is laden with infection, with tuberculosis and other contagious diseases, she cannot protect her children from this danger.

She can send her children out for air and exercise, **BUT** if the conditions that surround them on the streets are immoral and degrading, **she cannot protect them** from these dangers.

Alone, she cannot make these things right. **Who or what** can?

The city can do it—the **city government** that is **elected by the people to take care** of the interests of the people.

And **who** decides what the city government shall do?

FIRST, the officials of that government; and, **SECOND, those who elect them.**

Do the women elect them? NO, the men do. So it is **the men** and **not the women who are really responsible** for the

Unclean Houses	Bad Plumbing
Unwholesome Food	Danger of Fire
Risk of Tuberculosis and Other Diseases	
Immoral Influences of the Street	

In fact, **MEN are responsible for the conditions** under which the children live, but we hold **WOMEN responsible for the results** of those conditions. If we hold women responsible for the results, must we not, in simple justice, **let them have something to say** as to what these conditions shall be? There is **one simple way of doing this.** Give them the same means that men have. **LET THEM VOTE.**

Women are, by nature and training, housekeepers. Let them have a hand in the city's housekeeping, even if they introduce an occasional house-cleaning.

NATIONAL WOMAN SUFFRAGE PUBLISHING COMPANY, Inc.
PUBLISHERS FOR THE
NATIONAL AMERICAN WOMAN SUFFRAGE ASSOCIATION
505 Fifth Avenue   New York City

nity, may we not say that city housekeeping has failed partly because women, the traditional housekeepers, have not been consulted as to its multiform activities? The men of the city have been carelessly indifferent to much of its civic housekeeping, as they have always been indifferent to the details of the household. They have totally disregarded a candidate's capacity to keep the streets clean, preferring to consider him in relation to the national tariff or to the necessity for increasing the national navy, in a pure spirit of reversion to the traditional type of government, which had to do only with enemies and outsiders.

It is difficult to see what military prowess has to do with the multiform duties which, in a modern city, include the care of parks and libraries, superintendence of markets, sewers and bridges, the inspection of provisions and boilers, and the proper disposal of garbage. It has nothing to do with the building department, which the city maintains that it may see to it that the basements are dry, that the bedrooms are large enough to afford the required cubic feet of air, that the plumbing is sanitary, that the gas pipes do not leak, that the tenement house court is large enough to afford light and ventilation, that the stairways are fireproof. The ability to carry arms has nothing to do with the health department maintained by the city, which provides that children are vaccinated, that contagious diseases are isolated and placarded, that the spread of tuberculosis is curbed, that the water is free from typhoid infection. Certainly the military conception of society is remote from the functions of the school boards, whose concern it is that children are educated, that they are supplied with kindergartens, and are given a decent place in which to play. The very multifariousness and complexity of a city government demand the help of minds accustomed to detail and variety of work, to a sense of obligation for the health and welfare of young children, and to a responsibility for the cleanliness and comfort of other people.

Housekeeping Traditionally a Woman's Task

Because all these things have traditionally been in the hands of women, if they take no part in them now they are not only missing the education which the natural participation in civic life would bring to them, but they are losing what they have always had. From the beginning of tribal life, they have been held responsible for the health of the community, a function which is now represented by the health department. From the days of the cave dwellers, so far as the home was clean and wholesome, it was due to their efforts, which are now represented by the Bureau of Tenement House Inspection. From the period of the primitive village, the only public sweeping which was performed was what they undertook in their divers dooryards, that which is now represented by the Bureau of Street Cleaning. Most of the departments in a modern city can be traced to woman's traditional activity; but, in spite of this, so soon as these old affairs were turned over to the care of the city, they slipped from woman's hands, apparently because they then became matters for collective action and implied the use of the franchise. Because the franchise had in the first instance been given to the man who could fight, because in the beginning he alone could vote who could carry a weapon, it was considered an improper thing for a woman to possess it.

Is it quite public-spirited for woman to say: "We will take care of these affairs so long as they stay in our own houses, but if they go outside and concern so many people that they cannot be carried on without the mechanism of the vote, we will drop them; it is true that these activities which women have always had are not at present being carried on very well by the men in most of the great American cities, but, because we do not consider it 'ladylike' to vote, we will let them alone"?

Because women consider the government men's affair, and something which concerns itself with elections and alarms, they have become so confused in regard to their traditional business in life, the rearing of children, that they bear with complacency a statement made by the Nestor of sanitary reformers that one-half of the tiny lives which make up the city's death-rate each year might be saved by a more thorough application of sanitary science.

Suffrage Aids the Home

Woman suffrage, instead of being incompatible with child-welfare, leads toward it, and is, indeed, the next great service to be rendered for the welfare of the home.

Julia Lanthrop, for the National American Woman Suffrage Association, c. 1912.

Because it implies the use of the suffrage, they do not consider it women's business to save these lives. Are we going to lose ourselves in the old circle of convention, and add to that sum of wrong-doing which is continually committed in the world, because we do not look at things as they really are? Old-fashioned ways, which no longer apply to changed conditions, are a snare in which the feet of women have always become readily entangled. It is so easy to be stupid, and to believe that things which used to exist still go on, long after they are past; to commit irreparable blunders because we fail to correct our theories by our changing experience. So many of the stumbling blocks against which we fall are the opportunities to which we have not adjusted ourselves! We keep hold of a convention which no longer squares with our genuine insight into life, and we are slow to follow a clue which might enable us to solace and improve the life about us, because it shocks an obsolete ideal.

Why is it that women do not vote upon these matters which concern them so intimately? Why do they not follow these vital affairs, and feel responsible for their proper administration, even although they have become municipalized? What would the result have been could women have regarded the suffrage, not as a right or a privilege, but as a mere piece of governmental machinery, without which they could not perform their traditional functions under the changed conditions of city life? Could we view the whole situation as a matter of obligation and normal development, it would be much simplified. We are at the beginning of a prolonged effort to incorporate a progressive, developing city life, founded upon a response to the needs of all the people, into the requisite legal enactments and civic institutions. To be in any measure successful, this effort will require all the intelligent powers of observation, all the sympathy, all the common sense which may be gained from the whole adult population....

We certainly may hope for two results if the municipal franchise be granted to women: (1) An opportunity to fulfill their old duties and obligations with the safeguards and the consideration which the ballot alone can secure for them under the changed conditions; and (2) the education which participation in actual affairs always brings. As we believe that woman has no right to allow the things to drop away from her that really belong to her, so we contend that ability to perform an obligation comes very largely in proportion as that obligation is conscientiously assumed.

Government and Human Welfare

Out of the medieval city, founded upon militarism, there arose in the thirteenth century a new order, the middle class, whose importance rested, not upon birth or arms, but upon wealth, intelligence and organization. They achieved a sterling success in the succeeding six centuries of industrialism, because they were essential to the existence and development of the industrial era. Perhaps we can forecast the career of woman, the citizen, if she is permitted to bear an elector's part in the coming period of humanitarianism, in which government must concern itself with human welfare. She would bear her share of civic responsibility, not because she clamors for her rights, but because she is essential to the normal development of the city of the future.

"Woman suffrage will destroy the present
non-partisan power of women and give us
nothing worth having in its place."

Women's Suffrage Would Harm Governmental Reform

Margaret C. Robinson

Margaret C. Robinson was a prominent civic leader in
Massachusetts in the early twentieth century. She served as president of the Public Interest League of Massachusetts and was an
editor of *Anti-Suffrage Notes*, a publication of the Anti-Suffrage
League, a popular organization with more than 10,000 members.
In the following viewpoint, Ms. Robinson argues that women can
have far more influence on governmental and social reform
through the women's clubs and charitable organizations to which
they already belong than through the vote.

As you read, consider the following questions:

1. What evidence does the author give to show that social
   reform can be accomplished by women without the vote?
2. Why, according to the author, do some selfish and unprin-
   cipled persons want women to vote?
3. Why does the author believe women's moral force is more
   important than any political or physical force?

Margaret C. Robinson, "Woman Suffrage a Menace to Social Reform," *Anti-Suffrage
Essays by Massachusetts Women*, 1916.

The truth of our anti-suffrage doctrine that woman suffrage will destroy the present non-partisan power of women and give us nothing worth having in its place is constantly confirmed by the current happenings in suffrage states. We have now, in the eastern and middle states, a body of non-political women workers of incomparable value, and one is amazed at the wrong-headedness which would deprive society of their influence. Under present conditions the intelligent woman interested in public affairs brings the full force of her influence to bear upon legislation; her influence is a moral influence—it is direct and can be used with men of all political parties. The possession of this unprejudiced, unrestricted power is something which anti-suffragists value so highly that the threat of the suffragists to destroy it is a very serious grievance.

It is suprising that social workers and club women in larger numbers are not awake to this danger; but, as has well been said, deciding wisely on this question is not a matter of intelligence but of information; and it is easier to accept suffrage theories and the *mis*information which suffrage orators generously supply as to how suffrage *will* work than to study the happenings in suffrage states and learn for oneself how it *does* work.

Women Too Ignorant of Politics

Social workers and club women know their present strength and how many good laws they have helped to put on the statute books. What they seemingly do not realize is how quickly this power will be gone when they divide into political parties. Many of them are apparently too ignorant of politics to understand that *as voters* it is only those men for whom they will vote that they can influence.

A despatch from Topeka, Kansas, describing the recent campaign in that state says that three years ago the Kansas Federation of Women's Clubs lined up solidly for suffrage, and won it—and that they have not been lined up solidly for anything since! Instead of throwing their influence as a unit for good legislation, as women's clubs are wont to do in male suffrage states, these women are divided into Republicans, Democrats, Progressives, and Socialists, and the friction among them is greater than ever before....

Non-Voting Women a Strong Influence

In an article on the "Legislative Influence of Unenfranchised Women," by Mary R. Beard, which appeared in the "Annals of the American Academy of Political and Social Science," for November, 1914, Mrs. Beard, although an ardent suffragist, admits that women without the vote have been a strong influence toward good legislation. She says:

"National as well as state legislation has been affected by women, if the testimony of men like Harvey W. Wiley is accepted.

In his campaign for pure food laws, he stated repeatedly that his strongest support came from women's organizations. That support was not passive and moral, merely expressed to him privately, but these women inundated congress with letters, telegrams, petitions, pleading for the passage of the laws in question. These communications were presented to congress by their recipients who often urged as their reasons for supporting pure food laws the appeals of women whose interest in food should not be ignored....

Mrs. Beard also says:

"The woman's influence lies not in physical force, but in the occasional subservience of the mind of man to the actual presence of a moral force."

Platform Virtue

I fail to see in women any evidence of the character that is needed in our public life. I fail to see that they are even on the right track to attain it. I think there is no school so eminently unfit for the development of character as that of the public platform, which women are seeking more and more. I think there is a grave danger to the moral force of womanhood in woman's increasing participation in organized effort, in public life. To say nothing of the wire-pulling, of the unscrupulousness in attaining an end, of the unfairness, of the love of office, of the insincerity which reveal themselves in the large organizations of women, with discouraging and startling resemblance to the methods of their weaker brethren, I hold that there is certain to come a deterioration which I like to name "Platform Virtue."

Annie Nathan Meyer, *The North American Review*, January 1904.

The influence of this moral force is so strong and has come to be so well recognized that certain types of politicians and commercial interests rebel against it. They wish to destroy it, and as the best means to that end they advocate woman suffrage! That is not at all in line with what one is told at suffrage meetings. We are told that women need the ballot in order that they may improve the conditions in the home, that they may help the working girl, and put through good legislation. But the rank and file of suffragists are being deceived in these matters, for suffrage works, and will work directly the other way. The New York World has committed a great indiscretion and has let this cat out of the bag. The World recently came out for suffrage and gave its reasons. One of them is that a few women, representing perhaps ten per cent of the sex, have under present conditions too much influence. These women, the World says, "have maintained at times a reign of terror over legislative bodies, in consequence of which half the

53

country is now bedeviled by some form or other of harem govern-ment, and legislators are forever making ridiculous concessions to women agitators." These "women agitators" are, of course, the club women, social workers, and others interested in social welfare. In order to make it unnecessary for legislators to make "ridiculous concessions" to this type of woman, the World advocates—what? Giving the vote to all women! It has certainly hit upon the most effective expedient, and it is because the vote will do exactly what the World claims for it, that anti-suffragists are so opposed to it. The World says that most of the reasons urged in favor of suffrage are fantastic and unreal, that women are not purer and more noble than men, and that they are not so wise as men in general affairs. It admits that they will not purify politics—indeed, that they will confuse and disorganize govern-ment, without reforming it; but nevertheless it believes in woman suffrage because it will destroy the power of the ten per cent of women whose influence is now so strong!

Suffrage Will Destroy Woman's Influence

The question for intelligent women to decide is whether or not they *want* this influence destroyed. If they wish to give up the moral influence which a body of women, educated, public-spirited, non-partisan, can wield—an influence so strong that legislators feel obliged to make what the World calls "ridiculous concessions" to it—if in its stead they wish to depend on political influence gained through the ballot, which can be applied only to one party, which can be entirely offset by the votes of women who are ignorant, boss-controlled, and whose votes are purchasable—if they prefer that, they will get their wish if woman suffrage wins. That is exactly how it is working out in the suf-frage states....

Dance Hall Girls

There is no lack of testimony that the wrong-minded women do vote. On November 4, the day after election, the San Francisco Examiner said: "McDonough Brothers had several automobiles busy all day long hauling Barbary Coast dance hall girls and the inmates of houses on Commerical Street to the different booths, and always the women were supplied with marked sample ballots."

They were outvoting the women reformers!

What is the result? What is happening to moral conditions in San Francisco since women vote? The American Social Hygiene Association pointed out last spring that there had been an *increase* in the number of questionable dance halls, and the "Survey" of April 10 stated that danger signals were being flashed all over the country to young people bound for the exposition, as there was much unemployment, and the city's moral condition gave cause

Courtesy of the Social Welfare History Archives, University of Minnesota, Minneapolis, Minnesota.

for anxiety.

A later report, by Bascom Johnson, counsel of the Social Hygiene Association, who was sent to San Francisco for further investigation, appears in full in the September issue of "Social Hygiene." It is far more serious than previous reports. Within the exposition are several concessions, maintained despite protests specifically against them, which are deplorably vicious. In the city itself conditions are appalling, the policemen being there apparently to prevent anything from interfering with the orderly and profitable traffic in vice.

Summing up his report, Mr. Johnson says, *"in spite of announcements of officials to the contrary,* San Francisco remains one of the few large cities of this country where prostitution is frankly and openly tolerated. The natural and inevitable result has been that San Francisco has become the Mecca of the underworld, and that for every such addition to her population the problem is rendered that much more difficult."

Male Suffrage Gives Women More Power

These are the conditions in a city where women vote!...

If California were still under male suffrage—if the thousands of dissolute women in San Francisco who will vote as the party in power dictates did not have the vote—the moral influence of the ladies of the Y.W.C.A. and the W.C.T.U. would be much more likely to be a factor in the situation. If these ladies vote at all, their vote is divided between the Democrats, Republicans, Progressives, and Socialists, and is therefore of much less importance than the big vote which can be controlled. Dr. Helen Sumner, sent by the suffragists to study conditions in Denver several years ago, states that "the vote of these women to whom the police protection is essential is regarded as one of the perquisites of the party in power."...

Another danger connected with woman suffrage is this—the character of the women chosen for the positions of responsibility will change.

The Woman's Journal of March 20, 1915, speaking of Mayor Harrison, of Chicago, says: "If he had occasion to appoint a welfare worker for women and children, he did not appoint a woman who had experience for the work and could do it well, but picked out a woman who would be a cog in his political machine."

Naturally! It is when women are outside politics that they are appointed on their merits. When they have the vote those are naturally chosen who are cogs in the political machine....

Social Reforms Inconsequential

Miss Jane Addams, in a suffrage speech in Boston, claimed that by means of the ballot women in Chicago have accomplished several important reforms. These were:

1. Covered markets had been secured where food might be kept clean.
2. A court for boys of 17 and under 25 had been established.
3. Public wash-houses have been established.
4. The garbage dumps have been abolished.

The record of accomplishments of Chicago women voters as presented by Miss Addams is not impressive, for the reforms she cites have been accomplished in other cities without votes for women.

What the women accomplished in Chicago *before* they got the vote makes a much more impressive showing. It is to them, says the Chicago Tribune, that Chicago owes the kindergarten in the public school, the juvenile court and detention home, the small park and playground movement, the vacation school, the school extension, the establishment of a forestry department of the city government, the city welfare exhibit, the development of the Saturday half-holiday, the establishment of public comfort stations, the work of the Legal Aid Society, and the reformation of the Illinois Industrial School. This is a long and brilliant list of women's achievements, not to be matched by the voting women of any state. Chicago women were working together when these things were accomplished—now they are fighting each other in rival political parties....

Don't Neglect Reform

Anti-suffragists ask women not to turn their attention to politics and neglect civic reform; not to make this appalling mistake, which will set back the social progress of our cities for many years; not to make powerless, through woman suffrage, as the New York World wants to do, the women who are now working for social betterment....

Government Rests on Force

If the feminists are allowed free sway, there will be a total destruction of wifehood and the home, a total destruction of all the tender relations and associations that home involves, but there will never be a relegation of man to a subservient position, there never will be a society in which women will rule men. Granting that they have no other superior quality, men possess the dominating brute strength, and in the last analysis government rests on force.

The Man-Suffrage Association Opposed to Extention of Political Suffrage to Women, 1914.

Men who believe in fair play will refuse to force political life upon all the women of their states because a small fraction think they want it. Those who care for the political welfare of their states will decline to adopt this innovation, which assuredly cannot stand the tests of rational criticism and of experience. If they value in the slightest degree the assistance which educated, public-spirited women are able to give in securing enlightened legislation, they will certainly not favor votes for women; for what woman suffrage does is to take the power out of the hands of these women, who without the vote exert a strong moral influence toward good legislation, and put the power gained through an increase in the electorate into the hands of the bosses who can control the largest woman's vote.

Female Vote Easily Manipulated

"Practical politicians" are learning this lesson rapidly. The New York Commercial calls attention to the fact that in our cities the female vote is more easily manipulated than the male. This fact does not escape the bosses, and they are rapidly coming into line for woman suffrage. While woman suffrage was largely an untried theory suffragists could maintain with some plausibility that woman's vote would be cast for moral and humane legislation, and would purify politics; but with the actual conditions in Chicago, San Francisco, Reno, Denver, and Seattle what they are, this theory no longer holds water, and it is becoming increasingly evident that the way to do away with the moral influence of women in public life is to give the vote to all women.

Recognizing Stereotypes

A stereotype is an oversimplified or exaggerated description of people or things. Stereotyping can be favorable. However, most stereotyping tends to be highly uncomplimentary and, at times, degrading.

Stereotyping grows out of our prejudices. When we stereotype someone, we are prejudging him or her. Consider the following example: Before the 1985 Summit Conference between US President Reagan and Soviet Premier Gorbachev, one of Mr. Reagan's cabinet members stated that women would not be interested in what went on at the conference. They would only be interested, he said, in what Mrs. Reagan and Mrs. Gorbachev were wearing. The cabinet member prejudged women's political contribution to the summit based on a stereotype of women's abilities and interests. He didn't consider that many women are actively interested and involved in political issues.

The following statements relate to the subject matter in this chapter. Consider each statement carefully. *Mark S for any statement that is an example of stereotyping. Mark N for any statement that is not an example of stereotyping. Mark U if you are undecided about any statement.*

If you are doing this activity as a member of a class or group, compare your answers with those of other class or group members. Be able to defend your answers. You may discover that others will come to different conclusions than you. Listening to the reasons others present for their answers may give you valuable insights into recognizing stereotypes.

If you are reading this book alone, ask others if they agree with your answers. You too will find this interaction very valuable.

S = *stereotype*
N = *not a stereotype*
U = *undecided*

1. In the splendid civilization of Athens, women held a very subordinate place.

2. The danger of inconsiderate and rash legislation would be increased immensely if women, the most impulsive and excitable half of humanity, had an equal voice in the making of laws.

3. Women, immersed in their homes and their kitchens, have less sense of political responsibility than do men.

4. Woman has shown herself possessed of the same courage, intelligence, and moral elevation as man.

5. Women compose one-half of the human race.

6. The man is usually better informed with regard to State government, but women are better informed about house government, and she can learn State government with as much facility as he can learn how to instruct children, properly feed and clothe the household, care for the sick, play on the piano, or make a house beautiful.

7. The primary duty of the husband is to be the breadwinner for his wife and children.

8. A city is in many respects a great business corporation, but in other respects it is enlarged housekeeping.

9. Men are as carelessly indifferent to the housekeeping tasks of a city as they are to those in their own homes.

10. Having the vote will masculinize women.

11. The woman's influence lies not in physical force, but in the occasional subservience of the mind of man to the actual presence of a moral force.

12. If women are allowed to vote, they will not purify politics; indeed, they will confuse and disorganize politics without reforming it.

13. Without the vote, women accomplish great things together; with it, they will be divided by political parties and loyalties and be unable to accomplish anything.

14. Women have traditionally been housekeepers only because society demanded it.

15. Juries and judges are always prejudiced in favor of women in any case in which a woman is involved.

16. In 1910, two-thirds of the wage-earning women in the US ceased to be wage-earners by age thirty-five.

Bibliography

The following list of books, periodicals, and pamphlets deals with the subject matter of this chapter.

Annals of the American Academy of Political and Social Science
Special issue: "Significance of the Woman Suffrage Movement," supplement to May 1910.

Bax E. Belfort
The Fraud of Feminism. London: Grant Richards, 1913.

L.P. Brockett
Woman: Her Rights, Wrongs, Privileges and Responsibilities. Salem, NH: Ayer Publishing Company, 1869.

Mari Jo Buhle & Paul Buhle, ed.
The Concise History of Woman Suffrage. Urbana, IL: University of Illinois Press, 1978.

Horace Bushnell
Women's Suffrage: The Reform Against Nature. Washington, DC: Zenger Publishing Company, 1976.

Eleanor Flexner
Century of Struggle: The Woman's Rights Movement in the United States. Cambridge, MA: Columbia University Press, 1965.

Sharna Gluck, ed.
From Parlor to Prison: Five American Suffragists Talk About Their Lives. New York: Monthly Review, 1985.

Elizabeth Griffith
In Her Own Right: The Life of Elizabeth Cady Stanton. New York: Oxford University Press, 1984.

Sarah Grimke
Letters on Equality of the Sexes and the Conditions of Women. New York: Burt Franklin, 1838.

A.H. Hirsch
The Love Elite: The Story of Woman's Emancipation and Her Drive for Sexual Fulfillment. New York: Julian, 1963.

Inez Hayes Irwin
The Story of the Woman's Party. New York: Harcourt, Brace, 1921.

Aileen Kraditor
The Ideas of the Woman Suffrage Movement, 1890-1920. New York: Columbia University Press, 1965.

Elizabeth Cady Stanton, et al.
The Concise History of Woman Suffrage: Selections from the Classic Work of Stanton, Anthony, Gage and Harper. Urbana, IL: University of Illinois, 1978.

Should Women Work Outside the Home?

Introduction

Before industrialization and urbanization of the United States began in the 19th century, a serious debate about whether women should "work" never occurred. From earliest colonial times, the family had formed the basic economic unit of American society, and all its members worked together. Whether they lived on farms or in villages in the East and Midwest, on plantations in the South, or in moving settlements on the advancing frontier, women and men and children ploughed fields, tended cattle, spun wool, kept shop, made soap, and fought their enemies together. Faced with struggles for simple survival, there were few absolute divisions of labor by sex. Each family member contributed what he or she could to the family's well being.

But advances in agriculture, transportation, and industry reduced the amount of labor necessary for individual family sustenance. Families began migrating from rural areas to towns and cities. There they joined millions of immigrants who had come to the United States to find work and a better standard of life. This labor pool plus technological innovations and accumulating capital combined to change the United States in a relatively brief period from an agrarian to an industrial economy, permanently altering the nature of work: In urban industrial America more women remained in the home to raise families and perform a diminishing number of household tasks while men worked outside the home.

The debate over whether women should "work," defined as paid employment, began almost as soon as it became possible for middle-class and upper middle-class women *not* to work. Immigrant women, black women, and poor women worked at least until they were married; single women, widows, and those whose families were dependent on them might work for most of their lives. But the relatively small number of affluent women represented the ideal to which most American women and men aspired. The new ideal woman of the late 19th century remained in the home to raise children, meet her family's emotional and other personal needs, and consume the array of goods now being produced in industrial America.

The debate over women's work changed in the 20th century

to reflect changing social conditions: During wartime, society generally agreed that women's labor was a necessary contribution to the national effort; but during the Great Depression and the periods following wars, women were urged to return to their primary work—in the home—and to leave the work of factory, office, and field to men.

Today, statistics show that nearly all women will work for at least some portion of their lives, and that increasing numbers of them work throughout their lives. Whether these women work from sheer economic necessity, to help their families improve their standard of living, or for personal satisfaction, women are now a permanent part of the workforce. With this change, debate about whether women *should* work has shifted to one about the conditions under which they *will* work. Concerns today focus on child care, equal pay—especially equal pay for comparable work—equal access to occupations traditionally occupied by men, and the means for women to achieve success in the business world.

"[Wage earning] subordinates the higher interests of the family to the end of money-making."

Women's Work Is the Home

Flora McDonald Thompson

One impact of the industrial revolution was to make it easier for women to work outside the home. The abundance of new occupations not requiring brute strength inspired debate about the appropriateness of women working in industry. In the following viewpoint written in 1904, Flora McDonald Thompson, a journalist and mother, discusses in vivid detail the dangers this trend posed for both women and society.

As you read, consider the following questions:

1. According to the author, in what ways are women treated differently in the workplace because they are women?
2. Why does the author think that women's work is not "cost effective"?
3. Why does the author state that women wage earners are a "social menace "?

Flora McDonald Thompson, "The Truth About Women in Industry," *North American Review*, May 1904.

The common assumption is that by engaging in men's work women secure independence. That there are upwards of 3,000,000 women wage-earners in the United States, that women have entered all classes of occupation, that women form seventeen per cent of the industrial strength of the people, are facts popularly quoted as indicating the economic progression of the sex. Now, the truth of the matter, as statistics show, is that the woman wage-earner is under one aspect an object of charity, under another an economic pervert, under another a social menace....

The Business Jungle

The law of the business world, to which woman is unavoidably subject on entering general industry, is not the Golden Rule. It is the law which demands the greatest production at the least cost. Strictly speaking, business has absolutely nothing to do with the humanities—absolutely nothing to do with the individual save as a contributor to the wealth of the nation. In so far as woman's work serves business interests, business conditions inevitably are adjusted to her interests. Injustice to her in this connection is business suicide; it is killing the goose that lays the golden egg. But in so far as she is of trifling importance to business, or in so far as she represents any sort or degree of loss to business, she necessarily is ground under the inflexible rule of business law.

Numerically, women wage-earners, including all above ten years of age, are 17.22 per cent of the industrial population. This numerical strength, however, small as it is, is still less as a force in production because the industrial energy of woman is constantly depleted by marriage. At the age when maturity gives the laborer most power in production, women are withdrawn from the economic into the domestic sphere. Says the Chief of the Massachusetts Bureau of Labor Statistics: "The great cause that reduces the number of women in industry is marriage. Thus, the permanency of woman in industry is as a class, not as an individual."

In consequence of this, the woman who is a unit of production has no effect other than to confuse economic problems. She eternally eludes classification with reference to the volume of her production and its cost by fitfully disappearing from the economic order as the attraction of sex makes demands on her. Her aim in industry is not a livelihood, the laborer's aim and the basis of calculation from which economic equations are formed. She works as a makeshift pending marriage, and thus she tends always to sink to a level with the lowest order of labor, unskilled—the worth of which is reckoned not according to its power, but according to the shifting stress of the necessities of the laborer.

There are, however, other elements than wages which must be considered before we can determine what is the cost of woman's contribution to production and whether or not it pays.

At the outset, there instantly appears increased cost of production in the item of all the conveniences required for women working in factories and business houses. In the better mercantile institutions, these advance from bare necessaries to comfort, and even to luxury, in the matter of toilet rooms and lunch rooms, a few proprietors going so far as to serve hot tea, coffee and soup free to employees. These provisions are significant of their economy and purpose, as one is a familiar visitor in toilet rooms of mercantile institutions and daily witnesses one or more female employees stretched on a couch, worn out, sick—thus demonstrating that, as a class, women workers not only increase the cost of production, but diminish its efficiency. The cheapness of woman labor offsets in a measure the increased cost, but such are the demands of marriage, and such the physical unreliability of the sex that to substitute cheap woman labor for men is to substitute a less for a greater efficiency, a fluctuating for a constant force in production—it is, in short, mere money-saving, not economy.

"No More Girls" on Job

"No more girls for me," said this man, brusquely; "it's too hard to discharge them if they don't suit. When a man fails to come up to specifications, you can tell him so and that settles it; but with a girl—" Here he frowned and then sighed, as if he had been through some particularly disagreeable experience. "Well, I had one not long ago," he went on, "and she couldn't spell. That seemed to her a trifling matter, but not so to me. However, I put up with her work for a while simply because she was a woman, but finally I had to let her go. And what do you suppose she did? Why, sir, she came into my private office and wept on my desk until she had me unfit for work for all the rest of the day. I felt as if I had been through a melodrama in real life. That settled me, and I'll take no chance of repeating the experience."

Elliot Flower, *The Arena*, June 1902.

Moreover, as women engage in men's work, they withdraw an indispensable force from household production, which has the effect of increasing the cost of living while at the same time debasing the value of labor. The wages of women being fixed without reference to the cost of living, they tend, in competing with men, to reduce wages below what it costs to live. Thus, as they abandon the economy of the household for wage-earning, they put labor in the anomalous position of having living expenses increase in inverse ratio to wages. This is a perversion of the economic law of wages, which have always a tendency to increase as the cost of living increases. Women, however, disturb this relation by engaging in wage-earning, and in this instance they have the particular effect of depleting subsistence. Plainly, if wages are less than the cost of living, labor is poorly sustained—insufficiently nourished. Thus, both directly and indirectly, woman in industry, considered with strict reference to economy, operates both to increase the cost of production and to diminish the efficiency of labor....

Displacing Men

The effect of cheap woman labor is naturally to displace men. The report of the United States Department of Labor shows that exactly as the percentage of women increased in all occupations from 1887 to 1890 the percentage of men decreased. The apparent evil herein resulting is disclaimed by economists who adhere to the principle that cheap labor is to the advantage of production. Horace G. Wadlin, Chief of the Massachusetts Bureau of Labor Statistics, says:

> Displacements of men in industry due to advance of women is similar to the effect wrought by the introduction of machinery. It is temporary, and the hardship resulting is also temporary.

This is an error, because woman's wage-earning offers no compensation for the hardship it entails upon men in the benefits of facilitated production such as follows upon the use of machinery. Woman labor has solely the economic effect I have shown—to increase cost and diminish efficiency in production. And this effect is permanent, Mr. Wadlin to the contrary notwithstanding. By marriage the industry of woman is rendered so fitful and elusive of adjustment to economic principle that it defies establishment as a constant force to be counted on, as labor may reckon with machinery. It appears to-day unexpectedly substituting the cheap woman for the higher-priced man, and to-morrow it disappears in matrimony, leaving both its employer and its male rival at a disadvantage, the only definite result it has accomplished being that it has attached a lower wage to the performance of a certain amount of work.

In addition to the evil which woman labor thus imposes upon men, the reduction of men's wages it brings about is attended with no diminution of men's responsibility. The man remains liable for the support of the family, even though his wife and daughter, competing with him in business, should lower his wages to the starvation point. Woman labor is an economic element as abnormal as convict labor, and it is equally pernicious for the reason that legitimate labor is taxed for its support.

But are the woman's interests served? What has this industrial revolution accomplished for the sex?

It has secured her a competence averaging less than one dollar a day. It has undermined her health. It has trained her in the work of a machine, and made her unskilled in all the labor which supplements the office of wife and mother in the family. It has taken her out of the home....

The full significance of this I have learned from my own experience. I can best describe it in egotistic fashion.

Trained to a profession and not trained in household industry, on entering the domestic relation I find my situation to be this: I know next to nothing about domestic economy; I have not money enough at my command to pay for my education in this neglected branch, so I do what seems the only thing possible. I hire a capable woman to manage my house, and by working at my profession I earn money that compensates my family for the money loss entailed by my domestic inefficiency. But when I have thus settled my financial accounts with my family, I am still the cause of irreparable loss to them, and thereby to society. This proceeds from my being under the rule of competition in my professional work.

"*We can't go on meeting like this over a business lunch—couldn't you find time for an occasional evening at home with me and the children?*"

© Punch/Rothco

I am subject to business law. An editor will not wait for copy because my child is sick. A newspaper must go to press in spite of the fact that I have a baby in arms. Because I have been falsely educated in serving editors and writing for the press, instead of with a view to the fact that one day I would probably have a baby in arms and a child calling me to work by his bedside, I have had to organize my household labor on a scale of expense which compels me to earn money or precipitate the family into business confusion. Therefore, it is the editor and the paper going to press that I am bound to heed. My baby must develop in the arms of the most capable nurse I can hire; my sick child must do with the service of a hired attendant also. I am in industry. I must abide by its laws. If I neglect my work, there are others ready to seize it. And they will get it. The editor will not be touched by any exhibition of fine maternal solicitude that may be the occasion of my neglect of business. "Business is business."

Family's Needs Second to Business

This is the horror of wage-earning for women—it reduces her office in the family to a convenience of business. It makes of home a limited, cooperative boarding-house, where the several members of the family eat, sleep and are otherwise equipped and repaired for the pursuit of their individual interests in life outside. It subordinates the higher interests of the family to the end of money-making. Children are so many ethical problems that seriously embarrass the business success of the mother. They must be organized and disciplined accordingly. The arrangements for their development have always to include and provide for the mother's business obligations. Thus wealth comes to condition human character....

Since marriage is a state to which all women in the course of nature, barring accident, attain, it is to effects as determined by marriage that one must look in defining the principles which should govern the action of women. Facts concerning the wage-earning of wives, therefore, do not describe conditions of one class of women only; they represent the final equation of the matter in its bearing upon the sex. Therefore:

The practice of so-called economic independence has achieved for women financial results indicated in the fact that her average earnings are less than one dollar a day.

The effect of the practice upon economic interests is to lessen efficiency and to increase the cost of production.

The effect upon the woman herself is to impair her physical fitness for the maternal function, and to subject her to a false system of education, which mentally and morally unfits her for her economic office in the family.

The effect upon society is to promote pauperdom, both by increasing the expense of living and by robbing men of the responsibility which gives them force and success in their natural office of dispenser of wealth to the family.

In a word, the truth about woman in industry is, she is a frightful failure.

> *"Although the exclusion of womankind from the world's active work, and her subordination to man, have been a sociological necessity,...it has ceased to be beneficial."*

Women's Work Should Not Be Restricted to the Home

Vernon Lee

Vernon Lee is the pseudonym of Violet Paget, who was a prolific English novelist, essayist, and playwright. The following viewpoint written in 1902, is excerpted from her review of Charlotte Perkins Gilman's famous study *Women and Economics.* In the viewpoint, Ms. Paget describes the disservice society performs by encouraging women to work only in the home as wives, mothers, and consumers.

As you read, consider the following questions:

1. What does the author mean when she agrees with Charlotte Perkins Gilman that women are "over-sexed"?
2. What does the author believe are the prices paid for women's economic dependence?
3. How does the author think men will benefit if women become economically independent?
4. Does Ms. Paget see any solution to "the Woman Question"?

Violet Paget (as Vernon Lee), "The Economic Dependence of Women," *North American Review,* July 1902.

Although the exclusion of womankind from the world's active work, and her subordination to man, have been a sociological necessity—the price paid for the lengthened infancy, the increased educability of man, and also for that solid familial organization which alone permitted an accumulation and multiplication of human inventions and traditions; that, although the *regression*, or, at all events, the stagnation of one half of the human race has been inevitable and beneficial in the past, it has ceased to be beneficial, and is ceasing to be inevitable, in the present. A particular automatic arrangement of historical evolution has done its work; like slavery, like servage, like feudalism...it has grown to be an impediment to progress. For the prolonged infancy and youth of genus *homo* can now no longer be endangered; and a large proportion of human education has, since thousands of years, passed from the care of the mother to that of the community as a whole, or of portions—guilds, priesthoods, universities, and so forth—of the community; while, on the other hand, the inventions and traditions have been stored, multiplied, and diffused far beyond the powers of family education. The benefit has long, long ago been obtained beyond all possibility of loss; but the price is still being paid for it.

The Price of Keeping Women at Home

Now, what is that price? The stagnation or regression...of the female mind.... The removal of womankind from the field of action and reaction called "the universe at large" to the field of action and reaction called "the family circle"; the substitution, as a factor of adaptation and selection, of the preference of the husband or possible husband for the preferences, so to speak, of the whole of creation. In other words, the sequestration of the capacities of one half of the human race, and their enclosure inside the habits and powers of the other half of the human race.... The work which womankind might have accomplished during those hundreds and hundreds of years if she had not had a man to work for her; the work which might have been given by two halves of the human race, instead of being given by one only....The woman did do work throughout that time. Not merely the essential work, direct and indirect, of rearing a new generation and, in a measure, keeping up the acquired standard of civilization; but also the work, less essential indeed to the race, which enabled the man not merely to seek for food away from the home, but also to be as idle as he required (or at least as he liked) while in it. The woman, save among the exceptionally wealthy, has always been a chief domestic servant; and even nowadays she is so, to a greater or lesser extent. The woman, therefore, has worked; but—and here comes the subtle distinction on which the whole economic and sociological part of the subject reposes—she has worked not for the consumption of the world at large, and subject to the world's selection of good or bad, useful or useless, work; but for the consumption of one man and subject to that one man's preferences. The woman has worked without thereby developing those qualities which competition has developed among male workers. She has not become as efficient a human being as her brothers; whatever her individual inherited aptitudes,...she has not been allowed to develop them in the struggle for life; but has been condemned, on the contrary, to atrophy them in forms of labor which can require only the most common gifts, since they are required equally of every woman in every family.

But this is by no means the whole of the price which the human race has had to pay for the needful "division of labor" between its two halves. Negatively, the position of women has prevented

His Wife: "Good bye, dear. Write often, if it's only a check."

W.T. Swomley, 1902.

their developing certain of their possibilities; positively, it has forced them to develop certain other of their possibilities; it has atrophied the merely human faculties, which they possess rudimentarily in common with men; it has, on the other hand, hypertrophied the peculiarity which distinguished them from man; hypertrophied their sex.

First and Foremost, Females

There is one particular sentence in [Charlotte Perkins Gilman's book] *Women and Economics* which converted me to the cause of female emancipation: "Women are over-sexed."...

Over-sexed does not mean over-much addicted to sexual indulgence; very far from it, for that is the case not with women, but with men, of whom we do not say that they are *over-sexed*. What we mean by *over-sexed* is that, while men are a great many things besides being males—soldiers and sailors, tinkers and tailors, and all the rest of the nursery rhyme—women are, first and foremost, *females*, and then again females, and then—still more females....

That women are *over-sexed* means that, instead of depending upon their intelligence, their strength, endurance, and honesty, they depend mainly upon their sex; that they appeal to men, dominate men through the fact of their sex; that (if the foregoing seems an exaggeration) they are economically supported by men because they are wanted as wives and mothers of children—that is to say, wanted for their sex. And it means, therefore, by a fearful irony, that the half of humanity which is constitutionally (and by the bare facts of motherhood) more chaste, has unconsciously and inevitably acquired its power, secured its livelihood, by making the other half of humanity less chaste by appealing through every means, material, aesthetic and imaginative, sensual or sentimental, to those already excessive impulses and thoughts of sex. The woman has appealed to the man, not as other men appeal to him, as a comrade, a competitor, a fellow-citizen, or an open enemy of different nationality, creed, or class; but as a possible wife, as a female....

Waste of Male Productive Energy

Now, the chief point made by the author of *Women and Economics*, the point which, as it converted myself, ought to convert many others from indifference to the Woman Question, is concerned with the misapplication and waste of the productive energies and generous impulses of men, thanks to the necessity of providing not only for themselves and their offspring, but for a woman who has been bought up not as a citizen, but as a parasite, not as a comrade, but as a servant, or—well, consider the word even in its most sentimental and honorable sense—as a lover. The economic dependence of women (however inevitable and useful in the past) has not merely limited the amount of productive bodily and mental work at the disposal of the community, but it has very seriously increased the mal-distribution of that work and of its products....

It is, in reality, [the wife]...who decides the "standard of living"; the wife,...already accustomed both to a certain degree of expenditure as a reality, and, what is quite as important, to a certain expenditure as an ideal in the future....No, no, it is not the children who ask for carriage horses, toilettes, and footmen, or (in more sordid spheres) for the..."home for happy people," with its one overworked drudge and its preoccupation about the husband's dinner. It is not even the children who clamor for nurse-maids and governesses and expensive schools: it is the wife....

Perverted Consumers

Again, the consuming female, debarred from any free production, unable to estimate the labor involved in the making of what she so lightly destroys, and her consumption limited mainly to those things which minister to physical pleasure, creates a market for sensuous decoration and personal ornament, for all that is luxurious and enervating, and for a false and capricious variety in such supplies, which operates as a most deadly check to true industry and true art. As the priestess of the temple of consumption, as the limitless demander of things to use up, her economic influence is reactionary and injurious. Much, very much, of the current of useless production in which our economic energies run waste—man's strength poured out like water on the sand—depends on the creation and careful maintenance of this false market, this sink into which human labor vanishes with no return. Woman, in her false economic position, reacts injuriously upon industry, upon art, upon science, discovery, and progress. The sexuo-economic relation in its effect on the constitution of the individual keeps alive in us the instincts of savage individualism which we should otherwise have well outgrown. It sexualizes our industrial relation and commercializes our sex-relation. And, in the external effect upon the market, the over sexed woman, in her unintelligent and ceaseless demands, hinders and perverts the economic development of the world.

Charlotte Perkins Gilman, *Women and Economics*, 1898.

The virtuous woman of the well-to-do classes, and of the classes (more numerous and important) aspiring or pretending to such well-to-do-ness, alters, discards, throws away those objects which are no longer consonant with "what one *has* to have," and whose continued use would therefore suggest the horrid thought that the family was not really well-off; in eminently business countries the thought that the husband's *business* was not thriving. "It is good for trade," remark the more responsible among these ladies....It is good for trade: and so is a town being burnt down, or swallowed up by an earthquake, or washed away by a tidal wave. It makes room for more objects (dresses, crockery, furniture, houses, or human beings); but, meanwhile, you have wasted those that were already there, and all the labor and capital they have cost to produce.

Loss of Moral Spirit

But the spirit of wastefulness is by no means the worst correlative among women of the spirit of rapacity, of "getting wealth, not making it,"...which the economic dependence of the wife develops (as a virtue, too!) in the husband. An enormous amount of the hardness in bargaining, the readiness to take advantage, the willingness to use debasing methods (such as our modern hypnotizing advertisement system), the wholesale acceptance of intellectual and moral, if not material, adulteration of work and its products—correspond in the husband to what is honored as thrift, as *good management*, in the wife. It is more than probable that the time wasted, the bad covetousness excited, the futile ingenuity exercised by the women who crowd round the windows of our great shops and attend their odious "sales," are really the result of a perverted possibility of virtue.

For the man's virtue is to *make money*; the woman's virtue is to *make money go a long way*. And, between the two virtues, we are continually told that a business house cannot give better wages and shorter hours because it would be "crowded out of the market"; and we are told also, by more solemn moralists still, that nations cannot do without war, lest they lose their "commercial outlets," or fail to secure those they have not got.

Who can object? All these people are good husbands and good wives; the home is the pivot of our morality. And the most disheartening thing is, that all this is true.

Resolving the Problem

How do you propose to remedy it? By what arrangements do you expect to make the wife the economic equal of her husband, the joint citizen of the community?

I propose nothing, because I do not know. All I feel sure of is, that if people only want a change sufficiently strongly and persistently, that change will work out its means in one way or another. Which way? is a question often unanswerable, because the practical detail depends upon other practical details which the continuance of the present state of things is hiding from us, or even forbidding. And because, moreover, we are surrounded on all sides by resources which become available only in connection with other resources, and only under the synthetic power of desire. The lids of boiling kettles went on rising all through Antiquity and the Middle Ages; but the notion of using that expansive movement of steam could not occur until the people had already got roads and mariner's compasses and mechanical mills, and until people were beginning to find stage-coaches and sailing vessels and wind-mills and water-mills a little unsatisfactory. The integration of women as *direct* economic, and therefore *direct* moral and civic, factors in the community, is not a more difficult question of the integration of the laboring classes into the real life of nations; and yet the "social question" will find, some day, its unexpected solution; and the "Woman Question" will, very likely, have to be settled beforehand.

"Women must boldly announce that no job is more exciting, more necessary, or more rewarding than that of housewife and mother."

Being a Housewife and Mother Is Woman's Greatest Work

Agnes E. Meyer

Agnes Meyer, the mother of five children and grandmother of eight, graduated from Barnard College and later served as one of its trustees. She spoke and wrote with deep conviction about the primacy of traditional women's work. She wrote articles about education and served on national presidential commissions on higher education and on children and youth. In the following viewpoint, taken from a speech she delivered at Howard University in 1950, Ms. Meyer urges women to avoid selfishness and competitive materialism and instead to concentrate their powers on their most important work: bearing and raising children.

As you read, consider the following questions:

1. Why does the author believe that being a housewife and mother is so important to women and society?
2. What, according to Ms. Meyer, has caused so much confusion and unhappiness among women about their role in the world?
3. What skills does the author think housewives and mothers need?

Agnes E. Meyer, "Women Aren't Men," *The Atlantic Monthly*, August 1950. Reprinted with permission.

Women have many careers but only one vocation—motherhood. As a result their most successful careers are motherhood-substitutes such as teaching, nursing, social work, as well as medical, psychiatric, and other scientific professions that protect the child and the family. A woman confronting the world has no greater resources than those she finds within herself. Education can do no worse than to destroy those instinctive resources. It can do no better than to enhance them. When woman sublimates her mother-instinct in a career, she can achieve a rich, beneficent, and rewarding life. But only if she follows her vocation can she live in the fullest sense of the word. It is for woman as mother, actual or vicarious, to restore security in our insecure world—not the economic security on which we now lean far too much, but the emotional security for which the world longs as much as it longs for its daily bread.

Women's Responsibility for Moral Decay

We should look critically at woman's evolution in our industrial society, for the record that confronts us on every side as to woman's influence is not reassuring. The mounting divorce rate, the appalling number of youthful crimes, the deliberate neglect of children in many homes, and the looseness of sexual morality among young and old—these are merely some of the inescapable signs of a decaying moral structure in areas for which women have a prime responsibility.

The industrial revolution which has transformed our whole society created a transformation in the life of women far more profound than in the life of men. Two world wars and a depression have uprooted family life and created a nation-wide turmoil whose disorders our public and private welfare agencies have tried in vain to counteract. At the same time woman's traditional responsibilities were augmented by challenging social and political demands. She fought successfully for the vote, for equal rights in every field of endeavor. She was forced through economic necessity and through choice into the competitive maelstrom of our free-enterprise system. About 17 million women now have daily jobs and many more are doing part-time work.

It is no wonder that women have become confused and to a great extent disoriented. None of us—not even those of us old enough to date back to the stable pre-war society of the late nineteenth and early twentieth century which gave us a happy and secure childhood—have lived through the pandemonium of the later years without a tremendous internal and external struggle for integrity.

The shattering of the social structure has disastrously isolated the individual; it has also accelerated the spirit of competition inherent in our free-enterprise system to an almost unendurable intensity. To the extent that there is a world trend toward socialism, I am convinced, it is psychic as well as economic. Many people are tired and frightened to a point where they can no longer endure their social isolation and the burden of an individual destiny. Only the democratic nations have the vitality, the sense of responsibility, and the moral fortitude to accept the burden of individual freedom in a world shattered by two world wars. It is an exacting but never a dull life. It is a life of constant individual decisions, of irrevocable choices made every day, every hour, for good or for evil.

Crucial Role of Women

It is precisely because of this temporary moral, mental, and social isolation of the individual in a democratic society that the role of woman has become of crucial importance. For woman is the cement of society. Since time immemorial it has been woman who has held the family, society, and life itself together. She did it instinctively to protect herself during pregnancy and to protect her children during their long period of helplessness. Through this fundamental need for family solidarity it is woman who has

"THAT'S IT! SNEAK ON OFF TO WORK!"

developed the art of human relationships and an appreciation of the vital importance of human behavior. Whether the conditions were primitive or whether society attained the extreme refinement of the eighteenth-century aristocracy, it was woman who created the moral atmosphere of these diverse conditions. And today woman must look back with a clear comprehension to the moral force she once exerted in the social structure and realize that she can and must save our civilization from destruction by achieving new moral standards that will conform to the very different conditions of the present day.

Now that we have amassed so much factual knowledge of the importance of the home as the basis of society, of the importance of marital relationships, of child guidance and education in general, the role of wife and mother has become infinitely more exacting and difficult. Instead of apologizing for being a "mere housewife," as so many do, women should make society realize that upon the housewife now fall the combined tasks of economist, nutrition expert, sociologist, psychiatrist, and educator. Then society would confer upon the status of housewife the honor, recognition, and acclaim it deserves. Today, however, the duties of the homemaker have become so depreciated that many women feel impelled to work outside the home in order to retain the respect of the community. It is one thing if women wish to work or must do so to help support the family. It is quite another thing—it is a destructive influence—if society forces women into the labor market in order that they may respect themselves and gain the respect of others.

Exacting and Rewarding Roles

Women must boldly announce that no job is more exacting, more necessary, or more rewarding than that of housewife and mother. Then they will feel free to become once more the moral force of society through the stabilization of the home. Then the influence they once wielded in society instinctively and unconsciously will become stronger than it ever has been, because they will go about the task with mind and emotions, knowledge and experience, the conscious and the unconscious forces, working in unison. With all the scientific knowledge we have amassed, women can and should be the standard bearers of a civilization higher in every respect than any we have ever known before. But they can only do this if they will accept the fact that their functions as women are very different from those of men. What modern woman has to recapture is the wisdom that just being a woman is her central task and her greatest honor. It is a task that challenges her whole character, intelligence, and imagination.

If we look at the social scene about us we find very hopeful indications that women, especially the young married women, have begun to realize these fundamental truths. The high birth rate is in itself a promising symptom. But further than that, many of these young women are carrying out their duties toward their husbands, their children, and the physical maintenance of the home with joyous intelligence and great ability. It is fair to say that there have probably never been in any civilization so many ideal marital partnerships in which husband and wife respect each other's sphere of activity, and in which both share the responsibility for the education of the children.

Housewife's Central Role

But it is foolish to imagine that the complex roles and relationships sustained by the housewife can be abolished or assumed by outside agencies. Her role is nothing less than the central activity of the human community. All the other work—the business and politics and entertainment and service performed in the society— finds its ultimate test in the quality of the home. The home is where we finally and privately live, where we express our individuality, where we display our aesthetic choices, where we make and enjoy love, and where we cultivate our children as individuals. All very pedestrian, perhaps, but there is not very much more in civilized life.

George Gilder, *Sexual Suicide*, 1973.

On the other hand, it is no less true that there have never been so many women who are dissatisfied with being women and therefore with being wives and mothers. There have never been so many women who are unnecessarily torn between marriage and a career. There have never been so many mothers who neglect their children because they find some trivial job more interesting. I know this from wide contact with neglected children. The most pathetic are those who come from well-to-do homes. The poor child whose mother has to work has some inner security because he knows in his little heart that his mother is sacrificing herself for his well-being. But the neglected child from a well-to-do home, who realizes instinctively that his mother prefers her job to him, often hates her with a passionate intensity. There are the children who frequently get into the worst difficulties because they are the most deeply hurt and resentful.

Destroying Decent Instincts

What ails these women who consciously or unconsciously reject their children? Surface influences of a competitive, materialistic world have obscured the importance of women's role as the repository of continuity and of purposeful living derived from their biological and social functions. Our technological civilization has atrophied their emotions, and nothing is more horrible than a woman whose instinctive reactions have been destroyed. They are far more egotistical than men, more fiercely aggressive, more insensitive not only to the beauty but to the decency of life. They have become masculine without even knowing it. In their defense it must be said that they are the victims of a general decline of emotional spontaneity in our civilization. Our scientific age is afraid of feeling. Why else should there be such a flood of books on youthful crime and delinquency, which repeat with a monotonous insistence that what little children need most in order to become stable personalities is the feeling of being wanted by their parents? What kind of civilization have we built when fathers and mothers need to have it drilled into them by psychiatrists, sociologists, and other experts that they are creating social monsters because they do not love the children they have brought into the world?

I am not trying to drive all women back into the home. The married woman who is rebellious about family life does her children more harm by staying home in such a frame of mind than by leaving them to some kindly relative or sending them to boarding school. It is the frame of mind of such women that is wrong, that must be understood and changed. For these women are equally disastrous as an influence in their working environment. God protect us all from the efficient, go-getter businesswoman whose feminine instincts have been completely sterilized. Wherever women are functioning, whether in the home or in a job, they must remember that their chief function as women is a capacity for warm, understanding, and charitable human relationships. Women are throwing their greatest natural gift out of the window when they cease to function as experts in cooperative living.

It is distressing, therefore, to hear the oft repeated plaint that woman must be a personality first and a woman only secondarily. This cliche revives in a new form the dualistic conflict between nature and spirit, body and mind, the conscious and the unconscious, which weakens all personality, whether male or female, but is especially disastrous to woman at a time when an arid and strictly academic education has already dangerously widened the gap between her emotional and intellectual capacities. Are women people? Only to the extent that they fuse their inherited and acquired characteristics into a dynamic, harmoniously functioning unity which alone is worthy of being called personality.

Service More Important Than "Success"

Another fallacy about women which is receiving far too much currency is the accusation that they have lost the adventurous spirit of "their older sisters" who battled successfully against male domination. Agnes Rogers recently wrote an article in *Harper's* magazine and a similar one in the *American Scholar* deploring the fact that women are only too often content with minor positions in the business world. "Their willingness to accept the status of useful but humble cog in an enterprise directed by men is baffling to me," she said. She wants them to conquer their "humility and lack of confidence."

Now I fail to see any exaggerated humility in modern women. On the contrary, I find too much emphasis on success and too little upon service. In my opinion, humility is the greatest possible asset in any human being, particularly in women. True, humility is the understatement of a powerful personality. It is innocence triumphant, which Emerson has described as "the most powerful critic of all that passes through its alembic." It is the ability to understand reality as it confronts us. This ability, so characteristic of woman's inherent personality, to adjust herself to outward circumstances, to the husband in marriage, to the employer and fellow workers in business and industry, is not a sign of weakness but of strength. The woman who tries to control situations by force and by aggressively overplaying her hand in every human relation is the weak woman trying to overcompensate for her weakness.

"Skyscraper Spinsters"

These are the "skyscraper spinsters." Every big city in America has thousands of them; well educated, well-dressed, well-groomed and well-lost. And although many of them reach the top in competition there is never one who is completely satisfied with what she's done or where she's got. The ones with the courage to face facts often know reasonably early that they got off at the wrong floor, but even so it's too late to go back. They realize, too, that while they have won material success and economic security they have abandoned the most valuable thing in life—the demanding, sacrificing, richly rewarding and completely fulfilling full-time job of wife and mother.

Irene Corbally Kuhn, *American Mercury*, November 1954.

These are the worried, restless, immature females who complain bitterly that there are not enough women in high executive positions in the business world and in government. These aggressive, frustrated women actually make the role of woman in business and public life more difficult because more suspect. They are precisely the female types under whom neither women nor men want to work. The balanced, mature woman who knows her inner worth does not run around the world complaining of the injustice of men. She is quietly expanding her area of influence. This wise, subtle, and effective type of woman meets with appreciation wherever she is active, not because she is *demanding* recognition, but because her gifts are recognized as extremely rare and invaluable....

But youth is only too apt to think that it has to be aggressive if it is to make its way in our competitive society. That is untrue for women, whether young or old....What the world needs today is not more competition but woman's native genius for sympathetic cooperation. Competition is so acute because society has crumbled and left the individual atomized and unprotected. Unless we women succeed in modifying this competitive spirit through more effective cooperation between public and private endeavor, between management and labor, between the contending religious sects, between the family and the community, between one individual and another, then there is little hope for our democratic civilization. This is women's great opportunity—to ease the acute and dangerous tensions of American life.

I am not asking women to overdo self-sacrifice to a point of self-abasement. We all know extreme feminine types who use this masochistic weapon not out of a desire to serve, but to conquer and subdue their victims. Women must learn to keep self-respect and self-sacrifice, the social and the biological functions, in balance. Such women have the most friends because they defend their own personalities while giving free play to the expansion of other personalities. Those are the women who are called blessed because they constitute the happiness of their families and of the whole community.

Such women, moreover, are not concerned with the modern cry for equal rights because they are too sure of themselves and of what they have to give to the world. They seek not parity but partnership with men.

"The educated individual should have a community, a national, a world viewpoint; but that is pretty difficult to get and hold when you are continually involved with cleaning toilets."

Housewives Are Slaves

Edith M. Stern

Edith M. Stern, a graduate of Barnard College and a freelance writer, described herself as a "struggling housewife." She wrote several books and articles on topics relating to domestic problems including *Mental Illness: A Guide for the Family.* In the following viewpoint, taken from an article Ms. Stern wrote in 1949, she states that the condition of the housewife should have been outlawed when the Emancipation Proclamation outlawed slavery.

As you read, consider the following questions:

1. Why does the author call the housewife the "forgotten worker"?
2. What does the author see as the costs of women's intense devotion to being housewife and mother?
3. How, according to Ms. Stern, does the persistence of housewifery affect the liberation of women?

Edith M. Stern, "Women Are Household Slaves," *The American Mercury,* January 1949.

> HELP WANTED: DOMESTIC: FEMALE. All cooking, cleaning, laundering, sewing, meal planning, shopping, weekday chauffering, social secretarial service, and complete care of three children. Salary at employer's option. Time off if possible.

No one in her right senses would apply for such a job. No one in his right senses, even a desperate widower, would place such an advertisement. Yet it correctly describes the average wife and mother's situation, in which most women remain for love, but many because they have no way out.

A nauseating amount of bilge is constantly being spilled all over the public press about the easy, pampered existence of the American woman. Actually, the run of the mill, not gainfully employed female who is blessed with a husband and from two to four children leads a kind of life that theoretically became passe with the Emancipation Proclamation. Its confinement makes her baby's play pen seem like the great open spaces. Its hours—at least fourteen a day, seven days a week—make the well known sunup to sundown toil of sharecroppers appear, in comparison, like a union standard. Beside the repetitious, heterogeneous mass of chores endlessly bedeviling the housewife, an executive's memorandum of unfinished business is a virgin sheet.

Housewifery is a complex of housekeeping, household management, housework and childcare. Some of its elements, such as budgeting, dietetics, and above all, the proper upbringing of children, involve the higher brain centers; indeed, home economics has quite as respectable an academic status as engineering, and its own laboratories, dissertations and hierarchy of degrees. Others of its facets, and those the most persistent and time-consuming, can be capably handled by an eight-year-old child. The role of the housewife is, therefore, analogous to that of the president of a corporation who would not only determine policies and make over-all plans but also spend the major part of his time and energy in such activities as sweeping the plant and oiling machines.

Industry, of course, is too thrifty of the capacities of its personnel to waste them in such fashion. Likewise, organized labor and government afford workers certain standardized legal or customary protections. But in terms of enlightened labor practice, the housewife stands out blackly as the Forgotten Worker.

Few Benefits for Housewife

She is covered by no minimum wage law; indeed, she gets no wages at all. Like the bondservant of another day, or the slave, she receives maintenance; but anything beyond that, whether in the form of a regular "allowance" or sporadic largesse, is ruggedly individualistic. Indeed, paradoxically, the more service she renders, the more hard labor she performs, the less munificent are her rewards! Which is the more likely to get a new fur coat:

the housewife who does her own washing, lugs her groceries from the chain store and makes all the children's clothes, or she who patronizes a commercial laundry, markets by telephone and shops at Modes for Moppets?

No state or county health and sanitation inspectors invade the privacy of the home, as they do that of the factory; hence kitchens and domestic dwellings may be ill-ventilated, unsanitary and hazardous without penalty. That many more accidents occur in homes than in industry is no coincidence. Furthermore, when a disability is incurred, such as a bone broken in a fall off a ladder or legs scalded by the overturning of a kettle of boiling water, no beneficent legislation provides for the housewife's compensation.

Lonely Disappointment of Housewifery

No one can estimate the shock which getting married and having a child gives to this American educated woman. From the exhilarating threshold of the world with all its problems and possibilities, from the daily companionship of men and other women, she is catapulted into a house—a house, furthermore, from which she has no escape. Her husband disappears into the outside world on business of his own, while for hours and days at a time she has no companion except her child, and the hands with which she had planned to remake the world are, incredibly enough, in the laundry tubs, the dishpan, and the scrub bucket. And so her first experience of what it means to be a mother, however much she may love her baby, is an experience full to overflowing with confusion, disappointment, humiliation, and above all, loneliness.

Della D. Cyrus, *Atlantic Monthly*, March 1947.

Rest periods are irregular, about ten to fifteen minutes each, a few times during the long day; night work is frequent and unpredictably occasioned by a wide variety of factors such as the mending basket, the gang gathering for a party, a sick child, or even more pressing, a sick husband. The right to a vacation, thoroughly accepted in business and industry, is non-existent in the domestic sphere. When families go to beach bungalows or shacks in the woods Mom continues on almost the same old treadmill; there are still little garments to be buttoned and unbuttoned, three meals a day to prepare, beds to be made and dishes to be washed. Even on jolly whole-family motor trips with the blessings of life in tourist camps or hotels, she still has the job considered full time by paid nurses and governesses.

Though progressive employers make some sort of provision for advancement, the housewife's opportunities for advancement are nil; the nature and scope of her job, the routines of keeping a family fed, clothed, and housed remain always the same. If the male upon whom her scale of living depends prospers, about all to which she can look forward is a larger house—and more work. Once, under such circumstances, there would have been less, thanks to servants. Currently, however, the jewel of a general houseworker is virtually extinct and even the specialists who smooth life for the wealthy are rarities.

Housewife Carries On, No Matter What

Industry even has a kind of tenderness towards its women workers that is totally lacking towards women workers in the home. Let a plant employee be known to be pregnant, and management and foremen, who want to experience no guilt feelings to unborn innocents, hasten to prevent her doing any kind of work that might be a strain upon her. In the home, however, now as for centuries, a "normal" amount of housework is considered "healthy"—not to mention, since no man wants to do it, unavoidable. There may be a few proscriptions against undue stretching and heavy lifting, but otherwise, pregnant or not, the housewife carries on, turning mattresses, lugging the vacuum cleaner up and down stairs, carrying winter overcoats to the attic in summer and down from it in the fall, scrubbing kitchen and bathroom floors, washing woodwork if that is indicated by the season, and on her feet most of the time performing other such little chores beside which sitting at an assembly line or punching a typewriter are positively restful.

Despite all this, a good many arguments about the joys of housewifery have been advanced, largely by those who have never had to work at it. One much stressed point is the satisfaction every good woman feels in creating a home for her dear ones. Well, probably every good woman does feel it, perhaps because she has had it so drummed into her that if she does not, she is not a good woman; but that satisfaction has very little to do with housewifery and housework. It is derived from intangibles, such as the desirable wife-husband and mother-child relationships she manages to effect, the permeating general home atmosphere of joviality or hospitality or serenity or culture to which she is the key, or the warmth and security she gives to the home by way of her personality, not her broom, stove or dishpan. For a woman to get a rewarding sense of total creation by way of the multiple, monotonous chores that are her daily lot would be as irrational as for an assembly line worker to rejoice that he had created an automobile because he tightens a bolt. It is difficult to see how clearing up after meals three times a day and making out marketing lists (three lemons, two packages of soap powder, a can of soup), getting at the fuzz in the radiators with the hard rubber appliance of the vacuum cleaner, emptying wastebaskets and washing bathroom floors day after day, week after week, year after year, add up to a sum total of anything except minutiae that laid end to end reach nowhere.

Something else enjoyed by slaves, but not by housewives, was work in some measure appropriate to their qualifications. The more intelligent were selected as house servants; the huskier as field hands. Such crude vocational placement has been highly refined in industry, with its battery of intelligence and aptitude tests, personnel directors and employment counselors. Nothing of the kind is even attempted for unpaid domestic workers. When a man marries and has children, it is assumed that he will do the best work along lines in which he has been trained or is at least interested. When a woman marries and has children, it is assum-

ROTHCO
ORIGINAL

"NO, SHE WOULDN'T BE INTERESTED IN A JOB. SHE HASN'T WORKED SINCE WE GOT MARRIED."

ed that she will take to housewifery. But whether she takes to it or not, she does it.

Such regimentation, for professional or potentially professional women, is costly both for the individual and society. For the individual, it brings about conflicts and frustrations. The practice of housewifery gives the lie to the theory of almost every objective of higher education. The educated individual should have a community, a national, a world viewpoint; but that is pretty difficult to get and hold when you are continually involved with cleaning toilets, ironing shirts, peeling potatoes, darning socks and minding children. The educated should read widely; but reading requires time and concentration and besides, the conscientious housewife has her own five-foot shelf of recipes and books on child psychology to occupy her. Most frustrating of all, education leads one to believe that a project attempted should be systematically carried through to completion. In housewifery there is inevitable hopping from one unrelated, unfinished task to another; start the dinner—get at the mending—collect the baby—take down the laundry—finish the dinner is about the maximum height of efficiency. This innate incoherence of housewifery is like a mental patient's flight of ideas; nothing leads quite logically from one thing to another; and the woman schooled like her husband to think generally and in sequence, has a bad time of it intellectually and emotionally as a result.

Buried in the Homemade Cakes

Perhaps even more deplorable is the loss to society when graduate nurses, trained teachers, lawyers, physicians, artists and other gifted women are unable to utilize their prolonged and expensive educations for the common good. Buried in the homemade cakes the family loves, lost among the stitches of patches, sunk in the suds of the week's wash, are incalculable skilled services.

But just as slaves were in the service of individual masters, not of the community or state or nation in general, so are housewives bound to the service of individual families. That it devolves upon a mother to tend her children during helpless infancy and childhood—or at any rate, to see that they are tended by someone—is undeniable. But only a psychology of slavery can put women at the service of grown men. Ironically, the very gentlemen scrupulous about opening a door for a lady, carrying her packages, or helping her up onto a curb, take it for granted that at mealtimes, all their lives long, ladies should carry their food to them and never sit through a meal while they never get up. A wife, when she picks up the soiled clothing her husband has strewn on the floor, lugs his garments to the tailor, makes his twin bed, or sews on his buttons, acts as an unpaid body-servant. If love is the justification for this role, so was love a justification for antebellum Mammies.

Free individuals, in a democracy, perform personal services for themselves or, if they have the cash, pay other free individuals to wait on them. It is neither freedom nor democracy when such service is based on color or sex.

No Liberation for Housewives

As long as the institution of housewifery in its present form persists, both ideologically and practically it blocks any true liberation of women. The vote, the opportunity for economic independence, and the right to smoke cigarettes are all equally superficial veneers over a deep-rooted, ages-old concept of keeping woman in her place. Unfortunately, however, housewives not only are unorganized, but also, doubtless because of the very nature of their brain-dribbling, spirit-stifling vocation, conservative. There is therefore little prospect of a Housewives' Rebellion. There is even less, in the light of men's comfortable setup under the present system, of a male-inspired movement for Abolition!

"The working woman must learn to rein in the traits that are stereotypically labeled 'female,' since this behavior is what men have learned to devalue and deride."

Working Women Should Be Like Men

Robert E. Gould

Robert E. Gould is a physician and professor of psychiatry at New York Medical College. His long-standing interest in the changing roles of men and women contributed to his book *Men in the 80s: Old Questions, New Answers*. In the following viewpoint, Dr. Gould, who is generally sympathetic to feminism, states that in order to succeed in the business world, women must take special steps to overcome male dislike and rejection. He urges women to suppress their femininity in the workplace.

As you read, consider the following questions:

1. What, according to the author, must women do to succeed in the world of work?
2. How does the author believe childhood experiences affect behavior at work?
3. Do you agree with Dr. Gould that most men dislike and reject women?

Robert E. Gould, "Why Can't a (Working) Woman Be More Like a Man?" *Working Woman*, April 1985. Reprinted with permission from *Working Woman* magazine. © 1985 Hal Publications, Inc.

Where are the men who really like being with women? There's a sad but simple reason why they seem so scarce: Most men really don't like women. Nonsense, you say? Exaggerated? Well, let's look into it. Shall we forget about all the books, movies, plays and cartoons depicting the war between the sexes? And all the comedians who make a living poking fun at men and women trying to relate? These are only jokes, you say, but Freud made it painfully clear that jokes are deadly serious. Like dreams, they express deep feelings that we find unacceptable on a conscious level.

But what about the women's movement, you ask? Hasn't it wrought profound changes in the male psyche—especially in men's ability to see women as equals, peers and therefore colleagues and friends, as well as lovers and mates? There is no question that the women's movement has made dramatic changes in how women view themselves. In some ways, the consciousness of men has been raised, too; they now are used to seeing more women with paying jobs. But is there a noticeable difference in the way men treat and think about women?

A new survey by Peter Dubno, professor of behavioral science and management at the New York University Graduate School of Business Administration, indicates that despite all the feminist gains of the past two decades, male graduate-business students still feel significantly more negative about women executives than do female graduate students. The students were from three graduate schools of business, and the survey was taken in three different years—1975, 1978, 1983. There was no change over the eight years—male students' attitudes about women as managers were consistently negative. Conclusion: Women can expect to continue to suffer discrimination and stereotyping for some time to come.

Learning to Reject Women

How come men have changed so little? Why do I feel that basically most men really don't like women? The origins of these feelings go back to earliest childhood, which is why they are so difficult to eradicate. From the color of the nursery—blue for him, pink for her—and the thrill of a baby boy being bounced and tossed into the air while his sister is held ever so gently, boys learn that girls belong to some other species, maybe from another planet.

Boys learn to be boys: (1) by doing what is prescribed for them, (2) by *not* doing what is prescribed for girls and (3) by not hanging around with girls. When boys gravitate toward girls and girls' play, other boys will make fun of them by calling them "sissy," "wimp" or, worse, "faggot." Boys learn quickly to maintain a separate culture and to assert a superiority over the other sex. It is part of their learning-to-be-men that they reject what girls stand for: passivity, submissiveness, cheering from the sidelines and being emotional, irrational, unadventurous, dependent. Since these traits are unacceptable, any such feelings that boys harbor either must be repressed or cast out.

One of the ways boys do this is by developing a hypermasculine or macho stance; another is to hold girls continually in contempt because their feminine traits are, by definition, contemptible ones. Boys also discover that masculinity equals power equals first-class citizenship, while femininity equals second-class.

The Corporate Game

Q: *Are women less skilled at playing the corporate game?*

A: Yes. First of all, the whole societal conditioning that women have undergone has not given them the same advantages that men have had. One of the classic examples, of course, is sports, where young boys begin to learn very early the importance of competing, of playing as a team. Many women, obviously, have not had that chance, although it's changing with more women in amateur and professional sports.

Many women have been socialized to be very honest and very forthright and therefore bring a certain naivete to the world of business. They tend to fall victim to certain myths that lead to disappointment and to expectations that won't be realized. One of those myths is the idea that the business world will be fair. Yet how many of us, for example, have been in the position where a boss will take credit for work we have done? Or how many of us have been promised a promotion or a raise, only to find months later that we aren't going to get it?

Similarly, many women believe the old myth that hard work equals success. But that is true only if you are meeting the boss's definition of hard work. People have to learn what is the right kind of hard work and the right style of doing it.

Lawrence D. Schwimmer, *U.S. News & World Report*, February 8, 1982.

What makes this task more difficult—and loaded with emotional dynamite—is that from their earliest years, boys are dependent upon their mothers, who are, of course, women. The mother is both dominant and nurturing, and thus presents a formidable figure to every son who must deny his dependency on his mother in order to become a man. This creates even more pressure to assume a macho image to maintain distance from the "other" sex—the one that Mother belongs to and that therefore must be renounced.

The barriers grown men raise against relaxing and feeling comfortable with women are rooted in these early years of not seeing women as equals, of excluding them from their "man's" world.

Since the culture nurturing these traits is pervasive, virtually

95

all of us are affected. Personal experiences, temperament, genetic and hormonal influences determine how easily any individual boy or girl can transcend this social typecasting. But all boys on some level (conscious or unconscious) are somewhat uncomfortable dealing with girls. Even parents who try to raise their children in a nonsexist way are overwhelmed by the contradictory messages around them from television, movies, commercials and other adults. Yes, men learn to translate sexual attraction into "love" of a romantic kind, but "liking" based on shared experiences and respect for "female" ways of thinking and behaving is not taught to little boys. And the process of re-education in the adult male is formidable—if he even dares to undertake it.

Is it really, then, so hard to believe that men do not like women? The amazing thing is that some men manage to transcend their cultural training and feel that the female sex is fully equal to the male.

The need for men to hold the upper hand, to be dominant, is perhaps even more necessary when the woman has a fairly prestigious or well-paying job. In my psychiatric practice, I find that men often equate their money-making ability with a sense of manliness and power. In recent decades, the idea of masculinity has shifted from the old Hollywood image of the physically tough cowboy, private eye, soldier, adventurer to a new kind of conquering hero: the man who makes his "killing" by making big bucks. Money has come to replace symbolically many of the physical feats that once marked men as real men.

And since few men can really feel secure with the masculine image they have been forced to project, money is important in separating the boys and girls from the men. Still, money has its shortcomings. For one thing, one can lose it; for another, one can make it too easily. Even women can make it, and so it is a pretty insecure peg on which to hang a masculine image.

Learning to Succeed

How can we change men's attitudes in the workplace? How does a woman become more acceptable to her male colleagues?

As a psychiatrist interested in basic change, not cosmetic cover-ups, I would like to see all men go to therapists who would "work though" their early mistraining and eradicate ingrained stereotypical thinking. This is not about to happen. So it's up to women, as with any minority group, to instigate change in the thinking and behavior of the group in power. What does this mean in practical terms?

The working woman must learn to rein in the traits that are stereotypically labeled "female," since this behavior is what men have learned to devalue and to deride.

For instance, she must not give way to emotion. Geraldine Ferraro's posture during the [1984 Vice Presidential] debate is instructive. Under stress and provocation, she maintained her "cool" and won admiration from many men and women. Behaving "like a man" is what gained her this large measure of public acceptance. She had the facts at hand, was not intimidated and held her own against Bush.

Hard work is another avenue to equal treatment. Working harder and longer hours than a man in the same job indicates stamina, determination and ambition. It's sad but true that a woman has to do more and better than a man to overcome the ingrained anti-female executive, old-boy network, all-male club attitudes of men.

The 'Femininity' Fix

A problem that virtually all women face in the workplace is treading the fine line between maintaining femininity (read "attractiveness to men") and asserting oneself in the traditional (masculine) competitive manner to move up the ladder. Without assertion, a woman may be overlooked in the pack. With it, she risks being called "pushy," "unfeminine" and that ultimate hostile put-down: "a castrating bitch."

How to stay afloat in these stormy waters? Appearance and presentation of self are of the utmost importance. There was a time when a man could not hold a good position in most major corporations if he sported a beard or nonmatching pants and jacket. This holds double for businesswomen—even today. The idea is not to wear clothes that spell out "sex object," but also not to dress so severely that one looks unfeminine or mannish.

Male Power

If there is one change I would make to myself it would be to have my voice surgically altered to a brassy baritone. Women's voices get ignored because they're soft.

Christine Lunt, *Working Woman*, April 1985

Men in boardrooms cannot conduct business comfortably with women in pink sweaters. Suits with skirts, white blouses, something resembling a tie—a scarf—will do. The look is feminine but not too sexy; not quite like a man, more like a boy apprentice. Breasts should neither be accentuated nor strapped flat, 1920s style.

Why is this so important? Men have been conditioned to react sexually to women who dress and look a certain way. In World War II, soldiers in their barracks drooled like Pavlov's dogs over Hollywood pinups. Lest you think things have changed, consider the West Point Cadet Class of 1983.

As part of the first integrated class of male and female cadets, the men of '83 were taught to regard the women as colleagues and fellow soldiers. It seemed to be working until a parade ground ceremony called for the women to wear skirts rather than the fatigues and trousers they wore during training. Discipline broke down when male cadets saw "fellow soldiers" showing their legs. The result: Women's dress uniforms were switched to pants to help keep the men in line, so to speak.

Needless to say, starting a sexual relationship with someone in the office is risky. It can threaten the authority structure of the organization and subject the participants—especially the woman— to malicious gossip. Should you marry up, they'll say you slept your way to the top....If you marry down, both you and your husband will have to deal with the perceived blow to his "fragile male ego." If she has more power or status there will be those who call him "Mr." Jane Doe....

Stepping Softly

Getting ahead means not falling back on old-fashioned giggling or flirting. But it also means making men feel comfortable when you assert authority. In dealing with men at a lower level, especially those who report to them, women have to take care that they do not reestablish a "mother/son" relationship (as previously noted, this is a relationship that boys have had to rebel against to establish their "masculinity").

A woman can soften her authority—and hence her "mother" role—by challenging men gently and avoiding direct criticism or edicts. Often, putting a directive in a questioning way ("Don't you think you can trim the budget by cutting some fat in this or that area?") takes the edge off its being a flat dictation of woman to man as to what should be done.

Some men feel uncomfortable even today when a woman takes them to lunch. Some women may have to pay the maitre d' privately or establish charge accounts rather than pay openly.

Now, I expect some women reading these lines will be feeling uneasy because some of the tactics described smack of manipulation. But men, too, have to play certain roles in relation to women and to other men. There are rules in every game, and only geniuses, artists and people of independent wealth can flout them.

Women have to raise men's consciousness by winning their acceptance in the workplace. Exposing them to women who function as well as men is a forceful step in the right direction. But those women must behave in a nonthreatening way that allows the men they work with to see them as colleagues rather than as women who arouse their discriminatory reflexes.

For the future one hopes that the changes occurring in the workplace will eventually make it less necessary for men and women to play roles instead of being themselves. Changes in society outside the workplace are key—nonsexist child-rearing, in which male and female children see fathers and mothers sharing tasks equally could put a stop to gender-related stereotypes....

But before one thinks the millennium is just around the corner, remember that tradition dies hard. Male and female roles, though forced on us, seem "natural" to many people. An uphill fight is winnable but not inevitable (backlash and defeats are in evidence.) Attack in the workplace (the adult present) *and* in the playgrounds (the early formative years)—a pincer movement—is necessary if changing women are to change men into recognizing them as fully equal partners.

"It no longer makes sense for women to dress and act and work according to men's unreal expectations."

Working Women Should Be Themselves

Mary Kay Blakely

Journalist and essayist Mary Kay Blakely is a contributing editor for *Ms.* magazine. In the following viewpoint, she responds directly to Robert E. Gould, author of the previous viewpoint. Ms. Blakely says that since it is men who apparently have a problem with working women, it is men who should solve the problem by accepting the reality of a work world half-filled with women. It should not be women's place, she argues, to meekly try to blend into the woodwork. In fact, according to Ms. Blakely, the workplace—and society—would benefit if men acted more like women in some respects.

As you read, consider the following questions:

1. What does the author believe is the final barrier to women's equality in the workplace?
2. What, according to the author, is the lesson women should learn from vice presidential candidate Geraldine Ferraro's conduct in her television debate with Vice President George Bush?
3. Why does the author urge women to continue to express their feelings in the workplace and elsewhere?

The exclusive men's club of the corporation used to be protected by what have now become embarrassing cliches: "Women are not qualified," or "Women don't have enough experience," or "Women can't handle the job." Each of these excuses has been effectively dismantled by the impressive resumes, outstanding employment records and brilliant success stories that have made news for the last ten years. Now we learn that women who have leaped all those hurdles and are ready for the usual reward—a top job in their field—are facing one more barrier. The current—and presumably final—reason women are having such trouble getting into senior management positions is that the men who deal out the promotions aren't comfortable having women as colleagues. "Most men really don't like women," Dr. Robert Gould regretfully reports in a disturbing look at some of the reasons. The solutions, however, are even more disturbing. Although he is obviously sympathetic toward women's prolonged struggle for equal treatment, he stops just short of recommending a sex-change operation....

The detachment with which Dr. Gould can dispense his advice is possible, of course, because he is viewing the problem with the unpanicked leisure of a scientist, rather than with the excruciating pain of a victim. He assigns the blame to sex roles, history, economics, education and the most commonly cited perpetrator of mental disorders, the "formidable figure" of mother. What about communism? Isn't there some way to pin this national disgrace on the Russians? Everyone is responsible, it seems, except the bigoted men themselves—the ones who clearly benefit from discrimination against women.

The Bluebird Theory

While psychology is fond of assigning female "weakness" as the reason men feel so superior to women, there is another way to look at it. My friend Harriet Miller, the director of Fort Wayne Women's Bureau in Indiana, proposes "The Bluebird Theory."

According to Harriet, the problem began back in first grade, when children were divided up into separate reading groups. To avoid the cruelty of labeling the slow learners, the groups were given names like "Cardinals" or "Robins" or "Bluebirds." Everyone knew that the Bluebirds were the slow group, of course, and with its heavy concentration of boys, the bright girls in the Robins and Cardinals were cautioned against flaunting their superior reading ability. Parents and teachers enlisted the help of the girls to "make the Bluebirds feel good about themselves."

The plan worked admirably. The Robins and Cardinals fussed over the Bluebirds on the playground at recess, fluttering about and flattering them.

No one ever imagined that the Bluebird conspiracy would eventually backfire so totally. With all this cosseting, the Bluebirds learned to feel very good about themselves—so good, in fact, that many grownup Bluebirds now run the country.

Their self-confidence has brought them into the boardrooms of America, while the Robins and Cardinals still flutter and flatter modestly from their positions as assistants and "support staff." The problem, Harriet explains, is that "the Bluebirds still haven't learned how to *read*."

Whatever the reason for the slowness of some men to grasp the great social changes of the last two decades, we are left with "the simple, pervasive and infuriating fact that the bulk of men are insufferably clumsy in their confrontations with the other sex," columnist Sydney Harris says.

"Dominance makes a ruling group stupid," Harris writes. "The male has set up an image of the 'female' (much as the antebellum Southern white did of the 'darky'), and women by now simply are refusing to live up, or live down, to this uncomfortable distortion of reality."

Men Should Express Emotions

It no longer makes sense for some women to dress and act and work according to men's unreal expectations, to dedicate ourselves to making men feel good about themselves. If these women-hating men cannot unlearn their patterns, they *ought* to feel uncomfortable. With any luck, this discomfort will cause them to pick up a newspaper and read about what's going on in America.

Women and Male Standards

Too many women with good jobs are wearing imitation male suits and little ties in meek acceptance of male standards at the expense of female ones.

Kati Marton, *New York Times*, June 12, 1985.

In the meantime, it's preposterous for the rest of us to deny what we know—the hard truths about sexism we've studied and labored to learn. What's more, it could backfire. For example, Dr. Gould advises working women to "rein in the traits that are stereotypically labeled 'female' since this behavior is what men have learned to devalue and to deride." He cites Geraldine Ferraro's factual, unemotional debate with Vice-President George Bush. Her cool detachment, he believes, won the respect of reluctant supporters.

In fact, all the commentaries following the debate expressed disappointment that Ferraro "held back"—TV viewers had only a partial glimpse of the candidate's whole power. The "real" Ferraro—the passionate and intelligent woman on the campaign trail—was ill advised to "act like a man" for the TV audience. Analysts called it a careful, but flattening, performance. An argument could be made that she lost ground by accepting a narrower definition of her considerable charisma.

It might be worth remembering, too, that the most unforgettable line in the debate, was when Ferraro abandoned that "cool." It came right after Bush's attempt to ridicule her competence in foreign affairs. Instead of enduring the insult calmly, she responded heatedly: "Don't patronize me, Mr. Vice-President." In that remark, she was insisting that even when men don't respect us, we can still respect ourselves.

Rather than recommending that women repress their emotions, it makes far more sense for women to insist that men express theirs. The discoveries of the last 20 years offer firm evidence that men's habit of emotional supression is not only unhealthy, it's actually dangerous. As Philip Slater, author of *The Pursuit of Loneliness*, notes, "Hardly a day passes without some man or boy hacking up his sweetheart for letting him down gently. The truth is that men don't handle 'scorn' at all well, mainly because they don't allow themselves to express hurt, vulnerable feelings directly."

Often, the very men in the office who denigrate women for "emotionalism" are the ones who bark at their staffs and sink into sullen moodiness themselves. I once worked for a man who ripped his phone out of the wall and threw it through a $400 plate glass window. It's a good thing he wasn't "emotional"—he was simply "angry." Before convincing more women to "act like a man," we might take the time to price a large box of Kleenex against the cost of replacing a plate glass window.

Working Harder

Suggesting that women try to win men's respect by working harder and longer hours is similarly futile. The only equality this approach guarantees is that women will one day reach men's rate of heart disease. For one thing, women who've succeeded in the professions already *are* working that hard.

Since studies show that women are still doing most of the work at home as well, there are no more working hours left in us, unless we learn to work in our sleep.

Furthermore, doing "more" than men has not earned their respect—it's only increased their sense of entitlement. "I don't know how she does it," a lawyer said of his working wife, who gets up earlier and goes to bed later than he every day. (Here's a clue: She does it because he won't.)

When women adopt even more workaholic habits, unsupportive colleagues usually aren't converted by our dedication. They don't recognize "commitment"—they recognize a fool. And women don't end up feeling admired. We end up feeling used.

The most remarkable advice, perhaps, concerns appearance.

That Woman Must Be On Drugs by Nicole Hollander, St. Martin's Press, Inc., New York. Copyright © 1981 by Nicole Hollander.

Women should dress "like a boy apprentice"? Imagine applying that phrase to real women. Should Congresswoman Pat Schroeder take her place among her colleagues in the House of Representatives as "a boy apprentice"? Should San Francisco Mayor Dianne Feinstein pose at press conferences as "a boy apprentice" so that voters won't recognize that she's a woman? Of course not.

And disguising our breasts under pinstripes or other suitings will hardly obscure for men the fact that we have them.

The real problem is not the breasts, but rather the effect that breasts have on a particular part of the male anatomy. Instead of focusing exclusively on breasts, perhaps we should spend just a fraction of a second on penises. I suspect it is really the unpredictable rising and falling of that much-protected organ that terrifies men when women are around.

Far more damaging than the actual dress of women are men's fantasies about us. While most women know better than to show up for work with visible cleavage, they inevitably pass some reminder on the way to or from work of the way men currently think of us. Consider the magazine racks that litter the business districts of every city—the innumerable bared breasts and spread legs....It hardly matters what women actually wear; we are undressed in the eyes and thoughts of men.

There's really nothing women can do about the fact that some men in boardrooms "cannot conduct business comfortably with women in pink sweaters...." And what good would banning pink sweaters do? For some men, it's a pink sweater; for others, a slingback shoe or a stray curl circling about an ear. There's no sure way for a woman to guess what image a man may find erotic.

The solution is not to dress women in West Point uniforms "to keep the men in line, so to speak." If men in boardrooms can't control their fantasies in the presence of women, I suggest they simply remain seated, possibly with a *Wall Street Journal* covering their laps, until the particular crisis has passed....

Enlisting Male Help

Ours is the first revolution in history that requires its proponents to foment change without hurting anyone's feelings.

I don't share Dr. Gould's assertion that it's only women who must change the discriminatory barriers against us. Exactly ten years ago, my friend Rich Wanush, the department head of a large city agency, received a memo from a woman who worked across the hall. The memo was attached to an article called "Why Corporate America Fears Women." It was a reprint of an address by Jean Way Schoonover to a national conference of insurance executives, which thoughtfully outlines ten reasons why men resist working with women and ended with a passionate argument for the end of sexism.

Rich, a man with a reputation for supporting women, read the article, then called the woman across the hall. "What do you want me to do with this?" he asked.

"I want you to bring it up with the mayor," she said frankly. The mayor was her boss, a man who operated from a mindless swamp of cliches and tasteless jokes and idiotic conversational droppings about women. In his first two years in office, he'd managed to offend most of the female reporters, staff members and community leaders with whom he came into contact. This same stuff went on behind closed doors with men, of course.

The woman across the hall decided it was time for men to speak up. Sending copies of the article to several friends, as well as the mayor, she gave them a framework for their discussion. She named the most useful thing men with a conscience could do: Help the Bluebirds with their reading.

For a few weeks, Rich agonized over just how to begin the discussion. The mayor, after all, was his boss, too. I know of his agony because his wife, Maryanne, and I did all we could to increase it, on weekends at the bridge table.

As a man of character, it wasn't too difficult for Rich to see that while the mayor's misogyny offended him, it paralyzed the career of the woman across the hall.

A network of women—at work, at home, at bridge—kept up the pressure, and the discussion finally did take place. It was followed by a few more exchanges. It altered the mayor's behavior ever so slightly. Now, not only the women in the office, but one man "couldn't take a joke" anymore. The audience for the mayor's bigotry was decreasing.

Caring for the Future

Will this tactic help all those women trapped in middle management by Bluebirds who can't—or won't—own up to their potential? If there are supportive men to mobilize, bringing the issue out into the open could be worth the risk. If not, they might consider a prayer...to resist the temptation to blame themselves or to assume a boy-apprentice pose and repress all that is female. And if a gold watch for the Bluebird blocking the path is not imminent, it might be time to take that other route to self-respect (and more money)—finding another job.

The most revolutionary act the Robins and Cardinals can perform is to change their flight patterns: No more tolerant acquiescence, no more pretense of acceptance. Keeping the Bluebirds feeling so good about themselves has only prevented them from learning to read—to read our expressions and their own emotions: to read the truths uncovered in the last 20 years; to read the responsibilities they have as human beings; and to read the future we want for our daughters and sons. The only genuine cure for the pervasive sexism that hurts us all is for the Bluebirds among us to start doing their homework.

Distinguishing Between Fact and Opinion

This activity is designed to help develop the basic reading and thinking skill of distinguishing between fact and opinion. Consider the following statement as an example: "In 1904 there were upwards of 3,000,000 women wage-earners in the United States." This statement is a fact which could be checked in an almanac or other source of employment statistics. However, consider another statement about women in the work force: "The truth of the matter is that the woman wage-earner is a social menace." Such a statement is clearly an expressed opinion. The belief that women who work outside the home harm society is an idea that many people would challenge.

When investigating controversial issues it is important that one be able to distinguish between statements of fact and statements of opinion. It is also important to recognize that not all statements of fact are true. They may appear to be true, but some are based on inaccurate or false information. For this activity, however, we are concerned with understanding the difference between those statements which appear to be factual and those which appear to be based primarily on opinion.

Most of the following statements are taken from the viewpoints in this chapter. Consider each statement carefully. *Mark O for any statement you believe is an opinion or interpretation of facts. Mark F for any statement you believe is a fact.*

If you are doing this activity as a member of a class or group, compare your answers with those of other class or group members. Be able to defend your answers. You may discover that others will come to different conclusions than you. Listening to the reasons others present for their answers may give you valuable insights in distinguishing between fact and opinion.

If you are reading this book alone, ask others if they agree with your answers. You too will find this interaction very valuable.

O = opinion
F = fact

107

1. The woman, save among the exceptionally wealthy, has always been the chief domestic servant.

2. The exclusion of womankind from the world's active work and her subordination to man have been necessary for society.

3. It is, in reality, the wife who decides the family's standard of living.

4. In 1904, 17.22 percent of the industrial workers in America were women.

5. Women only work while waiting to marry, and thus tend to sink to the lowest level of unskilled labor.

6. Upon the housewife fall the combined tasks of economist, nutrition expert, sociologist, psychiatrist, and educator.

7. The effect of cheap woman labor is naturally to displace men.

8. A report of the US Department of Labor shows that as the percentage of women increased in all occupations from 1887-1890, the percentage of men decreased.

9. There is no question that the women's movement has made dramatic changes in how women view themselves.

10. A new survey indicates that despite all the feminist gains of the past two decades, male graduate-business students still feel significantly more negative about women executives than do female graduate students.

11. When boys gravitate toward girls and girls' play, other boys will make fun of them by calling them "sissy" or "wimp."

12. The discoveries of the last 20 years offer firm evidence that men's habit of emotional suppression is not only unhealthy; it's actually dangerous.

13. Men don't handle "scorn" at all well, mainly because they don't allow themselves to express pain and vulnerability easily.

14. The women's movement is the first revolution in history that requires its members to work for change without hurting anyone's feelings.

15. Women have many careers but only one vocation—motherhood.

16. Two world wars and a depression have uprooted family life and created a nation-wide turmoil.

Bibliography

The following list of books, periodicals, and pamphlets deals with the subject matter of this chapter.

Caroline Bird — *Born Female: The High Cost of Keeping Women Down.* New York: David McKay, 1968.

Sandra Burman — *Fit Work for Women.* New York: St. Martin's, 1979.

Sarah Eisenstein — *Give Us Bread, But Give Us Roses: Working Women's Consciousness in the United States 1890 to the First World War.* London: Routledge and Kegan Paul, 1983.

Charlotte Perkins Gilman — *Women and Economics.* New York: Harper and Row, 1966. [1st edition- 1898]

Alice Kessler-Harris — *Out to Work: A History of Wage-Earning Women in the United States.* New York: Oxford University Press, 1982.

Maxine E. Margolis — *Mothers and Such: Views of American Women and Why They Changed.* New York: Columbia University Press, 1984.

Julie A. Matthaei — *An Economic History of Women in America: Women's Work, the Sexual Division of Labor and the Development of Capitalism.* New York: Schocken, 1983.

Alva Mydral and Viola Klein — *Women's Two Roles: Home and Work.* London: Routledge and Kegan Paul, 1956.

National Manpower Council — *Work in the Lives of Married Women.* New York: Columbia University Press, 1958.

Letty Cottin Pogrebin — *How To Make It in a Man's World.* Garden City, NY: Doubleday and Company, 1970.

Mary Shivanandan — *When Your Wife Wants to Work.* St. Meinrad, IN: Abbey, 1980.

Robert Smuts — *Women and Work in America.* New York: Columbia University Press, 1959.

Sharon Tiffany — *Women, Work and Motherhood: The Power of Female Sexuality in the Workplace.* New York: Prentice-Hall, 1982.

Virginia Woolf — *A Room of One's Own.* New York: Harcourt Brace Jovanovich, 1957.

Does Marriage Fulfill Women?

Introduction

Although 19th century feminists attacked political, economic, legal, and educational barriers to women's equality, most of them were reluctant to challenge the institution of marriage. Feminists worked for passage of more liberal divorce laws that enabled women to leave unhappy marriages and laws that protected women's property and other rights within marriage. Yet only a few of them blamed marriage and the family for women's oppression. They assumed, with the rest of society, that the vast majority of women would continue to marry and have children. Marriage was a given.

Even without direct challenge, however, the institution of marriage began to change. While industrialization altered patterns of work, taking men from the home and confining women to it, it also provided substantially more leisure for women, who began to develop interests outside the home. Many women used improved methods of fertility control to limit family size and many took advantage of educational opportunities to aspire to careers. By the late 19th century, the divorce rate was rising, the birth rate was falling, and some educated women were delaying marriage or refusing to marry at all.

These dramatic and—to many—frightening changes prompted extended discussion on the failure of the American woman to act responsibly toward her role as wife and mother. In the 1950s, the debate culminated in a backlash. A virtual cult of domesticity arose glorifying homemaking as an art and a science and blaming women who deviated from it for everything from juvenile delinquency to communism's threat to democracy.

In the 1960s and 1970s feminists angrily attacked the institution of marriage. Retaliating against the "burden" of domesticity under which most of them had been raised, feminists characterized housework as degrading. They compared woman's role in the family to that of "nigger" and "slave," directly blaming marriage and the family for women's continuing inequality. Only when women radically changed marriage and family relations or refused to marry at all, they theorized, could they be fully liberated.

111

In the 1980s marriage is still a given for most women, but many enter into it with far different expectations than did their grand-mothers. Some couples write marriage contracts detailing finan-cial obligations while others go so far as to specify which spouse carries out the garbage, washes the dishes, and changes the baby's diapers. A small but increasing number of men have chosen to become full-time homemakers while their wives are the primary wage earners. Many couples decide not to have children, focus-ing instead on careers, and many with careers pay day care centers or other women to care for their children during the day. Today, as many families are headed by single parents (most often women) as remain in the traditional nuclear mold of working father, homemaker mother, and dependent children.

These substantial changes in marriage and family life have not eliminated the controversies surrounding them. Reconciling the competing and often conflicting needs of men, women, and children remains a difficult task. The continuing struggle to pro-vide economic and emotional security, family stability, and per-sonal freedom is likely to remain an issue for decades to come.

"Marriage is woman's work in the world."

Women Should Devote Themselves to Marriage

Anna A. Rogers

Rising divorce rates in the early twentieth century caused many to make dire predictions about the future of marriage. If the divorce rate continued, they argued, it would lead to the end of the family and the ruin of society. In the following viewpoint, Anna Rogers places the blame for marital breakups "at woman's door." She argues that it is women's increased selfish and frivolous attitudes that are destroying marriage. Only by making their households their focus, Ms. Rogers argues, can women save society.

As you read, consider the following questions:

1. Why does the author suspect that women may be responsible for the increasing failure of American marriages?
2. What factors, according to the author, have contributed to women's "devouring ego"?
3. How does the author believe women can improve their marriages?

Anna A. Rogers, "Why American Marriages Fail," *Atlantic Monthly*, September 1907.

That a large percentage of marriages achieve very little beyond a bare working compromise with happiness is not to be seriously denied. Nor is it to be doubted that there are more matrimonial catastrophes to-day than there were a generation ago. In fact, every recent decade has shown a marked increase in the evil of divorce in the United States,—out of all proportion to the growth of population....

Since during the last fifty years more radical changes by far have come in the social status of women than in that of men, there is a chance that at her door may lie the cause of at least some of this fast-growing social disease....

A Woman's Work

Marriage is woman's work in the world—not man's. From whatever point it is viewed, physical or spiritual, as a question of civic polity or a question of individual ethics, it is her specific share of the world's work—first, last, and always; allotted to her by laws far stonger than she is. And the woman who fails to recognize this and acknowledge it has the germ of divorce in her veins at the outset....

Not a Dream

The wife who insists childishly upon treating marriage, either in theory or practice, as a beautiful dream, is forgetful of how very little is left of earnest lifework for a woman if she repudiates the dignified *duty* of wedlock placed upon her shoulders. Why should she not be taught the plain fact that no other work really important to the world has ever been done by a woman since "the morning of the world"? Only as a woman, with all that that entails upon her, is she alone, preeminent, unapproachable. And yet apparently her whole energy is to-day bent upon dethroning herself!

Men, at this stage of civilization, are not only the world's workers, breadwinners, home-builders, fighters, supporters of all civic duties,—they are also the world's idealists. All else is mere quibbling!

Whatever the future may develop, up to the present time no great religion, deserving the name, has ever been founded by a woman; no vital discovery in science ever made by her; no important system of philosophy; no code of laws either formulated or administered. Nor along the supposedly more feminine lines of human development has, as yet, any really preeminent work come from her. Upon literature, music, sculpture, painting, women have as yet made very few enduring marks....

The rock upon which most of the flower-bedecked marriage barges go to pieces is the latter-day cult of individualism; the worship of the brazen calf of Self.

It is admittedly not easy to remember that our lives are only important as integral parts of a big social system. Especially difficult is it for a woman to be made to realize this, because her whole life hitherto has been generally an experiment in individualism; whereas a man's since the first primitive times, has become more and more an experiment in communism. The inborn rampant *ego* in every man has found its wholesome outlet in hard work, generally community-work, which further keeps down his egoism; whereas the devouring *ego* in the "new woman" is as yet largely a useless, uneasy factor, vouchsafing her very little more peace than it does those in her immediate surcharged vicinity.

Nowadays she receives almost a man's mental and muscular equipment in school or college, and then at the age of twenty she stops dead short and faces a world of—negatives! No exigent duties, no imperative work, no manner of expending normally her highly-developed, hungry energies. That they turn back upon her and devour her is not to be wondered at. One is reminded of that irresistible characterization: "Alarm-clock women that buzz for a little and then run down."

Women Are Ignoring Their Obligations

In [the] process...[of] emancipation, [woman] has in a sense lost sight of the purposes of emancipation. Interested in acquiring new tools, she has come to believe the tools more important than the thing for which she was to use them. She has found out that with education and freedom, pursuits of all sorts are open to her, and by following these pursuits she can preserve her personal liberty, avoid the grave responsibility, the almost inevitable sorrows and anxieties, which belong to family life. She can choose her friends and change them. She can travel, and gratify her tastes, satisfy her personal ambitions. The snare has been too great; the beauty and joy of free individual life have dulled the sober sense of national obligation. The result is that she is frequently failing to discharge satisfactorily some of the most imperative demands the nation makes upon her.

Ida M. Tarbell, *The Business of Being a Woman*, 1912.

And so it comes to pass that this highly trained, well-equipped (and also ill-equipped) feminine *ego* faces wife-hood—the one and only subject about which she is persistently kept in the dark. And from the outset she fails to realize, never having been taught it, that what she then faces is not a brilliant presentation at the Court of Love, not a dream of ecstasy and triumph, not even a lucky and comfortable life-billet—she is facing her work at last! her difficult, often intensely disagreeable and dangerous, life-task. And her salary of love will sometimes be only partly paid, sometimes begrudgingly, sometimes not at all—very rarely overpaid—by either her husband or her children. One of the precise facts that young women should be taught, as they are taught physical geography, is that men, all men, have their high and low emotional tides, and a good wife is the immovable shore to her husband's restless life....

All People Imperfect

There are no genuine psychic bargains thrown out on life's counter. The really good spiritual things cost the most, as do the material things. Success in any undertaking, even marriage, is always both shy and obstinate, and hides behind quite a thorny hedge of persistence, hard work, unselfishness, and above all, patience, a quality, now gone out of fashion, which made of our grandmothers civilizing centres of peace and harmony; for they were content to use slow curative measures to mend their matrimonial ailments, and the "knife" was looked upon with horror. One finds so often in the women of that generation a strange quiet as of wisdom long digested; a deep abiding strength; an aloofness of personality that makes for dignity; sweet old faces that bear the marks of "love's grandeur." What is there to-day in all this fret and fuss and fury of feminine living, that compares with the power for good of these wonderful old women, fast disappearing?

We, of our day, on the contrary, hear much of such things as these: "Out upon your patience! If patience had not gone out of us women, we should still be sold in the market-places! From it were welded our chains, and the whole ignominy of the past."

Masculine Ideals

There is really only one serious objection to this sort of talk—it is not true. The abolition of all forms of slavery that the world has ever seen began in some *man's* brain, working from above down, not from beneath up! No great united action of women has led to their gradual emancipation. Big changes such as that have always been born in some man's big soul, an entirely impersonal masculine ideality working slowly toward the general good.

Girls are capable of great patience, energy, and persistence in the acquisition of education or what are known as accomplishments. And later on in life, if women, bent on social success, were as easily discouraged, as exacting, as irritable in the accomplishment of that task, as they often are in the undertaking of marriage, the list of the world's successful salons would indeed be a brief one. There is no doubt that the women of the day have the qualities that would make for success, even in marriage, if they elected to expend them in these commonplace ways....

Of one thing the young wife may be sure, that a man has neither the instinct nor the time to coddle his disappointments in marriage—*he puts on his hat!* This is his universal, silent, unlabeled argument, that the happiness of that home is not his business, but hers. If the fault is his, the brute expects patience; if it's hers, he expects self-control. If neither is forthcoming—well, that is her lookout! He wanted to be happy, he expected it, or else he would not have married her....

Keeping Romance Alive

Unjustly all our nymphs complain,
Their empire holds so short a reign,
Is after marriage lost so soon,
It hardly holds the honeymoon:
For if they keep not what they caught,
It is entirely their own fault;
They take possession of the crown,
And then throw all their weapons down.
Though by the politician's scheme,
Who'er arrives at power supreme,
Those arts by which at first they gain it,
They still must practice to maintain it.

Dean Swift, *Woman in Girlhood, Wifehood, Motherhood*, 1906.

Let the fault be his or hers, the main source of trouble lies in the undue development of youthful individualism. That the fault is generally hers, is of course not for a moment implied; but as the great French pessimist, in a mild mood, suggests, "Quarrels would not last long if the fault was only on one side."

On his side, nine times out of ten in this country, a man marries for love. Of course he idealizes her, and is absolutely sure that she is going to make him happy. Surely the greatest source of peril to the young wife lies in the distorted vision of her bridegroom's eyes, blinded by a passion for perfection! It would indeed be heaven if love's lens were after all the only just one, instead of being generally the most untrue!

The man's motives, if selfish, are generally as pure as are consistent with faulty humanity. At least he considers them a fair basis for a happy marriage; and he also thinks that, if he stays true and steadfast and sober, and clothes and feeds his wife, he has done his part. That he wants to continue loving her and being loved, wants happiness, goes without saying; was it not nominated in the bond?

Man's Helplessness

He is perfectly amazed when some strange, obscure element suddenly intrudes and turns his, as well as her, melody into discord; blackens his, as well as her, ideal. He is helpless, bewildered, frantic....

117

On the young wife's part, she has been brought up in ignorance of a man's make-up, of his latent brutalities in which is rooted his very strength to bear the burdens of life. Unprepared, undisciplined, uncounseled, impatient of a less thing than godhood itself, she often refuses even to try to adjust the yoke to her inexperienced shoulders, and more and more often throws it off, glorying in the assertion of her "persistent self." She has not been told that perfection does not exist; that the yoke of imperfection is laid on every pair of shoulders, his as well as hers; that no wife celebrates her golden wedding, smiling and content under her gray hair, who has not her secret history of struggle, bitter disappointment, loneliness, jealousy, physical and mental agony. It is safe to say that she also did not marry an angel, for the very simple reason that there are none—male or female—in the whole wide world. But she was blessed with that "passion of great hearts," patience, and she has been victorious in the battle of life,—the battle that we are all fighting, every one; not this weeping wife here, nor that one there, nursing her wrath.

"That marriage is a failure none but the very stupid will deny."

Women Should Not Marry

Emma Goldman

Emma Goldman is viewed by many people as a forerunner of the modern feminist movement. Emigrating from Russia in 1889, she was an anarchist, writer, lecturer, and advocate of free love and birth control. Starting in 1906, she helped establish *Mother Earth,* an anarchist newspaper. Imprisoned several times in the United States for her radical political activities, she was deported to Russia in 1919. In the following viewpoint, Ms. Goldman argues that marriage and love are not synonymous. Indeed, she argues, it is impossible to marry and maintain a loving relationship. Marriage is a contractual entrapment that both men and women should shun.

As you read, consider the following questions:

1. The author argues that marriage has been primarily an economic arrangement. How has this affected the nature of marriage?
2. Does Ms. Goldman have hope for the future relationships of men and women?

Emma Goldman, "Marriage and Love," 1917.

The popular notion about marriage and love is that they are synonymous, that they spring from the same motives, and cover the same human needs. Like most popular notions this also rests not on actual facts, but on superstition.

Marriage and love have nothing in common; they are as far apart as the poles; are, in fact, antagonistic to each other. No doubt some marriages have been the result of love. Not, however because love could assert itself only in marriage; much rather is it because few people can completely outgrow a convention. There are today large numbers of men and women to whom marriage is naught but a farce, but who submit to it for the sake of public opinion. At any rate, while it is true that some marriages are based on love, and while it is equally true that in some cases love continues in married life, I maintain that it does so regardless of marriage, and not because of it.

On the other hand, it is utterly false that love results from marriage. On rare occasions one does hear of a miraculous case of a married couple falling in love after marriage, but on close examination it will be found that it is a mere adjustment to the inevitable. Certainly the growing-used to each other is far away from the spontaneity, the intensity, and beauty of love, without which the intimacy of marriage must prove degrading to both the woman and the man.

Marriage: An Economic Arrangement

Marriage is primarily an economic arrangement, an insurance pact. It differs from the ordinary life-insurance agreement only in that it is more binding, more exacting. Its returns are insignificantly small compared with the investments. In taking out an insurance policy one pays for it in dollars and cents, always at liberty to discontinue payments. If, however, women's premium is a husband, she pays for it with her name, her privacy, her self-respect, her very life, "until death doth part." Moreover, the marriage insurance condemns her to lifelong dependency, to parasitism, to complete uselessness, individual as well as social. Man, too, pays his toll, but as his sphere is wider, marriage does not limit him as much as woman. He feels his chains more in an economic sense.

Thus Dante's motto over Inferno applies with equal force to marriage: "Ye who enter here leave all hope behind."

That marriage is a failure none but the very stupid will deny. One has but to glance over the statistics of divorce to realize how bitter a failure marriage really is.

As to the protection of the woman—therein lies the curse of marriage. Not that it really protects her, but the very idea is so revolting, such an outrage and insult on life, so degrading to human dignity, as to forever condemn this parasitic institution.

It is like that other paternal arrangement—capitalism. It robs man of his birthright, stunts his growth, poisons his body, keeps him in ignorance, in poverty and dependence, and then institutes charities that thrive on the last vestige of man's self-respect.

The institution of marriage makes a parasite of woman, an absolute dependent. It incapacitates her for life's struggle, annihilates her social consciousness, paralyzes her imagination, and then imposes its gracious protection, which is in reality a snare, a travesty on human character.

Marriage: A Hollow Sham

Either one goes on gradually liberating the divorce laws, until marriage stands exposed as a hollow sham in which no one would wish to engage, or one takes a short cut and abolishes marriage altogether.

Eva Figes, *Patriarchal Attitudes*, 1972.

If motherhood is the highest fulfillment of woman's nature, what other protection does it need save love and freedom? Marriage but defiles, outrages, and corrupts her fulfillment. Does it not say to woman, Only when you follow me shall you bring forth life? Does it not condemn her to the block, does it not degrade and shame her if she refuses to buy her right to motherhood by selling herself? Does not marriage only sanction motherhood, even though conceived in hatred, in compulsion? Yet, if motherhood be of free choice, of love, of ecstasy, of defiant passion, does it not place a crown of thorns upon an innocent head and carve in letters of blood the hideous epithet, "Bastard"? Were marriage to contain all the virtues claimed for it, its crimes against motherhood would exclude it forever from the realm of love.

A Church-Begotten Weed

Love, the strongest and deepest element in all life, the harbinger of hope, of joy, of ecstasy; love, the defier of all laws, of all conventions; love, the freest, the most powerful molder of human destiny; how can such an all-compelling force be synonymous with that poor little state and Church-begotten weed, marriage?

Free love? As if love is anything but free! Man has bought brains, but all the millions in the world have failed to buy love. Man has subdued bodies, but all the power on earth has been unable to subdue love. Man has conquered whole nations, but all his armies could not conquer love. Man has chained and fettered the spirit, but he has been utterly helpless before love. High on a throne, with all the splendor and pomp his gold can command, man is yet poor and desolate, if love passes him by. And if it stays, the poorest hovel is radiant with warmth, with life and color. Thus love has the magic power to make of a beggar a king. Yes, love is free; it can dwell in no other atmosphere. In freedom it gives itself unreservedly, abundantly, completely. All the laws on the statutes, all the courts in the universe, cannot tear it from the soil, once love has taken root. If, however, the soil is sterile, how can marriage make it bear fruit? It is like the last desperate struggle of fleeting life against death....

In our present pygmy state, love is indeed a stranger to most people. Misunderstood and shunned, it rarely takes root; or if it does, it soon withers and dies. Its delicate fiber cannot endure the stress and strain of the daily grind. Its soul is too complex to adjust itself to the slimy woof of our social fabric. It weeps and moans and suffers with those who have need of it, yet lack the capacity to rise to love's summit.

Not Marriage, But Love

Some day, some day men and women will rise, they will reach the mountain peak, they will meet big and strong and free, ready to receive, to partake, and to bask in the golden rays of love. What fancy, what imagination, what poetic genius can foresee even approximately the potentialities of such a force in the life of men and women. If the world is ever to give birth to true companionship and oneness, not marriage, but love will be the parent.

===

*"Marriage and motherhood are the most
reliable security the world can offer."*

===

Marriage Can Make
Women Secure

Phyllis Schlafly

Phyllis Schlafly is a conservative political activist who publishes
two influential newsletters, *The Phyllis Schlafly Report* and *Eagle
Forum Newsletter*. An outspoken critic of contemporary feminism
and perhaps the best-known opponent of the Equal Rights Amendment, Ms. Schlafly holds a master's degree from Radcliffe College
and a law degree from Washington University. In the following
viewpoint, she argues that even now, marriage and motherhood
compose the most satisfying career a woman could choose.

As you read, consider the following questions:

1. What forms of security does the author believe marriage
   and motherhood offer women?
2. What evidence do the prominent women quoted by the
   author bring to the question of security and fulfillment
   in marriage?
3. Why does the author believe the work of wives and
   mothers compares favorably with careers outside the home?

Marriage and motherhood have always been the number-one career choice of the large majority of women. Are they still a viable career for the modern woman? Do they represent servitude or fulfillment? Are they, as the women's liberation movement would have us believe, an anachronism from a bygone era, the institutionalized serfdom (or "legalized prostitution") from which women must be freed if they are to find their own identity and self-fulfillment?...

Marriage and motherhood are not for every woman, but before a young woman rejects it out of hand, she should give it fair consideration as one of her available options.

What does a woman want out of life? If you want to love and be loved, marriage offers the best opportunity to achieve your goal. Men may want, or think they want, a cafeteria selection of lunch-counter sex. But most women continue to want what the popular song calls "a Sunday kind of love." A happy marriage is the perfect vehicle for the Positive Woman. Marriage and motherhood give a woman new identity and the opportunity for all-around fulfillment as a woman.

Are you looking for security—emotional, social, financial? Nothing in this world is sure except death and taxes, but marriage and motherhood are the most reliable security the world can offer....

Motherhood Is a Rewarding Career

Do you want the satisfaction of achievement in your career? No career in the world offers this reward at such an early age as motherhood. In the business or professional world, a man or a woman may labor for years, or even decades, to acquire the satisfaction of accomplishment. A mother reaps that reward within months of her labor when she proudly shows off her healthy and happy baby. She can have the satisfaction of doing her job well— and being recognized for it....

"I'd Rather Scrub Floors at Home"

In unguarded moments, women's liberationists often reveal the womanly desires lurking behind their negative attitude toward men and marriage. One who heard me extol the rewards of marriage and motherhood could not restrain the tears in her eyes even in front of live television cameras. Another, with a glamorous network television job, whispered off camera: "I'd rather be scrubbing floors in my own home than working on this program." A third said, "If you find one of those nice guys who would like to support a wife, please bring him around; I'd like to meet him." A fourth conceded in a public debate, "I envy the happily married woman."...

Marriage and motherhood, of course, have their trials and tribulations. But what lifestyle doesn't? If you look upon your home as a cage, you will find yourself just as imprisoned in an office or a factory. The flight from the home is a flight from yourself, from responsibility, from the nature of woman, in pursuit of false hopes and fading illusions.

Women Are the Great Conservatives

By and large, women are the great conservatives where husband and children and home are concerned. They don't want their nests fouled. A few changes here and there to make things tidier and more comfortable—but that's all.

American women also want respect—and respect starts with a respect for oneself. The belief that one is second class will assure second-class treatment. We feel that the American woman is manifestly first class. She is gracious, strong, gentle, and courageous with the grace and good humor to see her life as it really is and not through a gauze of bitterness. She sees herself as man's partner and not his adversary in a sterile struggle for "supremacy." The little niceties that the lib sees as symbols of a lower status—the opened door, the lit cigarette, the seat on the bus—are just that: little niceties, gifts of deference from a man to a woman no more or less important [than] the chilled martini, the unsolicited neck rub, and the smile of encouragement.

Jeannie Sakol and Lucienne Goldberg, *Purr, Baby, Purr*, 1971.

If you complain about servitude to a husband, servitude to a boss will be more intolerable. Everyone in the world has a boss of some kind. It is easier for most women to achieve a harmonious working relationship with a husband than with a foreman, supervisor, or office manager....

An Ultimate Decision-Maker

If marriage is to be a successful institution, it must likewise have an ultimate decision maker, and that is the husband. Seen in this light, the laws that give the husband the right to establish the domicile of the marriage and to give his surname to his children are good laws designed to keep the family together. They are not anachronisms from a bygone era from which wives should be liberated in the name of equality. If a woman does not want to live in her husband's home, she is not entitled to the legal rights of a wife. Those women who preach that a wife should have the right to establish her own separate domicile do not stay married very long. That "equal right" is simply incompatible with a happy lifetime marriage.

The women's liberationists look upon marriage as an institution of dirty dishes and dirty diapers. They spend a lot of energy writing marriage contracts that divide up what they consider the menial, degrading chores.

If you think diapers and dishes are a never-ending, repetitive routine, just remember that most of the jobs outside the home are just as repetitious, tiresome, and boring. Consider the assembly-line worker who pulls the same lever, pushes the same button, or inspects thousands of identical bits of metal or glass or paper, hour after weary hour; the stenographer who turns out page after page of typing; the telephone operator; the retail clerk who must repeatedly bite her lip because "the customer is always right."

Many people take such jobs because they need or want the money. But it is ludicrous to suggest that they are more self-fulfilling than the daily duties of a wife and mother in the home. The plain fact is that most women would rather cuddle a baby than a typewriter or factory machine. Not only does the baby provide a warm and loving relationship that satisfies the woman's maternal instinct and returns love for service, but it is a creative and growing job that builds for the future. After twenty years of diapers and dishes, a mother can see the results of her own handiwork in the good citizen she has produced and trained. After twenty years of faithful work in the business world, you are lucky if you have a good watch to show for your efforts....

Submerging One's Identity

Among the dozens of fallacies of the women's liberation movement is the cluster of mistaken notions that traditional marriage is based on the wife's submerging her identity in her husband's, catering to his every whim, binding herself to seven days and nights a week inside the four walls of the home, stultifying her intellectual or professional or community interests, and otherwise reducing herself to the caricature of the dumb, helpless blonde, or a domestic servant.

What nonsense. It is true (and properly so) that the husband is naturally possessive about his wife's sexual favors, but he is seldom possessive of his wife's mind, time, or talents. A Positive Man is delighted to have his wife pursue her talents and spend her time however she pleases. The more she achieves, the prouder he is—*so long as* he knows that he is Number One in her life, and that she needs him.

A Man Needs To Be Admired

A man who fights the competitive battle every day does not want to compete with his wife on the same terms that he competes with other men and women in the business world. He wants the security of knowing that he doesn't have to compete against his wife. However, he is perfectly happy to have her compete against others if she wants to join in the competitive world—*so long as* he knows that she admires and needs him....

126

A cheerful disposition can guide you over countless obstacles. A wife's cheerful disposition will draw her husband like a magnet. Why would a husband want to stop off at the local bar instead of coming straight home? Unless he has already become addicted to alcohol, the subconscious reason is probably because everyone there is cheerful and no one is nagging him. If home is to have a greater lure than the tavern, the wife must be at least as cheerful as the waitress. The Bacharach/David lyrics are a good reminder to wives: "Hey, little girl, comb your hair, fix your makeup, soon he will open the door. Don't think because there's a ring on your finger, you needn't try any more."

A Woman's Task

The woman's task is not easy—no task worth doing is easy—but in doing it, and when she has done it, there shall come to her the highest and holiest joy known to mankind; and having done it, she shall have the reward prophesied in Scripture; for her husband and her children, yes, and all people who realize that the work lies at the foundation of all national happiness and greatness, shall rise up and call her blessed.

Myer Solis-Cohen, *Woman in Girlhood, Wifehood, Motherhood,* 1906.

One of the mistaken pieces of advice often given young people is "be yourself." Maybe you are a hard-to-get-along-with person with an irritable disposition who spends the evening reciting and reliving the troubles of the day and blaming them on others. Don't "be yourself." Be the person you would like to be—a cheerful person who sheds a little sunshine into an otherwise gloomy day, who sees the silver lining in every cloud, who keeps a sense of humor in the face of every reverse. A cheerful disposition will keep a happy marriage decades longer than a pretty face. Men may like to watch a beautiful woman like Greta Garbo in the movies, but she is not the type of woman men marry or stay married to. Men choose and love the cheerful over the beautiful and wealthy. Miss Garbo never married.

*"Marriage...cannot...offer emotional
security, for such security is the achievement
of the individual."*

Marriage Cannot Make
Women Secure

Germaine Greer

A native of Australia, Germaine Greer took honors degrees at the
Universities of Melbourne and Sydney and won a scholarship to
Cambridge University in England where she earned a Ph.D. Currently a professor at the University of Tulsa, Oklahoma, Ms. Greer
has made many appearances on television, written for numerous
periodicals and published several books. These include *The Ob-
stacle Race: The Fortunes of Women Painters and Their Work*, and
Sex and Destiny: The Politics of Human Fertility. The following viewpoint is excerpted from her widely discussed work, *The Female Eunuch.* In it, she argues that a woman can be fulfilled in marriage
only if she believes that marriage is a pact between equals, and
if she does not relinquish responsibility for her own happiness.

As you read, consider the following questions:

1. How does the author support her statement that there is no
   such thing as emotional security?
2. What forms of security does the author state women seek
   from marriage?
3. Do you agree with Ms. Greer that there is freedom
   in insecurity?

Germaine Greer, *The Female Eunuch*. New York: McGraw-Hill Book Company, 1971.
Reprinted with permission.

There is no such thing as security. There never has been. And yet we speak of security as something which people are entitled to; we explain neurosis and psychosis as springing from the lack of it. Although security is not in the nature of things, we invent strategies for outwitting fortune, and call them after their guiding deity insurance, assurance, social security. We employ security services, pay security guards. And yet we know that the universe retains powers of unforeseen disaster that cannot be indemnified. We know that superannuation and pensions schemes are not proof against the fluctuations of modern currency. We know that money cannot repay a lost leg or a lifetime of headaches or scarred beauty, but we arrange it just the same. In a dim way we realize that our vulnerability to fortune increases the more we rig up defenses against the unforeseeable. Money in the bank, our own home, investments, are extensions of the areas in which we can be damaged. The more superannuation one amasses the more one can be threatened by the loss of it. The more the state undertakes to protect a man from illness and indigence, the more it has the right to sacrifice him to the common good, to demolish his house and kill his animals, to hospitalize his children or take them into approved homes; the more government forms upon which his name appears, the more numerous the opportunities for him to be calumniated in high places.

Security Is Boring

Security is when everything is settled, when nothing can happen to you; security is the denial of life. Human beings are better equipped to cope with disaster and hardship than they are with unvarying security, but as long as security is the highest value in a community they can have little opportunity to decide this for themselves. It is agreed that Englishmen coped magnificently with a war, and were more cheerful, enterprising and friendly under the daily threat of bombardment than they are now under benevolent peacetime....

It is assumed that women especially need to feel secure, reassured of love and buttressed by the comforts of home. Women who refuse to marry are seen to be daring insecurity, facing a desolate old age, courting poverty and degradation. But husbands die, pensions are inadequate, children grow up and go away and mothers become mothers-in-law. Women's work, married or unmarried, is menial and low-paid. Women's right to possess property is curtailed, more if they are married. How can marriage provide security? In any case a husband is a possession which can be lost or stolen and the abandoned wife of thirty-odd with a couple of children is far more desolate and insecure in her responsibility than an unmarried woman with or without children ever could be. The laws which make divorce easier increase the insecurity of a wife. The gibe of emotional insecurity is a criticism of a woman's refusal to delude herself that she cannot be abandoned; it is hard indeed to rely upon an uncertain relationship which will become even more fragile if it is tested by demands for reassurance. The marriage service promises security: for the religious it is a sacramental sign and the security is security in heaven where husband and wife can be one flesh; for women who understand it as a kind of life-long contract of personal management by one man it is a patently unsatisfactory document. The safeguards and indemnities ought to be written into it at the outset as they are in management contracts and then it would have at least the value of a business document. A sacramental sign in an atheistic age has no value at all. It would be better for all concerned if its contractual nature were a little clearer.

"I'VE DECIDED TO BECOME A HUMAN BEING, SO I WON'T BE ABLE TO BE YOUR WIFE ANY LONGER!"

© Glasbergen/Rothco

If marriage were a contract with safeguards and indemnities indicated in it, it would still not provide emotional security. Its value would be in that it *did not appear* to provide it, so that women would not be encouraged to rely absolutely upon a situation which had no intrinsic permanence. The housewife is an unpaid worker in her husband's house in return for the security of being a permanent employee; hers is the *reductio ad absurdum* of the case of the employee who accepts a lower wage in return for permanence in his employment. But the lowest paid employees can be and are laid off, and so are wives. They have no savings, no skills which they can bargain with elsewhere, and they must bear the stigma

130

of having been sacked. The only alternative for the worker and the wife is to refuse to consider the bait of security and bargain openly. To do this a woman must have a different kind of security, the kind of personal security which enables her to consider insecurity as freedom.

The Search for Security

Women are asked to exercise the virtue of personal security even if they do not have it, for they are supposed not to feel threatened within their marriages and not to take measures to safeguard their interests, although they do do all the things: self-reliance is theoretically necessary within marriage so logically there is no reason to accept a chimeric security which must not be relied upon if it is to eventuate. The search for security is undertaken by the weakest part of the personality, by fear, inadequacy, fatigue and anxiety. Women are not gamblers even to the small extent that men are. Wives tend to limit their husband's enterprise, especially if it involves risks, and consequently the opportunities for achievement, delight, and surprise are limited.

> Marriage—having a home and a wife and children—has a very important place in life. A man wouldn't be complete without them—but I don't believe in tying yourself down until you've done something on your own first.
> Most people get the best job they can, work for promotion and when they're earning enough money meet a girl and marry her. Then you have to buy a house and a car, and there you are—chained down for the rest of your life. When you get to thirty-five you're frightened to try anything new in case you lose your security. Then it means living with all the regrets about things you wanted to do.

This is how Mike Russell, the twenty-one-year-old reporter on the *Edinburgh Evening News* saw marriage and security in 1964. What he identified was the function of the wife in screwing her husband into his place in the commercial machine. The welfare state justifies its existence by the promise of security and forces the worker to insure against his own restlessness and any accident that may befall him by taking contributions for his old age and illness out of his wages, at the same time as it uses some of his earnings to carry on developing the greatest threats to his continuing existence in the name of defense. A wife is the ally in such repression. The demands of home, mortgages, and hire-purchase payments support the immobilizing tendencies of his employment, militating against his desires for job control and any interest in direct action. If the correct level of remuneration is maintained, and the anomalies of the situation are not too apparent, the married man is a docile and reliable worker.....

If women would reject their roles in this pattern, recognizing insecurity as freedom, they would not be perceptibly worse off

131

for it. Cynics notice that economically unmarried couples are often better off on taxation deals and so forth than married ones. Spiritually a woman is better off if she cannot be taken for granted. Obviously informal relationships can be more binding than formal ones if patterns of mutual exploitation develop, and they usually do, but if women were to keep spontaneous association as an ideal, the stultifying effects of symbiosis could be lessened. The situation could remain open, capable of development into richer fields. Adultery would hold no threat if women were sure that the relationships they enjoyed were truly rewarding and not merely preserved by censorship of other possibilities. Loneliness is never more cruel than when it is felt in close propinquity with someone who has ceased to communicate. Many a housewife staring at the back of her husband's newspaper or listening to his breathing in bed is lonelier than any spinster in a rented room.

Freedom Engenders New Demands

Freedom...frightens. It presents us with possibilities we may not feel equipped to deal with: promotions, responsibility, the chance to travel alone, without men to lead the way, the chance to make friends on our own. All kinds of opportunities opened up to women very fast, but with that freedom came new demands: that we grow up and stop hiding behind the patronage of someone we choose to think of as "stronger"; that we begin making decisions based on our own values—not our husbands', or parents', or some teacher's. Freedom demands that we become authentic, true to ourselves. And this is where it gets difficult suddenly; when we can no longer get by as a "good wife," or a "good daughter," or a "good student."

Colette Dowling, *The Cinderella Complex*, 1981.

Much of the loneliness of lonely people springs from distrust and egotism, not from their having failed to set themselves up in a conjugal arrangement. The marriage bargain offers what cannot be delivered if it is thought to offer emotional security, for such security is the achievement of the individual. Possessive love, for all is seductiveness, breaks down that personal poise and leaves its victims newly vulnerable. Those miserable women who blame the men who *let them down* for their misery and isolation enact every day the initial mistake of sacrificing their personal responsibility for themselves. They would not have been any happier if they had remained married. When a man woos a woman he strives to make himself as indispensable as any woman is to any man: he may even determine to impregnate her to break down her self-sufficiency. In the struggle to remain a complete person and to love from her fullness instead of her inadequacy a woman

132

may appear hard. She may feel her early conditioning tugging her in the direction of surrender, but she ought to remember that she was originally loved for herself; she ought to hang on to herself and not find herself nagging, helpless, irritable and trapped. Perhaps I am not old enough yet to promise that the self-reliant woman is always loved, that she cannot be lonely as long as there are people in the world who need her joy and her strength, but certainly in my experience it has always been so. Lovers who are free to go when they are restless always come back; lovers who are free to change remain interesting. The bitter animosity and obscenity of divorce is unknown where individuals have not become Siamese twins. A lover who comes to your bed of his own accord is more likely to sleep with his arms around you all night than a lover who has nowhere else to sleep.

"The plain unvarnished fact is that every woman wants to marry."

Marriage Fulfills a Woman's Life

Midge Decter

Midge Decter is an outspoken social commentator who has been a writer and editor for many popular magazines including *Harper's*, *Saturday Evening Post* and *Commentary*. The following viewpoint is excerpted from her book *The New Chastity*, a scathing critique of contemporary feminism. In it, she chronicles a woman's development and concludes that a woman's entire life is geared toward the ultimate fulfillment, marriage and children.

As you read, consider the following questions:

1. What does the author give as the major reasons women want to be married?
2. How, according to the author, is a woman's status and condition altered by marriage?
3. In Ms. Decter's opinion, is a man equally affected by marriage?

However determinedly the women's movement has evaded the issue...the plain unvarnished fact is that every woman wants to marry. She may want in addition to be a doctor or a lawyer, to spend her days in travel or her nights being swept across a ballroom floor; she may dream of participating in great projects or quest for great power, long to be a celebrity or a recluse enjoying the ease of large stretches of solitude. But, except should some pathology, some unnatural fear or lust for punishment, erect a barrier between self and desire, she will want as a basic pinning for her life to be married. Women's Liberation in grudging acknowledgment of this fact says that women wish for marriage only because from the cradle on they are trained, if not simply blackmailed, to do so. The truth is, however—certainly, anyway, in the contemporary world—that marriage is an institution maintained and protected by women, for the sake of and at the behest of women, and in accordance with their deepest wishes. Men have, to be sure, for the most part willingly and in some measure perhaps even eagerly, supported them in this. For marriage is not without its very great benefit to men. Nevertheless, the true balance of the situation is that marriage is something asked by women and agreed to by men.

Marriage a Great Assurance

A woman wants to be married for the simplest and most self-evident of reasons. She requires both in her nature and by virtue of what are her immediate practical needs (if indeed the two can even be separated) the assurance that a single man has undertaken to love, cherish, and support her. As a sexual being, her true freedom and self-realization lie in a sustained and ever more easy, ever more emotionally intimate commitment to one man—a commitment in which she may know herself to be desirable and to be acceptable for who and what she simply, individually is. As a social being, her true sense of value lies in activity that flows essentially from her connection to a stable personal order. And as a spiritual being, her true fulfillment lies in the exercise of her special capacity for sustaining and refining and enriching the materials of everyday existence. Some degree of freedom and self-realization, of feeling valuable and fulfilled, she must achieve by herself; and some of it depends entirely on her ability to forge for her life the conditions in which the necessary outside intervention can propitiously entertain and be brought to bear. For this she needs a husband—one man—who will agree to keep her safe while she brings forth her gifts and who by accepting these gifts will not only provide the measure of their value, and so of hers, but will help her to her own sense of having contributed fully to the human estate....

When she is young and still, as they say, unmarriageable—an adolescent, for instance, or a student committed to completing her

135

education—a girl almost by instinct organizes her relations with members of the opposite sex around the principle of rehearsal for wifehood. There is, of course, her father, with whom, if he permits it, she may begin abstractly and inconsequentially to test certain of her powers over men in general. Quite apart from any of the Freudian implications that smolder beneath the surface of their connection with one another, her father is simply the man she sees most clearly under the aspect of domesticity. Whether she plays the game of rivalry with her mother—offering services, bestowing little sympathies she feels or wishes to imagine have been withheld from him—or whether she insistently or stormily demands of him some recognition of her own unique place in the household constellation, she uses him as a foil against which to undertake some of the definition of her private womanliness....

Following a Man's Leadership

Subjection is primarily a military term meaning to rank under *(Vine's Expository Dictionary)*. The leader is not necessarily smarter or better than his followers. He simply is appointed as the source of direction to get on with winning the war.

Likewise my husband and I accomplish much more if I subject myself to his leadership. There is no such thing as fifty/fifty teamwork even in our Christian marriage. We have enough of the old nature to make any such proposition a tug of war. And with four children—an eight-year-old who still believes she is in charge of the world, followed by three teasing boys—we need every bit of strategy we can muster.

Miriam Neff, *Moody Monthly*, November 1980.

As a young girl, she is likely to have three distinct sorts of intensive relations with boys: that of "girl friend," that of "serious friend," and that of "buddy." Each represents a separate aspect of the adult relation with one man toward which she truly aspires. In the aspect of girl friend, she seeks to find herself out as the object of and participant in sex. Here relations are bound to be troubled, for in order to receive she must give, and she is neither quite ready nor quite willing to give on the terms being offered. She and her boy friend tend to struggle—even if they are lovers they struggle—to negotiate some bargain that might be satisfactory to both. If he gives in to her, and makes the pseudo-marital commitment she demands of him, she will be uneasy, feeling him to be (probably with justice) somehow unmanly. She wants to learn, to be taught, how one day to become a wife—not to triumph. If, on the other hand, she gives in to him, she will be more than uneasy, despising herself (probably with justice) for violating her own genuine feelings about and response to sex merely to hold him. For her part, indeed, this particular struggle may never truly come to an end until she marries, when daily relations with her husband cease in this way to be political and so might be freed to become "merely," as Gatsby would say, "personal."

In the aspect of serious friend to some young man, she learns to take herself seriously—to think of others, to deal empathetically with the thoughts and problems and experiences of others, and to catch some kind of glimpse of the person those whom she respects might take her to be. Sex will not come into play in this kind of friendship, at least not admittedly, for in sex she must think of herself and explore her own experience; sexual experience, especially when she is young, is antithetical to the kind of exploration of the world out there that her loyalty and sympathy for such a male friend is meant to lead her to. But the seriousness must be provided by a man: her female friendships, no matter how intimate, will not serve her in this way. She might enjoy the best sort of relations with another female (though every woman knows how rare they are)—relations that call upon her best instincts, sharpen, even if only by competitiveness, her best talents, open and strengthen the lovingness of her nature—but they will teach her nothing about how to be serious as a woman. That only a man can teach, for it is a lesson, again, meant to be applied in marriage.

From her buddy, finally—the playmate with whom she is neither seriously nor sexually engaged—she discovers what she wishes to know about men. Since she and this kind of friend are relieved of any obligation toward one another but to amuse, and therefore of any delicate responsibility for the way they present themselves, they speak frankly, betraying for one another's enlightenment the secrets of their respective sexes. Buddydom is usually arrived at by the need of one or both to secure some intelligence from the enemy camp, that is, by the exchange of confidences about some fear or difficulty or hurt provoked by other members of the buddy's sex; and in the ensuing process of comforting, advising, or even just turning the matter at hand to sport, she is afforded some glimpse into the unguarded male mind. This friendship will, though she does not know it, be the most important of all in fixing her future course with her husband, for it is with her buddy that she discovers her capacity, or incapacity, to acknowledge the rightful existence of the terms of maleness.

Courtship as a Step Toward Marriage

Courtship, when she is prepared for it to happen, will ring a certain change in the balance of her conduct. In courtship—that is, the involvement with a man in which both he and she are conscious of a looming possibility of marriage—she will have shifted the ground for herself (perhaps only an inch, perhaps so minutely and subtly as to be invisible to the naked eye) and become a suitor.

The culture in which she lives offers scant recognition in its seemingly ceaseless analysis of marital love to the notion of pursuer and pursued; marriage nowadays is held to be a "relationship" in which uniquely shaped pieces of personality, character, social attitude, and sexual aptitude are fitted together and reconstituted into a new and entirely peculiar whole. Now Women's Liberation has added to the cultural babble its pronouncement that this whole is nothing more complex than crude but effective mechanism for the subjugation and exploitation of one of its halves by the other. In either case, one of the things obscured in the general discussion is the fact that no woman marries who does not very much want to and no marriage takes place except *because* she very much wants it to....

Most men fear getting married and most women do not. For men this fear seems to be natural, reaching far beyond the inevitable unease felt by both men and women at making so large and so singular a commitment and extending to something like fear of a confrontation with manhood, which is to say mortality itself. For women, on the other hand, fear of marriage is a sign that something is interfering precisely with their longed-for confrontation with womanhood. Whatever has been the surface of their dealings, then, in the end a man and woman will marry because he has in some way revealed his dependence on her and she has in some way indicated that he must now either marry or lose her. They will marry, in other words, because she has asked it of him and he has not dared refuse....

Women Are Biological Animals

We're very biological animals. We always tend to think that if one is in a violent state of emotional need, it is our unique emotional need or state, when in fact it is probably just the emotions of a young woman whose body is demanding that she have children....I know lots of girls who don't want to get married or have children. And very vocal they are about it. Well, they're trying to cheat on their biology.

Doris Lessing, *Harper's*, June 1973.

Their courtships are a good deal less romantic than those implied by such comic-strip revelations: carried on far more naturally and spontaneously within the interstices of an ongoing life, conducted with far greater frankness, both physical and psychological, and based upon the development of a perfectly easy intimacy. In many cases, indeed, bride and groom actually have been living and keeping house together for some time before the arrangement becomes official.

The modern couple is left to hunt around for some rationale for getting married at all. If their sex life is unhampered, for instance, and if each is, and is content to remain, economically self-supporting, what exactly are they doing licensing themselves at the hands of the state and going through some ceremony? They tend to tell themselves that they are undergoing a social approved formality for the sake, say, of their parents. But this sort of sudden accession to filial piety when offered in explanation only begs the question. Why should filial piety come into play in connection with marriage and so little else—such as, e.g., setting up housekeeping together? Another possible explanation they offer themselves is the necessity—also purely social, also imposed only from the outside—to legitimize their children. But children, after all, are not necessarily in the immediate offing; the couple may decide not to have any for years; they may decide not to have any at all. Their puzzlement is compounded by the fact that marriage itself has come to seem tentative and conditional: the current ease and frequency of divorce having the inescapable effect of clothing marriage with the aura of a mere love affair, which may be sustained or terminated depending entirely on the strength of the wife's or husband's personal satisfaction with it. Then why bother?

The answer to the question of why be married lies, of course, with the woman; but it is an abstract answer, or rather an answer she can articulate only abstractly. By marrying her, her husband has signaled his agreement to forsake all others and cleave unto her. He may renege on this agreement, but now no longer without genuine consequence. She is not just his girl friend any more.

Wifehood: A Definition of Self

The alteration she experiences will in fact, like her rationale for marriage, be largely abstract. It will involve her not so much in a change of feeling or behavior with respect to her husband, or of his with respect to her, as in a change of status. Her daily life, to be sure, might also be radically altered—she might become a full-time or a regularly part-time housewife or she might suddenly have become a good deal poorer or a good deal richer—but again not necessarily....She will nevertheless find that her life, her sense of herself, and above all the world's sense of her, have moved onto an altogether different ground. She is now, at least to a palpably significant degree, defined by the fact that she is a wife.

This will not at all be true for her husband. Whatever change marriage works in him will be private, concerned with the feeling of having shouldered new responsibilities or having been forced into a new kind of seriousness about his future. His being married may affect certain of his own habits of speech and mind, but it will have nothing to do with the way either he himself or the society around him assesses his status. A husband is an incidental thing to be, a limiting and conditioning circumstance in a man's life like any other....

She Is His

Thus he may not understand what his new wife is going through, what she is discovering about herself in marriage, just as he no doubt did not fully understand why getting married was so important to her in the first place. For her a great disproportion has set in between them. She is his, but he is not hers in anything like the same way.

She is understood to be his in several different respects. She takes his name, and in so doing undertakes to share some part of whatever will be his reputation and fate. Moreover, as the movement so bitterly complains, she will be expected to fit her own professional life, if she has one, as well as her social behavior to his needs as the family's major breadwinner. If he must live in a certain place, or in a certain style, or according to a certain routine, so must she. By marrying her, the sociologists tell us, he automatically confers upon her membership in his social class or—what may be more precisely to the point—his social milieu. But her belonging to him will make its most powerful effect upon her life in a way not generally even seen from the outside. She will be calling upon him for a kind of support and protection that naturally includes the elements of economic security and even, if need be, outright physical defense, but that beyond these serves far more importantly to hedge her spirit around with the fixed borders of care and love within which this spirit might expand and reach to its full growth; in exchange, she will hold him at the center of all her spiritual reaching, make his concerns her own and of at least equal importance with her own. This will make her extremely, and as she might sometimes feel, even excessively, vulnerable to his moods and feelings—and above all to the value he places on her offerings to him. Should he hold these offerings of little account to his well-being, or should he reject them, it will constitute for her more than a judgment on her competence as a wife: it will constitute a judgment on her very worth as a person and a woman. She has, then, freely granted him an enormous power over her. Often women who appear to be abused in one way or another by their husbands remain peacefully married while women who would seem to be treated with great courtesy and kindness grow restive and full of complaint. These apparently mysterious responses to their marriages on the part of such women are not mysterious at all, for each is responding to something far more essential to her than the appearances and manners of her day-to-day life. The husband who speaks harshly to his wife or is repeatedly and indiscreetly unfaithful to her may yet be betraying for her eyes alone how vital is the contribution of her womanly exertions to his survival, and therefore, no matter how badly he injures, he yet confirms her; he protects and supports her by needing her. Whereas a courtly husband might at the same time show her that he is largely untouched by her assumption of the responsibility for him and therefore, while appearing to honor, he in fact disconfirms her.

In other words, a woman stakes her very self on marriage. This is indeed precisely what she marries for.

"Marriage constitutes slavery for women."

Marriage Enslaves Women

Sheila Cronan

Under the broad term "feminism" are many subdivisions. One, the radical feminists, believes that women are an identifiable political class who have been oppressed and maligned by society. These people believe that in order to achieve equality with men, women must work to overthrow the patriarchy now in existence. In the following viewpoint, Sheila Cronan, one of the founders of Redstockings, a radical feminist organization, and a member of The Feminists, another radical women's group, discusses her opinion of marriage. She argues that women should never accept marriage, a male invention equivalent to slavery.

As you read, consider the following questions:

1. In what ways are marriage and slavery similar, according to the author?
2. Why does Ms. Cronan believe that women participate in the institution of marriage?
3. Do you think that some feminists would oppose the author's views on marriage?

Sheila Cronan, "Marriage," in *Radical Feminism*, ed. by Anne Koedt, et al., New York: Quandrangle Books, 1973.

Marriage has been a subject which has generated considerable controversy in the Women's Movement. So far as I know, no group other than The Feminists has publicly taken a stand against marriage, although I'm sure it has been a topic of discussion in most.

One widely held view in the Movement is represented in the following statement:

> We women can use marriage as the "dicatorship of the proletariat" in the family revolution. When male supremacy is completely eliminated, marriage, like the state, will wither away.
> —Kathy Sarachild, "Hot and Cold Flashes," 1969.

The basic assumption behind this concept, and one that I myself shared at one time, is that marriage benefits women. This idea is very much part of the male culture and is always being reinforced by men's complaints about marriage and by the notion that women are the ones who want to get married. We've all heard plenty of jokes about how women "snare" husbands, and popular songs with lines like "the boy chases the girl until she catches him." Mothers give their daughters advice on how to get their boy friends to marry them, etc. The propaganda tells us that marriage laws are operating in the interest of women and in fact exist to provide protection for the woman. From this assumption it is logical to conclude that we must retain the institution of marriage until such time as discrimination against women no longer exists and consequently "protection" is no longer necessary.

A Feminist Examination of Marriage

The Feminists decided to examine the institution of marriage as it is set up by law in order to find out whether or not it did operate in women's favor. It became increasingly clear to us that the institution of marriage "protects" women in the same way that the institution of slavery was said to "protect" blacks—that is, that the word "protection" in this case is simply a euphemism for oppression.

We discovered that women are not aware of what marriage is really about. We are given the impression that love is the purpose of marriage—after all, in the ceremony, the wife promises to "love, honor, and cherish" her husband and the husband promises to "love, honor, and protect" his wife. This promise, which women believe to be central to the marriage contract, is viewed as irrelevant by the courts. For example, in a well-known case...in New York State, a woman attempted to obtain an annulment on the grounds that her husband had told her that he loved her prior to the marriage and then afterward admitted that he did not and never would. This was held *not* to give grounds for annulment, despite the fact that the man committed fraud, which is normally grounds for nullifying any contract.

There is nothing in most marriage ceremonies specifically refer-

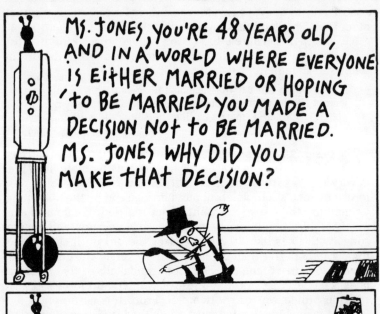

Ma Can I Be a Feminist and Still Like Men? by Nicole Hollander, St. Martin's Press, Inc., New York. Copyright © 1980 by Nicole Hollander.

ring to sex, yet the courts have held that "the fact that a party agrees to and does enter into the marriage implies a promise to consummate the marriage by cohabitation, so that failure to do so gives grounds for annulment on the basis of fraud in the inducement." An annulment was granted a New York man on the grounds that his wife was unable to have sex with him due to an incurable nervous condition.

But then, one might ask, how is this particularly oppressive to women? After all, men also enter into marriage with the understanding that love is central. Many of us, in examining our personal histories, however, have suspected that "love" has different meaning for men than it does for women. This has been substantiated by a study done by a man, Clifford R. Adams of Penn State University, who spent thirty years studying 4000 couples, researching the sub-conscious factors involved in mate selection. His conclusion was:

> When a man and a woman gaze into each other's eyes with what they think are love and devotion, they are not seeing the same thing...For the woman, the first things she seeks are love, affection, sentiment. She has to feel loved and wanted. The second is security, then companionship, home and family, community acceptance, and sixth, sex. But for the man sex is at the top of the list, not at the bottom. It's second only to companionship. The single category of love-affection-sentiment is *below* sex....

Marriage Is Slavery

The word "slave" is usually defined as a person owned by another and forced to work without pay for, and obey, the owner. Although wives are not bought and sold openly, I intend to show that marriage is a form of slavery....

Women believe that they are voluntarily giving their household services, whereas the courts hold that the husband is legally entitled to his wife's domestic services and, further, that she *cannot be paid* for her work....

Whereas the legal responsibilities of the wife include providing all necessary domestic service—that is, maintaining the home (cleaning, cooking, washing, purchasing food and other necessities, etc.), providing for her husband's personal needs and taking care of the children—the husband in return is obligated only to provide her with basic maintenance—that is, bed and board. Were he to employ a live-in servant in place of a wife, he would have to pay the servant a salary, provide her with her own room (as opposed to "bed"), food, and the necessary equipment for doing her job. She would get at least one day a week off and probably would be required to do considerably less work than a wife and would normally not be required to provide sexual services....

Women Agree to Slavery

The enslavement of women in marriage is all the more cruel and inhumane by virtue of the fact that it appears to exist with the consent of the enslaved group. Part of the explanation for this phenomenon lies in the fact that marriage has existed for so many thousands of years—the female role has been internalized in so many successive generations. If people are forced into line long enough, they will begin to believe in their own inferiority and to accept as natural the role created for them by their oppressor. Furthermore, the society has been so structured that there is no real alternative to marriage for women. Employment discrimination, social stigma, fear of attack, sexual exploitation are only a few of the factors that make it nearly impossible for women to live as single people. Furthermore, women are deceived as to what the nature of marriage really is. We have already seen how we are made to believe that it is in our interest. Also, marriage is so effectively disguised in glowing, romantic terms that young girls rush into it excitedly, only to discover too late what the real terms of the marriage contract are.

The marriage contract is the only important legal contract in which the terms are not listed. It is in fact a farce created to give women the illusion that they are consenting to a mutually beneficial relationship when in fact they are signing themselves into slavery.

The Only Way to Stay Married

Shutting one's eyes is an art, my dear. I suppose there's no use trying to make you see that—but that's the only way one *can* stay married.

Zoe Atkins, *Declasse*, 1919.

The fact that women sign themselves into slavery instead of being purchased has significance from another point of view. A purchased slave is valuable property who would not be merely cast aside if the master no longer liked him, but would be sold to someone else who would be obligated to care for him. Furthermore, the necessity for purchasing slaves ensured that only people with money could be slave masters, whereas almost any man can have a wife.

Divorce Not in a Woman's Interest

Given the existence of marriage and the fact that women work for no pay but with the expectation of security—that is, that their husbands will continue to "support" them—divorce is against the interest of women. Many of us suspected this for some time because of the eagerness with which men have taken up the cause of divorce reform (i.e., making it easier to get one). When a man "takes a wife" he is obtaining her unpaid labor in return for providing her with basic maintenance. After twenty years of marriage in which she has provided him with domestic and sexual services, given birth to and raised his children, and perhaps even put him through medical school and helped him build a thriving practice, he is free to cast her aside in order to replace her with someone more exciting. If there are minor children involved, he will pro-

146

bably be required to provide child support—which is only fair since they are his children. If he is well off financially and the judge is sympathetic to the woman, he may be required to pay alimony; if this occurs you can be sure he will complain bitterly and claim that it constitutes oppression for him. But what is alimony after all? Isn't it ridiculous to require an employer to give his employee severance pay when he in fact owes him twenty years'. back wages?...

Wives Are Owned

While wives are ''owned'' by their husbands in the same sense that slaves are owned by their masters—that is, that the master is entitled to free use of the slave's labor, to deny the slave his human right to freedom of movement and control over his own body—the scarcity of slaves resulted in their monetary value. Any man can take a wife and although he is legally required to support her, there is very little anyone can do if he is unable to fulfill this responsibility. Thus many women are forced to work outside the home because their husbands are unemployed or are not making enough money to support the family. This in no way absolves us from our domestic and child care duties, however.

Since marriage constitutes slavery for women, it is clear that the Women's Movement must concentrate on attacking this institution. Freedom for women cannot be won without the abolition of marriage. Attack on such issues as employment discrimination is superfluous; as long as women are working for nothing in the home we cannot expect our demands for equal pay outside the home to be taken seriously.

Marriage: A Model of Discrimination

Furthermore, marriage is the model for all other forms of discrimination against women. The relationships between men and women outside the marriage follow this basic pattern. Although the law does not officially sanction the right of man to force his sweet-heart to have sex with him, she would find it very difficult to prove rape in the courts, especially if they have had a regular sexual relationship. Also, it is not unusual for a man to expect his girl friend to type his term papers, iron his shirts, cook dinner for him, and even clean his apartment. This oppressive relationship carries over into employment and is especially evident in the role of the secretary, also known as the ''office wife.''

One of the arguments in the Movement against our attacking marriage has been that most women are married. This has always seemed strange to me as it is like saying we should not come out against oppression since all women are oppressed. Clearly, of all the oppressive institutions, marriage is the one that affects the most women. It is logical, then, that if we are interested in building a mass movement of women, this is where we should begin....

147

The Women's Movement must address itself to the marriage issue from still another point of view. The marriage relationship is so physically and emotionally draining for women that we must extricate ourselves if for no other reason than to have the time and energy to devote ourselves to building a feminist revolution.

Recognizing Statements That Are Provable

From various sources of information we are constantly confronted with statements and generalizations about social and moral problems. In order to think clearly about these problems, it is useful to be able to make a basic distinction between statements for which evidence can be found and other statements which cannot be verified or proved because evidence is not available or the issue is too controversial.

Readers should constantly be aware that magazines, newspapers and other sources often contain statements of a controversial or questionable nature. The following activity is designed to allow experimentation with statements that are provable and those that are not.

Most of the following statements are taken from the viewpoints in this chapter. Consider each statement carefully. *Mark P for any statement you believe is provable. Mark U for any statement you feel is unprovable because of the lack of evidence. Mark C for statements you think are too controversial to be proved to everyone's satisfaction.*

If you are doing this activity as a member of a class or group, compare your answers with those of other class or group members. Be able to defend your answers. You may discover that others will come to different conclusions than you. Listening to the reasons others present for their answers may give you valuable insights in recognizing statements that are provable.

If you are reading this book alone, ask others if they agree with your answers. You too will find this interaction very valuable.

> *P = provable*
> *U = unprovable*
> *C = too controversial*

1. Marriage and motherhood have always been the number-one career choice of the large majority of women.

2. If you want to love and be loved, marriage offers the best opportunity to achieve your goal.

3. If marriage is to be a successful institution, it must have an ultimate decision maker, and that is the husband.

4. It is true (and properly so) that the husband is naturally possessive about his wife's sexual favors, but he is seldom possessive of his wife's mind, time, or talents.

5. The laws which make divorce easier increase the financial insecurity of the wife.

6. Unmarried couples are often better off on taxation than married couples.

7. Many a housewife staring at the back of her husband's newspaper or listening to his breathing in bed is lonelier than any spinster in a rented room.

8. Lovers who are free to go when they are restless always come back.

9. Every recent decade has shown a marked increase in divorce in the United States—and all out of proportion to the growth of the population.

10. During the last fifty years, more radical changes by far have come in the social status of women than in that of men.

11. Up to the present time (1907), no great religion has ever been founded by a woman; no vital discovery in science ever made by her; no important code of laws either formulated or administered; no really preeminent work of literature, music, sculpture, or painting has come from her hands.

12. Nine times out of ten in this country, men marry for love.

13. One has but to glance over the statistics of divorce to realize how bitter a failure marriage really is.

14. The Gallup Poll repeatedly identified former Israeli Premier Golda Meir as "the most admired woman" in the world.

15. Abortions, widespread use of the Pill, and the large influx of women into the labor force are some causes for the plummeting birth rates.

16. Marriage does not offer emotional security.

Bibliography

The following list of books, periodicals, and pamphlets deals with the subject matter of this chapter.

Helen Andelin	*Fascinating Womanhood.* Santa Barbara, CA: Pacific Press, 1972.
Jessie Barnard	*The Future of Marriage.* New York: World, 1972.
Grace Baruch & Others	*Lifeprints: New Patterns of Love & Work for Today's Women.* New York: McGraw-Hill, 1983.
Carl Degler	*At Odds: Women and the Family in America from the Revolution to the Present.* New York: Oxford University Press, 1980.
Barbara Ehrenreich	*The Hearts of Men: American Dreams and the Flight from Commitment.* Garden City, NY: Anchor Press/Doubleday, 1983.
Adolph Guggenbuhl-Craig	*Marriage: Dead or Alive?* Dallas, TX: Spring Publications, 1977.
Harold H. Hardt, ed.	*Marriage: For and Against.* New York: Hart Publishing Company, Inc., 1972.
Terry Hekker	*Ever Since Adam & Eve: The Satisfactions of Housewifery and Motherhood in the Age of Do-Your-Own-Thing.* New York: William Morrow and Company, Inc., 1979.
Germaine Greer	*Sex and Destiny: The Politics of Human Fertility.* New York: Harper and Row, 1984.
Tim LaHaye	*Understanding the Male Temperament: What Every Man Would Like to Tell His Wife about Himself...But Won't.* Old Tappan, NJ: Power Books/Fleming H. Revell Company, 1977.
William J. Lederer	*Marital Choices: Forecasting, Assessing, and Improving a Relationship.* New York: W. W. Norton & Co., 1981.
Jean McCrindle	*Dutiful Daughter: Women Talk About Their Lives.* New York: Penguin, 1984.
Marabel Morgan	*The Total Woman.* Old Tappan, NJ: F.H. Revell, 1973.
Ann Oakley	*Subject Woman.* New York: Pantheon Books, 1975.

What Are the Roots of Male/Female Differences?

Feminism

Introduction

One of the familiar stereotypes of children is that little girls are "sugar and spice and everything nice" and that little boys are "noise with dirt on it." Observations of some children at play seem to confirm that many boys are indeed tougher, more active, and more difficult to control. Some girls at play seem quieter, gentler, and more responsive to adult direction. As adults, women tend to be smaller and to have more endurance in certain sustained physical activities such as running and swimming. Men tend to be larger, stronger, and, some say, more competitive than women. Some recent studies of the human brain have shown men to have superior visual-spatial capacities and women to have significantly higher verbal ability and greater manual dexterity. But if there is general agreement about any of these observable differences, there is serious and often angry disagreement about what causes them and how significant they are for individual males and females.

In the last ten years, there has been an enormous amount of research on sex differences and sex roles, and the results suggest only that the questions are more complicated than anyone had imagined. Anti-feminists find support in current research on the influence of hormones, which shows that hormones affect mental and psychological as well as physical development. They also point to the failure of experiments in non-sexist childrearing, noting that no matter how non-traditional parents try to be in the toys they give and the behaviors they encourage, most boys seem stubbornly to prefer trucks and guns while most girls choose to play house.

For their part, feminist scientists and social scientists have analyzed and successfully challenged much earlier research as being biased. They point out, for example, that "scientific" studies in the late 19th century "proved" that women, if educated, lost their ability to bear children. Psychologist Eleanor Maccoby noted that the often-cited studies of animal behavior "generalized wildly from a little monkey research." Most important, they point out that previous studies failed universally to account for the impact of environment, or society's expectations of men and women.

153

As research on sex differences and sex roles continues, the questions raised in the following viewpoints will continue to be debated. Particularly important is the question of whether it is possible or desirable to erase sex differences through non-sexist childrearing techniques. Individual parents will continue to wonder if they should encourage their sons to cry and their daughters to play baseball. Might children raised in non-sexist ways suffer from confusion in gender identity or grow to be healthier, happier adults?

" 'Inborn' differences between human males
and females can be shown to have a meaningful
function within an ecology which is built...
around the fact that the human foetus must
be carried inside the womb."

Male/Female Differences Are Innate

Erik H. Erikson

Erik H. Erikson is a renowned Danish psychoanalyst whose work
focused on problems of youth and identity. His essay called "Inner
and Outer Space: Reflections on Womanhood," from which the
following viewpoint is excerpted, provoked a major controversy
among feminists and anti-feminists. In this selection, Professor
Erikson describes an experiment he performed with preadolescent children, which, in conjunction with other information, led
him to conclude that there are innate differences between males
and females. The obvious anatomical differences, states Dr.
Erikson, echo inborn psychological differences.

As you read, consider the following questions:

1. What did Dr. Erikson observe that led him to believe that
   males and females are innately different?
2. What substantiating evidence did he observe in the films
   of the baboon colony?
3. Does Dr. Erikson wholeheartedly agree with Freud's
   dictum that "anatomy is destiny"?

Erik H. Erikson, "Inner and Outer Space: Reflections on Womanhood," *Daedalus*, Spring
1964. Reprinted by permission.

It was in the observation of preadolescent children that I was enabled to observe sex-differences in a nonclinical setting. The children were Californian boys and girls, aged ten, eleven, and twelve years, who twice a year came to be measured, interviewed, and tested in the "Guidance Study" of the University of California....Over a span of two years, I saw 150 boys and 150 girls three times and presented them, one at a time, with the task of constructing a "scene" with toys on a table. The toys were rather ordinary: a family; some uniformed figures (policeman, aviator, Indian, monk, etc.); wild and domestic animals; furniture; automobiles. But I also provided a variety of blocks. The children were asked to imagine that the table was a moving picture studio, the toys, actors and props; and they themselves, moving picture directors. They were to arrange on the table "an exciting scene from an imaginary moving picture," and then tell the plot. This was recorded, the scene photographed, and the child complimented....

Simple Differences

The differences themselves were so simple that at first they seemed a matter of course....This, is typical: the girl's scene is an *interior* scene, represented either as a configuration of furniture without any surrounding walls, or by a *simple enclosure* built with blocks. In the girl's scene, people and animals are mostly *within* such an interior or enclosure, and they are primarily people or animals in a *static* (sitting, standing) position. Girls' enclosures consist of *low walls*, i.e. only one block high, except for an occasional elaborate *doorway*. These interiors of houses with or without walls were, for the most part, expressly *peaceful*. Often, a little girl was playing the piano. In a number of cases, however, the *interior was intruded* by animals or dangerous men. Yet the idea of an intruding creature did not necessarily lead to the defensive erection of walls or the closing of doors. Rather the majority of these intrusions have an element of humor and of pleasurable excitement.

Boys' scenes are either houses with *elaborate walls* or *facades with protrusions* such as cones or cylinders representing ornaments or cannons. There are *high towers*; and there are exterior scenes. In boys' constructions more people and animals are *outside* enclosures or buildings, and there are more *automative objects* and *animals moving* along streets and intersections. There are elaborate automotive *accidents*, but also traffic channeled or arrested by the *policeman*. While high structures are prevalent in the configurations of the boys, there is also much play with the danger of collapse or *downfall; ruins* were exclusively boys' constructions.

The male and female spaces, then, were dominated, respectively, by height and downfall and by strong motion and its channelization or arrest; and by static interiors which were open or simply enclosed, and peaceful or intruded upon. It may come as a surprise to some, and seem a matter of course to others, that here sexual differences in the organization of a play space seem to parallel the morphology of genital differentiation itself: in the male, an *external* organ, *erectible* and *intrusive* in character, serving the channelization of *mobile* sperm cells; *internal* organs in the female, with vestibular access, leading to *statically expectant* ova. The question is, what *is* really surprising about this, and what only too obvious, and in either case, what does it tell us about the two sexes?...

Different Genes; Different Beings

The central fact is that men and women are different from each other from the gene to the thought to the act and that emotions that underpin masculinity and femininity, that make reality as experienced by the male eternally different from that experienced by the female, flow from the biological natures of men and women.

Steven Goldberg, *The Inevitability of Patriarchy*, 1973.

The play-constructing children in Berkeley, California will lead us into a number of spatial considerations, especially concerning feminine development and outlook. Here I will say little about men; their accomplishments in the conquest of geographic space and of scientific fields and in the dissemination of ideas speak loudly for themselves and confirm traditional values of masculinity. Yet the play-constructing boys in Berkeley may give us pause: on the world scene, do we not see a supremely gifted yet somewhat boyish mankind playing with history and technology, and this following a male pattern as embarrassingly simple (if technologically complex) as the play-constructions of the preadolescent? Do we not see the themes of the toy microcosm dominating an expanding human space: height, penetration, and speed; collision, explosion—and cosmic super-police? In the meantime, women have found their identities in the care suggested in their bodies and in the needs of their issue, and seem to have taken it for granted that the outer world space belongs to the men....

Sex Differences in Primates

In approaching the place of sexual differentiation in basic social organization, I will also call on a visual and nonverbal impression.

Recent motion pictures taken in Africa...demonstrate vividly the morphology of basic baboon organization. The whole wandering troop in search of food over a certain territory is so organized as to keep within a safe inner space the females who bear future offspring within their bodies or carry their growing young. They are protectively surrounded by powerful males who, in turn, keep their eyes on the horizon, guiding the troop toward available food and guarding it from potential danger. In peacetime, the strong males also protect the "inner circle" of pregnant and nursing females against the encroachments of the relatively weaker and definitely more importunate males. Once danger is spotted, the whole wandering configuration stops and consolidates into an inner space of safety and an outer space of combat. In the center sit the pregnant females and mothers with their newborns. At the periphery are the males best equipped to fight or scare off predators.

I was impressed with these movies not only for their beauty and ingenuity, but because here I could see in the Bush configurations analogous to those in the Berkeley play structures. The baboon pictures, however, can lead us one step further. Whatever the morphological differences between the female and the male baboons' bony structures, postures, and behaviors, they are adapted to their respective tasks of harboring and defending the concentric circles, from the procreative womb to the limits of the "productive" and defensible territory. Thus morphological trends "fit" given necessities and are therefore elaborated by basic social organization. And it deserves emphasis that, even among the baboons, the greatest warriors display a chivalry which permits the female baboons, for example, to have weaker shoulders and lesser fighting equipment.

Whether, when, and in what respects, then, a female in any setting is "weaker" is a matter to be decided not on the basis of comparative tests of isolated muscles, capacities, or traits but on that of the functional fitness of each item as part of an organism which, in turn, fits into an ecology of divided function.

Biological Sex Differentiation

Human society and technology has, of course, transcended evolutionary arrangement, making room for cultural triumphs and liberties as well as for physical and psychological maladaptation on a large scale. But when we speak of biologically given strengths and weaknesses in the human female, we may yet have to accept as one measure of all difference the biological rockbottom of sexual differentiation. In this, the woman's productive inner space may well remain the principal criterion, whether she chooses to build her life partially or wholly around it or not. At any rate, many of the testable items on the long list of "inborn" differences between human males and females can be shown to have a meaningful function within an ecology which is built, as any mammalian ecology must be, around the fact that the human foetus must be carried inside the womb for a given number of months; and that the infant must be suckled or, at any rate, raised within a maternal world best staffed at first by the mother (and this for the sake of her own awakened motherliness as well as for the newborn's needs), with a gradual addition of other women. Here years of specialized womanhours of work are involved. It makes sense, then, that the little girl, the bearer of ova and of maternal powers, tends to survive her birth more surely and is a tougher creature, to be plagued, to be sure, by many small ailments, but more resistant to some man-killing diseases (for example, of the heart) and with a longer life expectancy. It also makes sense that she is able earlier than boys to concentrate on details immediate in time and space, and has throughout a finer discrimination for things seen, touched, and heard. To these she reacts more vividly, more personally, and with greater compassion. More easily touched and touchable, however, she is said to also recover faster, ready to react again and elsewhere. That all of this is essential to the "biological" task of reacting to the differential needs of others, especially infants, will not appear to be a farfetched interpretation; nor will it, in this context, seem a deplorable inequality that in the employment of larger muscles she shows less vigor, speed, and coordination. The little girl also learns to be more easily content within a limited circle of activities and shows less resistance to control and less impulsivity of the kind that later leads boys and men to "delinquency." All of these and more certified "differences" could be shown to have corollaries in our play constructions.

Unique Gender Differences

Extensive documentation now exists that the sexes differ in brain structure and function. For example: the male canary sings, the female does not. Their behavior is different and so are their brains. With manipulation of sex hormones, the female becomes male-like: she sings and her brain develops male morphology....

Even the uniquely human function of speech and language appears to have a different neural substrate in the sexes.

S.F. Witelson, *New York Review of Books*, October 24, 1985.

Now it is clear that much of the basic schema suggested here as female also exists in some form in all men and decisively so in men of special giftedness—or weakness. The inner life which characterizes some artistic and creative men certainly also compensates for their being biologically men by helping them to specialize in that inwardness and sensitive indwelling (the German *Innigkeit*) usually ascribed to women. They are prone to cyclic swings of mood while they carry conceived ideas to fruition and toward the act of disciplined creation. The point is that in women the basic schema exists within a *total optimum configuration* such as cultures have every reason to nurture in the majority of women,

159

and this for the sake of collective survival as well as individual fulfillment. It makes little sense, then, when discussing basic sex-differences to quote the deviations and accomplishments (or both) of exceptional men or women without an inclusive account of their many-sided personalities, their special conflicts and their complex life histories. On the other hand, one should also emphasize...that successive stages of life offer growing and maturing individuals ample leeway for free variation in essential sameness.

Importance of Total Configuration

Thus only a total configurational approach...can help us to see the differences of functioning and experiencing in context rather than in isolated and senseless comparison. Woman, then, is not "more passive" than man simply because her central biological function forces her or permits her to be active in a manner tuned to inner-bodily processes, or because she may be gifted with a certain intimacy and contained intensity of feeling, or because she may choose to dwell in the protected inner circle within which maternal care can flourish. Nor is she "more masochistic" because she must accept inner periodicities...in addition to the pain of childbirth, which is explained in the Bible as the eternal penalty for Eve's delinquent behavior and interpreted by writers as recent as [Simone] de Beauvoir as "a hostile element within her own body." Taken together with the phenomena of sexual life and motherhood, it is obvious that woman's knowledge of pain makes her a "dolorosa" in a deeper sense than one who is addicted to small pains. She is, rather, one who "takes pains" to understand and alleviate suffering, and who can train others in the forbearance necessary to stand unavoidable pain. She is a "masochist," then, only when she exploits pain perversely or vindictively, which means that she steps out of, rather than deeper into, her female function....

One argument, however, is hard to counter. Woman, through the ages (at any rate, the patriarchal ones), has lent herself to a variety of roles conducive to an exploitation of masochistic potentials: she has let herself be incarcerated and immobilized, enslaved and infantilized, prostituted and exploited, deriving from it at best what in psychopathology we call "secondary gains" of devious dominance. This fact, however, could be satisfactorily explained only within a new kind of biocultural history which (and this is one of my main points) would first have to overcome the prejudiced opinion that woman must be, or will be, what she is or has been under particular historical conditions.

Am I saying, then, that "anatomy is destiny"? Yes, it is destiny, insofar as it determines the potentials of physiological functioning, and its limitations. But anatomy also, to an extent, co-determines personality configurations. The modalities of woman's commitment and involvement, for better *and* for worse, also reflect the ground-plan of her body. We may mention only woman's capacity on many levels of existence to (actively) include, to accept, to "have and hold"—but also to hold on, and to hold in. She may be protective with high selectivity, and overprotective without discrimination. That she must protect means that she must rely on protection—and she may demand overprotection. She too has her organ of intrusion, the nipple which nurses; and her wish to succor can, indeed, become intrusive and oppressive. It is, in fact, of such exaggerations and deviations that many men and also women think when the unique potentials of womanhood are discussed.

In all of this, however, the problem is not whether a woman is "more so" than a man, but how much she varies within womanhood, and what she makes of it within the leeway of her stage of life and of her historical and economic opportunities. For man, in addition to having a body, is *some*body; which means he is an indivisible personality *and* a defined member of a group. In this sense Napoleon's dictum that *History is destiny*...is equally valid. In other words: anatomy, history, and personality are our *combined destiny.*

"One can only conclude that the female is more completely and more negatively conditioned than the male."

Male/Female Differences Are Culturally Imposed

Kate Millett

Kate Millett is a feminist activist and author who received her Ph.D. from Columbia University. The author of several books including the immensely influential *Sexual Politics* from which this viewpoint is taken, Ms. Millett believes that the differences between males and females which are "proven" by scientific studies are more often a product of learning rather than being inborn. In the following excerpt, she debates the conclusions of Erik Erikson (see previous viewpoint). She argues that Professor Erikson began with false assumptions and did not thoroughly study the possibilities suggested by his experiment.

As you read, consider the following questions:

1. What conclusions does Ms. Millett believe are more likely than those Dr. Erikson drew from his experiment with toys and building blocks?
2. How does Ms. Millett say education, both formal and informal, affects male/female differences?
3. What dangers does the author perceive in views such as those presented by Dr. Erikson?

Recently, two new statements on sexual differences have appeared. Both argue from "nature" by presupposing congenital temperaments for the two sexes. Lionel Tiger has defined patriarchy and male dominance as the function of a "bonding" instinct inherent in the male....Erik Erikson's formulation that a relation to inner and outer space differentiates the sexes is more benign and probably more influential. Retaining a Freudian or psychoanalytic theory of female personality and the notion that this is innate, Erikson adds something new in suggesting "femininity" is socially and politically useful.

Erikson begins his famous essay "Womanhood and the Inner Space"[1] by deprecating that part of male achievement which has brought the race to the brink of destruction, appealing to women to save it....

Culturally Conditioned Traits

One finds it hard not to agree that the conduct of human affairs under male dominance has produced our present predicament (the essay was written under the shadow of the Bomb) and that the temperamental traits Erikson assigns to women would be eminently useful in the conduct of society. What Erikson does not recognize is that the traits of each group are culturally conditioned and depend upon their political relationship, which has been relatively constant throughout history regardless of contemporary crises. Instead, the entire emphasis of his essay, and the whole force of the experiment on which his theory is based, is to convince us that complementary masculine and feminine traits are inherently male and female. Erikson has perceived that much of what we know as masculine in our culture is and must be recognized as progressively antisocial and dangerous even to the preservation of the species, while much of what we know as feminine is directly related to its well-being. The logical recommendation to be made from this does seem to be a synthesis of the two sexual temperaments. Even acknowledging that, under the present circumstances of two sharply divided sexual cultures, we could achieve a human balance only through co-operation of the two groups with their fragmented collective personalities, one must really go further and urge a dissemination to members of each sex of those socially desirable traits previously confined to one or the other while eliminating the bellicosity or excessive passivity useless in either. But to do this is considerably beyond Erikson's scope, since he believes in the existence of innate sexual temperament and imagines the experiment [with toys and blocks] he relates is proof of it....

What the experiment does seem to illustrate, and with remarkable clarity, is that each group responded with extreme sensitivity to its conditioning; one to passive domesticity, the other to egoistic achievement, partly constructive (towers, machines, ornament) and partly destructive (cannons, accidents, ruins). Yet for all the efficiency of the socialization (perhaps somewhat facilitated by Erikson's standardized Hollywood movie equipment) not every youth responded as planned. Some unaccounted for number failed to conform: a girl who did outside scenes is dismissed as a "tomboy," a boy who was insufficiently aggressive would also register as a deviate (effeminate), popularly regarded as a graver danger. One must also recall the normative attitude in which sexual identity is viewed. In 1964, when this study was first publicized, sexual reaction had created a climate where failure to conform to sexual category was seen as unhealthy or disturbing....

Psychologists Blinded by Sexist "Norms"

It is an interesting but limited exercise to show that psychologists and psychiatrists embrace these sexist norms of our culture, that they do not see beyond the most superficial and stultifying media conceptions of female nature, and that their ideas of female nature serve industry and commerce so well. Just because it's good for business doesn't mean it's wrong....It *is* wrong;...there isn't the tiniest shred of evidence that these fantasies of servitude and childish dependence have anything to do with women's true potential;...the idea of the nature of human possibility which rests on the accidents of individual development of genitalia, on what is possibly today because of what happened yesterday, on the fundamentalist myth of sex organ causality, has strangled and deflected psychology so that it is relatively useless in describing, explaining or predicting humans and their behavior. It then goes without saying that present psychology is less than worthless in contributing to a vision which could truly liberate—men as well as women....

Psychology has nothing to say about what women are really like, what they need and what they want, essentially because psychology does not know. I want to stress that this failure is not limited to women; rather, the kind of psychology which has addressed itself to how people act and who they are has failed to understand, in the first place, why people act the way they do, and certainly failed to understand what might make them act differently.

Naomi Weisstein, *New England Free Press*, 1968.

As an experiment, there is so much in Erikson's report and in the implications he derives from it, which will not bear scrutiny, that its claim to be accepted as scientific evidence is negligible indeed. It does, however, tell us a good deal about Erikson, a man genuinely interested in peace and the "feminine" virtues, although apparently quite unable to conceive that since they are humanly valuable they should, logically, be equally valuable for both sexes.

Within the experiment no variable was employed, no attempt to reverse proceedings, both of which are essential when one is trying to prove inherency, since what is not arbitrary, imposed, irrelevant, acquired, or learned, will continue to be manifest despite other instructions or modifications in the situation. Erikson's whole theory is built on psychoanalysis' persistent error of mistaking learned behavior for biology....

Erikson believes he has answered objections by the disclosure that photos of his subjects' constructions were sex-identifiable to his colleagues. This is not very conclusive, since his teen-agers themselves proved so adept at taking such conspicuous cultural clues. The behavior of the subjects themselves is insisted on: "If the boys thought primarily of their present or anticipated roles, why, for example, is the policeman their favorite toy?" Why indeed...

Possibly the motive is revealed in Erikson's question—a policeman is an authority figure operating by physical force, and it is just this idea of himself that official educators such as public schools and the producers of textbooks wish to inculcate in the little male. Why boys choose policemen to align themselves with and girls do not is hardly a question; apart from the fact that they are taught to make sex-category identifications and policemen are not women, every child, or rather most of those in Erikson's test, is fully aware that boys are supposed to play with policemen and girls are not. What might be more productive to study is the child who has broken the magic circle of programmed learning so that one could isolate elements which helped in transcending the cultural mold. How, for example, does a tomboy arrive at the positive "aggression" of an outdoor scene, or a boy arrive at a peaceful scene; the one escaping the doll house which has been successfully inflicted on her peers, the other the malevolence inflicted on his.

Female Education

Eleanor Maccoby's informative article on female intelligence offers some clues to this sort of question by pointing out that the independence and ego-strength necessary for first-rate achievement in certain analytical fields is completely absent from the cultural experience of nearly every girl child. Other experiments have proven that the field orientation and dependency, the reliance upon approval and destructive attention which is the general course of female upbringing, produces in boys, a condition of passivity and infantilism considered extremely detrimental to achievement and even to maturity. The double standard of formal, and even informal, education decrees what is harmful to one group is beneficial to another. And so it is if one approves an arrested development for half the race at the level of "playing house." While it is indisputable that the games of both sexes were, as the result of Erikson's choice of materials, notably banal, those for the girls were, for all the sedate feminine virtue the investigator found in them, but the prediction of stereotypical domestic lives; those of the boys had the seeds of something that might become real achievement, architectural, technological and exploratory, as well as moronic violence and war.

Anatomy Is Only *Part* of Destiny

All anatomy does is to make some associative patterns *more likely* in one sex than the other if nature takes her course, and if nothing is done to change what would normally be learned. So, unfortunately, the facts of science cannot dictate what women should be and do. In fact, many women...are more masculine than the average man. Science certainly cannot assert that women can't behave like men or vice versa. Nature leaves society a choice, but it does bias the outcome if nothing is done to reverse normal learning.

David C. McClelland, in *The Woman in America*, 1964, 1965.

The pacific, rather than merely passive character which Erikson ascribes to the girls' play is of course most depressing in view of the fact it lacks all possibility of social implementation until the female "sphere" becomes not the doll's house inner space Erikson endorses, but the world. What is perhaps most discouraging of all is not even the masculine fixation on violence but the futility of the girls' sedentary dream, even its barrenness, for they sit awaiting the "intrusion of men and animals" (a remarkable combination) and doing nothing at all—not even the "nurturance" expected of them. [He asks,]

> Could the role of playing the piano in the bosom of their families really be considered representative of what these girls (some of them passionate horseback riders and all future automobile drivers) wanted to do most or, indeed thought they should pretend they wanted to do?

Unless we assume, as Erikson does, that the pianos in some obscure manner do pertain to inherent female nature as "natural reasons which must claim our interest," the very "spatial order" of their sex, one can only conclude that the female is more completely and more negatively conditioned than the male. And it seems she has to be in order to fulfill the far more limited existence or, in jargon, "role" which Erikson and his confreres would continue to prescribe for her. Erikson himself takes satisfaction from the more "limited circle of activities" which girls are permitted in society, and the "less resistance to control" they exhibit than do males. The latter phrase may be rendered in one word—docility....

There is a certain awkwardness in the fact that no matter how he tries to brighten the picture, Erikson is incapable of stopping at the right moment, but must always go on to exhibit his own distaste or misgiving for the situation he is trying to reinterpret in such positive terms. Even the possession of a womb becomes a detriment, leaving the female "unfulfilled" every moment she is not pregnant....

Erikson disclaims any intention to "doom" woman to perpetual motherhood or "deny her the equivalence of individuality and the equality of citizenship;" he is simply eager that she not "compete" or participate in the "active male proclivities" of civilization. Since "woman is never not-a-woman," as he states with assumed profundity, it is clear that once she has proven herself equal to "men's performance and competence in most spheres of achievement"— and it is said that she has—Erikson is content to assume that the potential equality of the sexes is proven, without requiring that their actual inequality be modified. He implies woman would do well to rely upon her "right to be uniquely creative" through maternity and think little further.... Erikson appears to believe women are "better" and therefore should offer a vicarious and remote moral assistance to the male. Yet...there is a fairly clear understanding that civilization is a male department. And since both masculine vanity and masculine uneasiness (lest "femininity" be lost...) prevent the male from acquiring the humanity attributed to woman, or woman from transcending her politically and socially powerless role, Erikson is...unlikely to realize his hopes.... Others, less sincere than Erikson, may find in his theory a splendid rationale to insure that the "outer space" of the technological future and every means of social and political control remain exclusively male prerogative. And to such an end fables about "inner space" are very expedient myth.

[1] Erik Erikson, "Womanhood and the Inner Space" (1964), *Identity, Youth and Crisis* (New York, W.W. Norton, 1968). First printed in *Daedalus*, The Journal of the American Academy of Arts and Sciences, Spring 1964.

"The differences between boys and girls [are]
so obvious and uniform as to be clearly innate."

Male/Female Differences Are Obvious

Michael Levin

Michael Levin is a professor of philosophy at City College of New
York. An ardent opponent of feminist attitudes, he has written
a forthcoming book called *Feminism and Freedom*. His articles are
frequently published in conservative journals. In the following
viewpoint, Mr Levin argues that feminists' attacks on innate sex
differences are ill-founded and ultimately dangerous.

As you read, consider the following questions:

1. What evidence does Professor Levin present to prove that
   sex differences are innate?
2. Why, according to the author, is it so important to
   feminists that sex differences be learned and not innate?
3. Why does Professor Levin object to use of the term "sex
   roles"?

Feminism in its contemporary form is an empirical doctrine leading to recomendations for social action. The doctrine has three main tenets:

1. Physical differences apart, men and women are the same. Infant boys and girls are born with virtually the same capacities to acquire skills and motives, and if raised identically would develop identically.

2. Men occupy positions of dominance because the myth that men are more aggressive has been perpetuated by the practice of raising boys to be mastery-oriented and girls to be person-oriented. If this stereotyping ceased, leadership would be equally divided between the sexes.

3. True human individuality and fulfillment will come only when people view themselves as *human* repositories of talents and traits, without regard to sex....

This tendency to dismiss the factual question of gender differences as irrelevant to the demand for gender equality is completely misguided. If there are important biologically-based differences between the sexes, the rest of contemporary feminism falls apart. Moral prescriptions and social programs cannot be concocted in an empirical vacuum. It is senseless to try to make the sexes conform to an "androgynous" ideal if they cannot conform to it. What is obviously unattainable cannot be the object of rational human effort. In this sense, if the factual assumption of feminism is wrong, the rest is irrational....

No Convincing Feminist Evidence

It would be good to examine the most rigorous presentation of the social-causation theory of sex differences. Unfortunately, despite the walls of books on "women" that line every bookstore, no such presentation exists. Contemporary feminism has yet to produce a single work that seriously challenges a skeptic.

We may dismiss the scores of works that simply *assert* the similarity of the sexes. We may dismiss the many memoirs of dissatisfied women and the meaningless agglomerations of anecdotes that feminists so often mistake for argument. We may dismiss accounts of exceptional women, for at issue is what is true of men and women on the whole. We may dismiss the extensive catalogue of books and articles forever demonstrating what no one denies: that men occupy more positions of power than women, that society judges male philandering less harshly than female, that popular films and literature have seldom shown women as leaders. The question is *why* these things are so.

The innate similarity of the sexes is sometimes supported by catchy but dubious analogies. In attempting to meet the worry that an army with women in combat-support positions would be at a disadvantage, a recent federal court decision ruling all-male

169

draft registration unconstitutional states:

> Oriental men are also significantly lighter and shorter than Caucasians on the average, but this in no way precludes their use in the military, nor has it precluded various Asian nations from fielding very effective fighting forces.

The Myth of Equality

Once women accepted the mythical idea that they were identical with men, it was automatic that they should revolt against every contrary fact; womanhood itself is such a fact. People, unfortunately, have an extravagant capacity to live by myths; they are able completely to delude themselves for centuries at a clip. But the difficulty with mythological faiths is that, sooner or later, reality catches up and the public cost is in keeping with the size of the common error.

A bright six-year-old could see that the same brain would produce differing climates and behaviors on the very different bodies of a man and a woman. Frantic psychologists, neurologists, endocrinologists, anthropologists and sane laymen have been trying to restore that simple truth to view ever since the theory of diploma-equality was inflated and distorted into the legend that equal school marks mean identical Everything.

Of course, if men and women *are* identical, the history of humanity is inexplicable. So, of course, they are not.

Philip Wylie, *American Scholar*, 1950.

Ignored here is the simple fact that those effective Oriental armies have been composed of Oriental *men*, who are indeed smaller and lighter than Occidental men, but pound for pound much stronger and tougher than women....And quite apart from the matter of physical strength, the decision makes no effort to show that women, Oriental or Occidental, are as aggressive or physically courageous as men. All the evidence—the experience of Israel in the first Arab war, and Russia and Germany in World War II—is negative. Yet it remains almost a reflex to dismiss the greater aggressiveness of men as socially caused. Here is Dr. Estelle Ramey:

> As an endocrinologist, I think virtually all the differences in male and female behavior are culturally, not hormonally, determined....It is said, for instance, that men are innately more aggressive than women. But conditioning, not sex hormones, makes them that way. Anyone seeing women at a bargain-basement sale—where aggression is viewed as appropriate—sees aggression that would make Attila the Hun turn pale.

It is hard to take this analogy seriously but harder to find anything more trenchant in the literature. Is Dr. Ramey suggesting that one woman would put another to the sword over a choice bit of lingerie, and then kill her relatives to avert a blood feud? In general, the most commonly cited examples of female aggressiveness unleashed—intransigence at faculty meetings, clawing up the corporate ladder—uniformly lack the steadfast murderousness that men have exhibited "where aggression is viewed as appropriate." During Rommel's North African campaign, German and English tank crews kept at their posts month after month while watching their comrades literally being blown to bits. No instance of female aggression parallels this, not even the seemingly obligatory inclusion of a female on bombings or kidnappings by leftist terrorists. War may be loathsome, but only males have ever been capable of waging it.

Strong Evidence for Sex Differences

Since today's feminism seems able to make people doubt what they have seen confirmed from childhood on, let us proceed to review some scientific evidence for "gender dimorphism." But I want to stress that the principal evidence is what anyone who watches little children can see. Not only are the differences between boys and girls so obvious and uniform as to be clearly innate, each of us has experienced the differences as innate while growing up.

But scientific evidence is wanted, so scientific evidence we shall have....

There is, first, a large body of work by John Money and other physiologists documenting the effect of hormones on human development. Most people know that much sex-distinctive behavior is triggered by hormones: the sound of a baby's voice, for instance, will release oxytocin in a woman, making it hard for her to resist attending to the baby. But the full story involves more. The male hormone testosterone not only affects postnatal behavior, but also plays a large role in shaping the central nervous system of fetuses. Given that some of the other differences between males and females to be mentioned below involve differences in neural processing, it seems that from the beginning boys and girls are built by their hormones to perceive and behave differently.

In the cognitive domain, R. Darrell Bock and Donald Kolakowski have documented "a pronounced difference in favor of males" in the ability to visualize spatially, the familiar capacity to imagine what three-dimensional objects look like when rotated. They calculate this difference to be 46 percent genetic in cause. By analyzing the existing statistical literature and their own experiments, they are able to demonstrate in particular that the ability to visualize spatially occurs in humans exactly as it would if it were determined by a sex-linked recessive gene. As with other sex-linked traits, the correlation for the presence of this ability is

171

especially high between sons and their mothers. What is significant about this latter fact is that it rules out "environmentalist" explanations for the superiority in this area of males, such as, for example, that fathers teach their sons to catch fly balls and handle tools....

Male and Female Brains

These gender differences in spatial abilities become more pronounced as children mature. Nor is this a matter of "culture taking over"; some ingenious experiments with left-handers, whose neural organization is the mirror-image of the usual, show that these sex-associated differences are induced by the now-familiar differences between the cerebral hemispheres.

Masculine Logic

In other words, the stereotype that sees the male as more logical than the female is unquestionably correct in its observation and probably correct in its assumption that the qualities observed conform to innate sexual limitations analogous to those relevant to physical strength. Society's socializing girls away from careers in mathematics may well be an acknowledgment of hormonal reality. An ability to deal with high-level abstractions *is* unfeminine in the statistical sense and it is on such statistical realities that social conceptions are—for all the reasons we have discussed—based. A woman who possesses such an ability possesses an ability that we *correctly* tend to associate with men. Her ability is "unfeminine" only in the sense that a six-foot woman's height is unfeminine (i.e., the quality of being six feet tall is usually associated, correctly, with men). Undeniably the female mathematical genius will meet discrimination (she will be discouraged where a man of equal ability will be encouraged), but this is an inevitable result of the fact that a mathematical genius who is a female will always be a very rare exception.

Steven Goldberg, *The Inevitability of Patriarchy,* 1973.

As a kind of synthetic union of these results, a number of investigators have found that the female brain responds more powerfully to almost any stimulus than does the male brain, a fact which would explain the common-sense observation that women are more "sensitive" than men, and more prone to stress. Similarly, the sex-linkage and high heritability of spatial-visualizing ability offers a non-sociological explanation of the "dominance" of men in painting and certain branches of mathematics. Finally, one might mention the more speculative suggestions of sociobiologists who have proposed interesting "models" in which gender dimorphism is an optimally adaptive evolutionary strategy.

These studies would be merely suggestive and not conclusive

if "sex-role stereotypes" were not the same in every culture. All over the world and at all times, little girls have differed from little boys, and men from women, in just the same ways. Unless one posits a mysterious grapevine or a still more mysterious conspiracy which tells parents everywhere how to condition their children, the conclusion is inescapable that females are born with a greater prepotency to be interested in people (for example) than are males.

Some contemporary feminists do admit the anthropological universality of "sex-role stereotyping," but they seem unable to appreciate how thoroughly it undermines their position. Alice Rossi, for example, dismisses the large number of societies that exhibit conventional gender differences with the remark that "Americans are impressed by large numbers." Others, like the anthropologist Marvin Harris, explain the universality of male dominance by reference to the rugged conditions of early human life, conditions under which the physically stronger male had to be the hunter and the woman the caretaker of the home. Unfortunately, this explanation concedes that men already were more aggressive, for hunting requires such psychological traits as aggressiveness and bravery as well as physical strength. A muscular man who would rather play with children is no help on a mastodon hunt. Moreover, despite the fact that societies seldom preserve non-functional atavisms, role differentiation has remained constant down to our own day, even though the hunt is no longer part of our lives.

Universal Sex-Role Differentiation

The universality of sex-role differentiation shows the theory of stereotyping to be as conceptually confused as it is empirically baseless. As Steven Goldberg, Mary Midgley, and others have pointed out, the theory simply ignores the question of *why* every society has chosen to do things the same way. Why do not at least 50 percent of human societies have tough, aggressive women and giggly, chatty men? A universal conspiracy will not do, and the only other explanation is that whatever conditioning does actually take place tags along after preexistent bents. More pertinently, such "conditioning" could not have persisted unless it meshed with a prepotency for it. The effort to condition girls to be nurturant would have lapsed long ago if girls were not more susceptible to it than boys. Given the universality of sex-role differentiation, the feminist's "taught" collapses into "innate": it is evidently an *innate* feature of human beings that they will train their male and female offspring differently.

The slogan "human beings have no instincts" can obstruct an appreciation of innate gender differences. This slogan is true enough, for adult humans at least, if "instinct" means a specific, stimulus-bound pattern of behavior. But if "instinct" is allowed to cover larger patterns of motivation, then humans certainly do have instincts. I buy insurance, an Eskimo stores blubber, and a Masai warrior repels an invader, all to protect our families. Naturally, I must learn the ways of my society to know the specific threats my family faces and the steps to meet them. But this does not mean I must *learn* to react if someone threatens my family.

Far greater mischief is done by the use of the term "sex role," a confused phrase which betrays the ideology underlying today's feminism. Aping sociologists, many feminists describe as "roles" any patterns of feeling or behavior they find objectionable. But consider how tendentious such talk is. A role is something you can adopt (by an act of will) and cast off; it is the opposite of behavior that expresses "the real you." And, indeed, many feminists dismiss romantic love, marriage, and all that flows from them as "inauthentic," in the apparent belief that if you strip away all these things you will find the real McCoy, people in their pure "humanness."...

People *Are* Male or Female

This whole view of persons as neuter monads, to which accidents of personality are arbitrarily fixed, is absurd. We come into the world not as bits of prime matter but as males or females: there is no prior state we are in or could aspire to. Strip away our characteristic feelings and behavior and you will find not persons in their pure essence, but nothing at all. Apart from our genetic endowment—which is already male or female—what *is* the abstract "humanness" we are supposed to become? We are never told, nor could we be.

If anything, it is an even greater error to suppose that the more of our character we could strip away, the freer we would be. Free action *is* action that flows from character; it is action arising from desires we approve of ourselves having. Some desires—compulsive, unwanted, or merely obtrusive—can indeed impede freedom. But it is as foolish to think that we are most free when we are uninfluenced by desire as to think that tennis is at its best when played without a net. "Pure persons" would be wraiths as incapable of freedom as are clouds.

*"The distinctions of human temperaments
and personality into feminine and masculine
have always been* creations.*"*

Proof of Male/Female Differences Is Dubious

Ruth Bleier

Ruth Bleier, trained as a physician and neuro-physiologist, is head
of women's studies at the University of Wisconsin in Madison.
Her book *Science and Gender,* from which the following viewpoint
is excerpted, evaluates the several strains of science which have
analyzed and offered explanations for gender differences. In this
viewpoint, she points out some of the weaknesses of theories
which explain male and female behavior as being the natural result
of biological differences. She writes that far from confining women
and men to specific "roles," human biology allows people to be
amazingly flexible and creative.

As you read, consider the following questions:

1. What aspects of Sociobiology does Dr. Bleier object to?
2. What evidence does Dr. Bleier offer to show the fallibility
   of Sociobiological interpretations of "innate" male and
   female behavior and temperament?
3. Does the author reject all aspects of biological interpretation of human behavior?

It seems anachronistic in the extreme that the nature-nurture, heredity-environment controversy need be addressed today as a serious intellectual issue. The theme, raised recurrently over the past century, remains frighteningly the same despite enormous advances in general scientific sophistication: Women's efforts to do other than what they are destined to do—by biology and evolution, by nature and temperament—threaten the health and survival of the human race. A theme stated explicitly by nineteenth-century physicians, it is today hinted at darkly by modern biological determinists who predict incalculable harm from "tampering" with nature....

Even though there has always been a strong current of biological determinist thinking in the sciences of human behavior, it surges at times of political and social upheaval. In the mid-nineteenth century, the antislavery, women's rights, and suffrage movements were accompanied by a flourishing of the recurrently discredited science of craniology; human brains were weighed, measured, and remeasured in an effort to find some index of quantitative inferiority of the brains of women and exslaves and other blacks. Anatomists in one decade found females to be deficient in the lobe of the brain believed to be the "seat" of intelligence. The next decade had to reverse the measurements when it was decided that another lobe accounted for "man's" highest achievements. After a half-century of pronouncements about female and "Negro" brains and futile efforts to demonstrate consistent quantitative differences, the science of craniology faded away. But there were many other physicians and scientists throughout the last half of the nineteenth century and up to the present who remained dedicated to the task of explaining why women and blacks are naturally fitted, biologically destined, for the social roles they indeed fill and, consequently, for social inferiority and economic dependence. It is in woman's nature to do the caring, tedious jobs.

In recent decades several important areas of biology have produced explanations and theories of sex differences in behaviors and characteristics: the field of sociobiology, the sciences of human cultural evolution, and research on the effects of sex hormones on the developing brain and on subsequent adult behavior....

Sociobiology

Even though the field of sociobiology has provided important insights into the social behaviors of animals, E.O. Wilson introduced Sociobiology in 1975 (the capitalized form will be used here to specify Wilsonian sociobiology) as the ultimate discipline of human behavior, the "new synthesis" that will "reformulate the foundations of the social sciences." Sociobiology considers all human behaviors, characteristics, social relationships and forms of social organization to be biologically, genetically, and evolutionarily determined. Human characteristics and relationships are explicitly programmed in our genes, having evolved over millions of years because they were adaptive for survival. The very fact of their existence proves they have to exist, otherwise they would not have evolved. Not only do Sociobiologists claim to establish the innateness of racism and wars, but also sex differences in social roles and position. Prominent in their writings is the specific attention they pay to the issues, concerns, viewpoints and goals of the contemporary women's movement. In fact, such issues become central to Sociobiological theory-making. "Sociobiology relies heavily upon the biology of male-female differences....Ironically, mother nature appears to be a sexist." (David Barash) Sociobiology announces certain characteristics of the female and male "nature" to be universal and then explains why they are universal: why women are genetically predisposed to be "attached" to home and nursery and men to business and professions; why men are hasty, fickle, and promiscuous and women are faithful and selective; why men are aggressive and dominant and women nurturant and coy....

Biology Shows Human Flexibility

Rather than a curse against women, biology is a promise to us. Biology shows us that the subjugation of women is anything but natural and fixed....

Even without our capacities to create and change specific cultures, biology tells us that we belong to an order stunningly flexible in its social arrangements and capable of great change within species. With this cultural capacity, possibilities expand. Biology tells us that there is nothing genetic stopping us from having full sexual and social expression.

Naomi Weisstein, *Ms.*, November 1982.

The significance of Sociobiological theories lies not only in the seriousness of the political implications but in the fact that Sociobiology uses shoddy and deceptive methodology....Their basic premises are flawed: the universal behaviors, characteristics, and sex differences of humans that they presume to explain as biological and innate are *not* universal either within or between cultures; the behaviors of animals *cannot* be taken to indicate innate behaviors of humans, "uncontaminated" by culture, since animals learn and have cultures; nor are the animal behaviors they describe universal. But, most importantly, it is *not* possible to tease apart genetic and other biological factors from environmental and learning factors in human development. This is, in fact, a meaningless way to view the problem, since, from conception the relationships between the actions of genes and the environment of fetus are inextricable. The very structure and functioning of the brain, the organ of mind and mediator of behavior, are influenced by environmental input both before and after birth. Thus, whatever the genetic and hormonal influences are on the development of our fetal and newborn brains, they are inextricable from the influences of the environmental milieu, from sensory input and learning. In addition, in its structure and function, the human brain is qualitatively and quantitatively different from the brains of other animals. Its capacity for learning, consciousness, memory and intent, motivation, intelligence, innovativeness, and flexibility frees us from predetermined and stereotypic behavior patterns, and it also has created cultures of staggering complexity and sophistication that affect our behaviors from the time of birth. No science or discipline can peel off layers of culture and learning and find an untouched core of biological *nature*. Rather than biology acting to constrain and limit our potentialities, it is, in fact, the supreme irony that our magnificent brains, with their nearly limitless structural and functional potentiality for learning, flexibility, and choice-making, have produced *cultures* that constrain and limit those potentialities.

Male/Female Distinctions Are Cultural

Distinctions of human characteristics and temperaments into *innate* male and female natures have been social, *cultural* constructs and are not *natural*. They are part of an ideology that attempts to make what are in fact social and political distinctions appear to be natural and biological and, therefore, to justify differences in social roles and also relationships of dominance and subordinance. Furthermore, that which can be "shown" to be natural easily becomes the norm that justifies rules and mores from which deviance warrants disapproval or punishment....

The basic premise of Sociobiology is that human behaviors and certain aspects of social organization have evolved, like our bodies, through adaptations based on Darwinian natural selection. It is important to understand Darwin's theory of evolution of the *physical forms* of animals by adaptation in order to understand its application by Sociobiologists to *behavior*. In its modern version, the theory assumes that by some genetic recombination or mutation, a particular anatomical characteristic appears anew in a species, let us say gray body color in a family of orange moths. If the gray color in the moths' particular ecological setting permits more gray than orange moths to survive predation and other causes of an early demise and therefore to reach sexual maturity so that more gray moths are reproduced than their relatives of the original orange color, then an increasing proportion of moths will be gray in successive generations. Over time, the genes for gray will be present in increasing numbers of moths and become a predominant feature of moths in *that* ecological setting. The new genetic feature for gray is then considered, in the language of Darwinian evolution, to be adaptive through natural selection, since it contributes to the maximum fitness of the moths, with *maximum fitness* being defined as the ability to leave many healthy descendants that are themselves able to reproduce and thus spread the genes for gray body color.

Sociobiologists suggest and assume that *behaviors* also evolve in similar ways so that "adaptive" and "successful" behaviors become based in our genes, and that certain genetic configurations became selected because they result in behaviors that are adaptive for survival. Our "innate" predispositions to display these behaviors constitute our human *nature*....

ROTHCO
ORIGINAL

"SUPPOSE EVE HAD COME BEFORE ADAM, WOW! WHAT A WORLD THIS WOULD HAVE BEEN!

© Hoppes/Rothco

All behavior of course reflects at least *some* component of gene action. Individuals of any species of animal behave within the limits of the broad range of biological capabilities defined by their genes. Humans walk rather than fly. Birds peck at their food. When we are frightened, our hearts beat faster. But what is really at issue in Sociobiological theory is not the physical capacity for behavior that biology provides but rather the genetic encoding of the entire range of complex human behaviors and characteristics that are expressed in a nearly infinite variety of ways by different individuals and cultures and often not expressed at all, such as altruism, loyalty, dominance, competitiveness, aggressivity. In addition, Sociobiology claims genetic encoding for such arbitrarily chosen and questionably sexually differentiated "traits" as coyness, fickleness, promiscuity, rapaciousness, or maternalism....

From the time of conception genes do *not* act in isolation from their environment, and even fairly stereotypical behaviors in animals, with few exceptions, represent interactions between experience or learning and biological mechanisms. What has evolved in response to environmental challenge is the brain and its capacities for learning and culture, not behaviors themselves. Behaviors are the *products* of the brain's functioning in interaction with the external world, and the innumerable patterns of social behaviors, relationships, and organization that characterize human societies have evolved through cultural transmission within specific historical contexts....

The Creative Potential of Culture

Paradoxically, it is the very culture that on the one hand has provided a powerful adaptive force for the exuberant evolutionary course of human behaviors and social organization, freeing our human history from the otherwise slow evolutionary course of the pre-human modes of behavior, that on the other directs, molds, and constrains the extraordinary potential our brains offer for a seemingly limitless flexibility of behaviors and relationships. This is not to say, however, that culture and learning are any more narrowly deterministic than are genes. Each of us is exposed to a unique set of environmental-social circumstances and interacts with them in uniquely creative ways. Every person does not, after all, conform to the stereotypical expectations that the dominant culture holds for the social category of which she is a member. Our intelligence and ingenuity ensure that neither genes nor culture can necessarily produce the lumbering robots Sociobiologists would have us believe we are.

The cultures of patriarchal societies have developed an ideology or a concept of *woman* and her *nature* within a political context in which women are an oppressed class, just as theories of the nature of the slave and more contemporary racial beliefs and theories have served important economic, social, and political functions for dominant classes. The constructed nature of woman is seen to suit her admirably for the tasks that our society has in fact required of her: the care, loving, and nurturing of its men and children.

The distinctions of human temperaments and personality into feminine and masculine have always been *creations*, and in our patriarchal cultures are a part of the ideology that attempts to make what are in fact social and political distinctions appear to be natural and biological. These presumably natural, biological differences between the sexes then provide the explanation and justification for the differences in social roles and for relationships of dominance and subordinance. It is not unreasonable to believe, in Kate Millett's words, that "sexual caste supersedes all other forms of inegalitarianism: racial, political or economic," and that the basic unit of oppression and exploitation is that between the sexes....

It is rather striking that women are *defined*, and seen as *constrained*, by our biology, while the biology of men presumably fits them to fill *every* role, except, of course, that of mothering and nurturing. The brain, however, knows no such distinctions. Limitations are placed on the fullest exploitation of its rich potential for thought, creativities, innovation, humaneness, and emotional expression not by hormones or mystical *natures* but by poverty of environment, experience, and opportunity and by the ideological contraints imposed, both crudely and subtly, by any individual, class, or social order that cannot permit autonomy in "others."

In attempting to discard the concepts of instincts, innateness, or biological predispositions in human behaviors, I may seem to be discarding biology altogether. Rather, my hope and intent is the discarding of the controversy and dichotomy between nature and nurture or biology and learning because the dichotomy is impossible, unresolvable, and scientifically meaningless. It is a controversy that serves to obscure social and political origins of inequality and to undermine change and, furthermore, cannot lead to an understanding of human behaviors. All factors affecting and determining human behaviors and relationships not only interact with each other in effecting responses but in the process change each other so one cannot separate out and measure proportions of influence.

Humans Are Unique

What can be considered the unique *nature* of humans is our capacities to learn, to exercise choice among alternative behaviors, to be self-conscious and intentional, and to use written and spoken language. But what we *do* with those capacities, our behaviors and characteristics, whether we are altruistic or aggressive or nurturing or analytical (and so on) are *learned*, just as we learn to go to war, to want babies, to parent, to be obedient, to be competitive, to dominate, or create. Our potential for creativity is a nearly limitless resource....It is within our human/biological capacities to liberate the human mind and behaviors from the cultural molds that confine them and only serve the best interests of a minority.

*"The family is built on the bond of sexual
attraction between male and female. No culture
has yet felt it could afford, by blurring all
distinctions between the sexes, to dissolve that
glue."*

Male/Female Differences Serve Society

Sara Bonnett Stein

Sara Bonnett Stein is the author of numerous non-fiction books
for children and for families. Her attitudes toward sex differences
and child-rearing were shaped in her own family and through her
extensive work in day care centers and nursery schools. In the
following viewpoint she argues that some sex differences are
innate and that fostering them in children is absolutely essential
to gender identity, on which reproduction itself depends.

As you read, consider the following questions:

1. In what ways does Ms. Stein believe that human evolution
   and culture are related?
2. Why, according to the author, are we not free to eliminate
   sex differences?
3. Why does Ms. Stein believe that "internal clues" to gender
   identity occasionally need a helping hand?

The bold experiment to raise nonsexist children is not working. Boys are not dressing baby dolls. Girls are not playing with trucks. This problem is baffling those who have devoted themselves to eradicating sexism and sex stereotypes in their families....

Park bench impressions and laboratory measurements concur: there are sex differences. But what is the point of them? Or are they, as feminists claim, beside the point?...

Culture Reinforces Nature

Culture did not descend on our ancestors or on us from an external source. We made it up—we still do—to safeguard the ways of life that work best for us based on our own experience. Like any other animal, we are made of stuff, organized in specific ways, wired to perceive certain patterns through certain senses. None of our inventions, no matter how impressive or innovative, completely transcends our human nature. Quite the opposite; culture serves to refine and express more exquisitely the potential of our raw material.

The more consistently and the more emphatically human culture expresses sex differences, the more ancient those differences must be and the more rooted in our biological past. The more fundamental our tendency to form couples, the more we should expect to find that tendency made urgent by the phenomenon of falling in love, ritualized in marriage rites, sanctified by religious systems, protected by law, and promoted by our grandparents. The more we have depended on men to band together, to run, throw, take risks, plan strategies, and venture far from home, the more we should expect to find informal customs and formal institutions that train boys for that destiny.

Nor is it correct to assume that our own culture, by elaborating and even exaggerating behavioral differences, has over these millions of years superseded the original biological basis that gave rise to it. Evolution is very conservative. Without environmental pressure that literally kills off those who behave in traditional ways or prevents them from having babies, a species changes only by a process of drift or barely changes at all. Until now, human ways of life and human culture have not been inimical to the ancient behaviors on which they are based, and so they are still with us. Theories that justify exploitation must certainly be fought, but today's battle, however it might improve the ways in which sexism is expressed, will not eradicate it from our culture.

Gender Identity Is Innate

We adults manage our culture, but we do not run it. We can attend to the details—specify what constitutes marriage or agree on what clothing we recognize as masculine and feminine—but we aren't biologically free to rid ourselves of coupling or gender identity. These limitations come wrapped within each baby and can't be shucked by growing up.

In what raw form might we expect to find the fundamental, biologically determined, anciently rooted behavioral differences between sexes? First, there are areas where we should not expect to find differences. We should be unable to find a yardstick by which we can measure differences in dependency, for dependency should prove to be a human condition, not a sexual one. We should be similarly unable to measure differences in nurturance, as our evolution relied on paternal as well as maternal bonds. We may, however, find that nurturance and dependency, while not differing in degree, differ somewhat in form.

Sex Differences Are Vital

Man's environment—civilized society—is a prodigious and precarious achievement. If one accepts that sex is nothing less than the life force in a community, one may conclude that particular sexual arrangements contributed to the birth of this prodigy. One may suspect that its maintenance depends on an intelligent ordering of our sexual relationships. And one may speculate that our current cultural stresses, which could conceivably destroy our democratic civilization, derive from and reflect sexual disorders. Sexuality is not simply a matter of *Games People Play*; it is one of the few matters truly of life and death to society.

George Gilder, *Sexual Suicide*, 1973.

There are three areas in which we should expect to find real distinctions between the sexes because they are tied to the ancient ways the family was provisioned—meat provided by far-ranging, tightly cooperating bands of male hunters, gathered foods provided by females who paced their work to fit the necessities of childrearing in smaller groups and at less distance from their homes. The first is the individual's center of activity; the second is the physical quality of that activity; the third is the social relations with other members of a person's own sex. Specifically, males should tend to explore toward the outskirts of the backyard or the community while females should tend to stay closer to home. Males should show more interest in, and spend more time at, practicing throwing, racing, tumbling, and leaping, as well as mock or real fighting. Females should be more interested and involved in small repetitive movements and less interested in fighting. Males should tend to gather in larger groups and to order themselves hierarchically within those groups, whereas females should form smaller groups that are more egalitarian in spirit. Although no overall differences in intelligence or temperament

184

should be expected, any slight differences, such as competitiveness or skill in spatial relations, that support these sex-linked patterns should be more commonly observed in one sex than the other. Finally, we should expect to find the building blocks of the most fundamental potential of all: a strong tendency in both sexes to respond differently to their own sex and to the opposite sex.

These are just the distinctions psychologists have measured and that describe your typical gang of ball-throwing, team-joining boys and your typical pair of arm-in-arm, doll-dressing girls.

"Typical" and Unique Individuals

The typical boy or girl we think we see when we observe children in a group, however, vanishes when we look at each child alone. When we come to know each boy and girl very well, we are struck with the uniqueness of each and find it difficult to reverse the process and bunch them back together again into a typical boy or girl. The same is true of the measurable traits we have discussed, for though the results of testing hundreds or thousands of children creates a striking profile for each sex, the profile says nothing about any given child and may in fact be a very poor fit. In either case, once we focus on the individual rather than the group, sex differences prove elusive.

How can we explain the fact that certain fundamental traits such as aggressiveness appear to be linked to one sex or the other, but that there is also such a great difference from one individual to another, regardless of sex, that we cannot predict whether any particular baby girl will be more or less aggressive than any particular baby boy? [Professor C.O.] Lovejoy's speculative reconstruction of human evolution points to the kind of differences researchers have found. A rigid distribution of traits by sex, however, could not have survived environmental pressures during those millions of years of evolution. No culture could survive if its women could only pick blueberries or its men could stick pigs. When men were skimmed from our own society to serve in World War II, women replaced them in every sort of job. Emergency shifts, or slow and gradual changes under less pressing circumstances, must have been taking place all through human history. Looking at our past, the difference between the sexes makes sense only if it constitutes an average—a statistical— difference with sufficient overlap and sufficient flexibility so that under the stress of environmental challenge, either sex can shift in either direction.

The very fact of such extreme variability and flexibility poses a problem for each society and for the children growing up in it. Every culture's basic unit is the family. However that unit is defined, whether marriage is monogamous or polygamous, families nuclear or extended, whether children are raised with their

185

parents or in communal groups, the family is built on the bond of sexual attraction between male and female. No culture has yet felt it could afford, by blurring all distinctions between the sexes, to dissolve that glue. Men and women may be similar in temperament, dress pretty much alike, even perform very much the same functions; but gender identity itself must not suffer lest heterosexuality suffer too. Underlying the bread-and-butter issue from which our brand of sexism probably arose 10 million or more years ago is the most fundamental point of all: reproduction. If each individual child has some potential for both masculine and feminine behavior, if that potential can be socially manipulated, and if a culture chooses to adapt—as some are suggesting we do now—by emphasizing "unisex," how can a child learn to evoke and respond to sexuality in the opposite sex? What would make the child bother to become his or her gender at all? The fact of being male or female when not interpreted to mean masculine or feminine might remain as meaningless as an infant's automatic smile when no one smiles back.

Complementary Differences

The differences between men and women are also emotional and psychological. Without woman's innate maternal instinct, the human race would have died out centuries ago....

An effort to eliminate the differences by social engineering or legislative or constitutional tinkering cannot succeed, which is fortunate, but social relationships and spiritual values can be ruptured in the attempt. Thus the role reversals being forced upon high school students, under which guidance counselors urge reluctant girls to take "shop" and boys to take "home economics," further confuse a generation already unsure about its identity. They are as wrong as efforts to make a left-handed child right-handed.

Phyllis Schlafly, *The Power of the Positive Woman*, 1977.

Regardless of parental ideology, trying to achieve and consolidate a sense of being one sex or the other has evolved along with us (because otherwise we would not be here to ponder on it) and is built into the pattern of child development. The child does not care whether he or she is born into a culture that defines femininity by ribbons or body scars, masculinity by crew cuts or pigtails, as long as it is clear which way to go. Apparently, we have a hard time being unclear. How many mothers can stop themselves from sitting with a leg tucked under—the female way in our culture; how many men can force themselves to sit that way instead of sprawled—the male way in our culture? Almost all our little boys soon sit sprawled and almost all our little girls soon sit tucked.

That sense of gender is not thrust upon the child by society. It comes from within the child, although it is simultaneously supported from without, just as the push to stand and walk arises internally, although we still extend a helping hand.

A Need to Teach Vital Differences

Without some internal clues, the helping hand would not be strong enough. To learn their native tongue, children rely on built-in patterns as well as on specific models and assistance echoed from outside. Those learning patterns fade after a certain age, and it is never again as easy to learn a language. Perhaps, in similar fashion, when children seek their gender, they use those remnants of sex-linked behavioral patterns that evolved so long ago and that now appear to us so obsolete; perhaps those templates also fade with age. Without the helping hand, the slim clues that cause boys to gang and girls to cluster are certainly not enough either. No one thing is. Biological bases can be overridden, statistical averages are only that, parents themselves have less influence than they think. Yet some combination of all three must be hard at work, for children vehemently, tenaciously, often in opposition to adult notions and in ways unique to childhood, seek out and loudly express their gender. What makes the "neutral" infant become a boy or girl?

Perhaps as we explore the answer to this question, we will salve another disturbing feeling: that for all the work that has gone into studying sex differences, the results are not satisfying. What we can measure and put on paper fails to capture the sense of difference we feel, the intuition that masculinity and femininity contrast with one another in profound ways for which there is no yardstick and which no cluster of traits defines—but that are the differences that make the greatest sense of all.

"Making sure that boys know they are better and that girls accept lesser status...is the basic agenda of...sex role learning."

Over-Emphasis on Male/Female Differences Damages Society

Letty Cottin Pogrebin

Letty Pogrebin is a magazine writer, author, and a founder and editor of *Ms. Magazine*. She and actress Marlo Thomas created a record, book, and television special, *Free To Be, You and Me*, that explored non-sexist childrearing. In the following viewpoint, which is taken from her classic book *Growing Up Free*, she vividly describes the damages inflicted by emphasizing sex differences and the benefits of non-sexist childrearing.

As you read, consider the following questions:

1. What does Ms. Pogrebin mean by "the cult of sex differences"?
2. In what ways does Ms. Pogrebin believe that the cult of sex differences damages both males and females?
3. How, according to the author, would children raised in a non-sexist society differ from those who weren't?

Letty Cottin Pogrebin, *Growing Up Free: Raising Your Child in the 80s*. New York: Mc-Graw Hill book Company, 1980. Reprinted with permission.

How can one dismiss the two distinct sexual essences that are distilled in every school of human thought: anthropology's hunter and childbearer, philosophy's masculine and feminine principles, religion's Man and Helpmeet, psychology's Oedipus Complex and Penis Envy, not to mention such age-old sexual dichotomies as carnal/spiritual, Science/Mysticism, and Yin/Yang?

And what about the polarities that inspire art and passion? Soft/strong in the poet's sonnet, light/dark in the painter's portrait, subject/object in the lover's pursuit—each seems to borrow its aesthetic tension from the original attracting "opposites," male and female.

Whether or not such expressions are the cause or the effect of sex differences, do we really want to live without them? Maybe the French are right: *Vive la difference.* So why not leave well enough alone?

Because it isn't well enough or good enough. In fact, the cult of sex differences hurts both sexes. It creates a gender caste system with reasoning that leaps from

the two sexes are different,

to

the two sexes are opposites,

to

one sex is better than the other.

Differences and "opposites" seem to cry out for hierarchical evaluation, which is where the trouble starts. When Dr. Samuel Johnson was asked who is more intelligent, men or women, he replied, "Which man and which woman?" But that respect for human individuality has been rare through the centuries. Most people find it easier to generalize, to earmark group traits and make sure everyone acts accordingly.

Cheating Children

By instructing a child to *act* like a girl or *act* like a boy, the cult of sex differences says "Conform," "Pretend," "Act"; it does not say "Be your best self." It makes children imposters within their own sex and strangers to their "opposites." It decrees a half-life for a girl and a half-life for a boy. In short, the cult of sex differences cheats children....

Here come the "buts"...

"But how will my son know he's a boy unless he learns all the ways he's different from a girl? And vice versa.

"But my daughter might turn out masculine if we don't teach her to be feminine." And vice versa.

In a society that favors either/or simplifications, such concerns make sense. But stop and think for a moment and they become suspect: Why do sex differences alone inspire such paranoia?

Parents show absolutely no concern about teaching children about everything *else* they're different from. No one asks, "How will my son know he's different from a dog, or my daughter know she's a person, not a houseplant?" No one worries that without intervention children might think they are chairs.

Pink and Blue

Many researchers contend that a child's awareness of gender is more decisive than biology in shaping sexual differences. "The real problem for determining what influences development in men and women is that they are called boys and girls from the day they are born," says biologist [Richard] Lewontin. He cites the classic "blue, pink, yellow" experiments. When a group of observers was asked to describe newborn infants dressed in blue diapers, they were characterized as "very active." The same babies dressed in pink diapers evoked descriptions of gentleness. When the babies were wearing yellow, says Lewontin, observers "really got upset. They started to peek inside their diapers to see their sex."

David Gelman and others, *Newsweek*, May 18, 1981.

Such rudimentary lessons in identity are considered unnecessary because humanness is perceived to be a "felt reality." Obvious. Basic. Certain. After humanness, being female or male is the most salient fact in every person's who-am-I or what-am-I profile.

If adults were not so hypertense about "femininity" and "masculinity," the same knowingness, the same "felt reality" that is taken for granted about one's human identity would develop in connection with one's gender identity. Since the anatomical, biological, and physical sex differences are among the most visually obvious human characteristics, gender is one of the earliest concepts children understand. By the time they can talk, they know girls from boys as surely as they know humans from dogs, chairs, and houseplants.

Learning Gender

A child learns that she is a girl or he is a boy sometime between eighteen months and three years of age, a period considered critical for the establishment of gender identification. During these months, children learn their gender label by hearing the word girl or boy applied to themselves over and over again. ("What a good boy you are!" "That's my brave little girl." And so on.) At the same time they learn to generalize sex labels by organizing information they see and hear about other people. ("He's a nice man." "She's a friendly woman." "Look, that boy is running after that girl!") We may not know exactly how children organize all this information but we do know how the sequence progresses.

By interviewing thousands of children—asking such questions as "Is this a girl doll or a boy doll?" "Are you a boy or a girl?" "Is this a picture of a woman or a man?"—developmentalists have been able to trace the stages of gender comprehension.

At twenty-four months, many children were not quite sure of their own gender but could identify the women and men even if the pictured females had short hair or wore trousers. By age three, almost all children were aware of their own sex as well as other people's.

In the three-year-old's mind, however, gender identity is still subject to a childhood phenomenon known as "magical thinking," the belief that under certain conditions, things can turn into other things on whim; for example, a cat could become a dog if its whiskers were cut off.

Ask a three- or four-year-old girl, "Could you turn into a boy if you wore a boy-style haircut or boys' clothing?" and she will nod confidently. By age five she may equivocate; sometimes gender is stable, other times not. But ask her at age six and she'll think you've lost your mind.

Unchangeable Gender Identity

Once the concept of "gender constancy" is absorbed, the healthy child knows that each person's sex is unchanging; the girl knows that she was a girl when she was a baby, will remain a girl no matter what she wears or does or plays with, will become a woman, not a man, when she grows up and a mother, not a father, if she has a child. This knowledge becomes a "felt reality" to children at about the same time that their minds make the link between genital differences and the girl-boy labels that go with them.

Once *core gender identity* has been established, it is "probably the most entrenched, unchangeable psychic structure in the human psyche." *So invincible are feelings of boyness or girlness after the critical period that if a child with male genitals somehow believes himself to be a girl* (parental and medical ignorance or ambiguous infant genitals have created such error in sex assignment), *it is easier to surgically change his body to match his belief than to try to psychologically change his gender identity to match his body.* (And the same is true for incorrectly assigned girls.)

With normal children under normal circumstances, once core gender identity is established, there is no reason why children should not spend the rest of their lives exploring the infinite variations of their who-am-I profiles. In a nonsexist society, that open vista would stretch out before us all. But in our present culture, the facts of biological and physical sex differences and the "felt reality" of gender identity are overlaid with layers and layers of irrelevant sex-linked rules.

It is not enough today to *be* a girl or *be* a boy; one must *play the part* of a girl or boy. Society reintroduces "magical thinking" in a new guise: Watch out, child; the haircut may not change her into a boy but it can make her *masculine*. The whiskers don't make the tomcat male, but without them he might turn *feminine*. Watch Out.

How sex differences can be touted as "natural" and at the same time must be hammered into us, is one of sexism's craziest contradictions. Nevertheless, the hammering is accomplished by a catechism of sex role rules and regulations expressed in absolutes and extremes and embodied in the sex role stereotype.

Cultural Sledgehammer

Literally, a stereotype is a printing block from which pages of type can be duplicated. The essential "permanence and unchangeableness" of these blocks are the features that have come to symbolize rigidity and regularity.

Stereotypes oversimplify human complexity. They bang people into shape with a cultural sledgehammer that flattens the wonder of individuals into monotonous group characteristics.

"She says, 'To hell with ballet, she's going to be a jockey.'"

Stereotypes assert themselves through caricature, name-calling, and idolatry: "Poles are dumb," "Children are destructive," "Blacks are lazy." All stereotypes are "a substitute for intimacy"—and sex stereotypes, in particular, are a *barrier* to intimacy. One doesn't describe a friend or lover in lumpish generalizations....

Because stereotypes are by definition extravagant overstatements blunt enough to be understood by children, they are also blunt enough to advertise their intent. What sex role stereotypes tell children and the rest of us is this:

Boys Are Better.

Girls Are Meant to Be Mothers.

These two messages—male supremacy and compulsory motherhood—are the raw essentials of a patriarchal system. In order for the system to perpetuate itself, children must be trained to play their proper roles and to believe the system natural and just.

Male Power Begins at Home

Male supremacy—the paradigm for white supremacy or any oppressive form of hierarchy—begins at home. Big Daddy is in charge in the family, and some men are expected to be in charge of other men (and all women) in the corporations, universities, governments, and playing fields of the nation. Boys, therefore, must be trained to become men who can exercise their rightful power and believe themselves worthy of it. Girls must be trained to admire and depend upon the men who exercise power, and to believe themselves unworthy of controlling their own or others' destinies.

Because male power is to be spread across all of public life, boys must be motivated to produce in all arenas—business, policy, art, academia, everywhere. Not only are the females to stay out of the action in those arenas, but they are themselves to be incentives that motivate males to strive for power, the sexual and ornamental rewards that the male controls and sometimes marries. As a wife, "his woman" further rewards him with offspring (she "gave" him a son) to carry on his name, the continuity of the patriarchal line, and to provide the larger patriarchal system with workers, soldiers, and more mothers. (History shows that in wartime and during periods of decreasing population and underemployment, motherhood has been vigorously promoted and abortion and contraception are more likely to be made illegal.)

Training Girls to Reproduce

For this gender arrangement to come into being, girls must learn to see themselves as sexual entities after puberty and be motivated to be mothers after marriage. Only when she is under male control (married) can a woman be exalted in motherhood (unwed mothers are not) and her child be officially recognized ("illegitimate" babies are not). A girl must be so well trained that she relinquishes the desire to *produce*—business, policy, art, and so on—in favor of *reproducing*. When she succumbs to the definition of her optimum self as Mother legitimatized by marriage, she locks male supremacy into place.

As Simone de Beauvoir has said, woman's "creation results only in repeating the same Life in more individuals," whereas man "remodels the face of the earth, he creates new instruments, he invents, he shapes the future." Man transcends. Woman repeats. Or, as I have chosen to formulate it for purposes of this discussion: *Boys are Better. Girls Are Meant to Be Mothers.* That's how children see it.

Thus, vastly oversimplified, we have the intent of sex stereotypes and the hidden agenda of sex roles. The name of the game is power and one's relationship to it: Someone wins because someone else loses. All the players learn the rules in childhood. The objective of the game for boys is to grow up to be President. The objective of the game for girls is to grow up to have a baby. For him, the one and only pinnacle position; for her, a destiny available to every female of every species on the face of the earth.

There is nothing wrong with the stereotype of the attractive young woman who becomes a mother—other than the fact that she is the *only* woman a girl is supposed to become.

There is nothing wrong with the fearless leader stereotype either, except that since it cannot be fulfilled by 99,999 out of 100,000 males, it dooms most boys and men to a deep sense of "masculine" failure, which must then be relieved by reaffirmation of the one manageable component of the male stereotype: superiority over women.

Secret Agenda of Sex Role Learning

Whoever he is and however he performs, at least he can feel strong if she is weak. Her "femininity" and his "masculinity" have been made such a seesaw of opposites that if she refuses to be powerless she "emasculates" him. His sex role and his phallic potency rise and fall in unison. If she agrees to be powerless, his "masculinity" rises and from his full height on the seesaw, he looks down and proclaims her "a real woman."

This dynamic springs from the original fallacy:

The two sexes are different;

the two sexes are opposites;

one sex is better than the other.

Making sure that boys know they are better and that girls accept lesser status and eventual reproductive duty is the basic agenda of patriarchy and the conscious or unconscious foundation of sex role learning.

"What is repugnant to every human being is to be reckoned always as a member of a class and not as an individual person."

Men and Women Should Be Judged as Individuals

Dorothy L. Sayers

English novelist and theologian Dorothy L. Sayers (1893-1957) was one of the first women to receive a degree from Oxford University. She is also author of the Peter Whimsey detective series. In this viewpoint, Ms. Sayers points to some of the absurdities that result when men and women are segregated too rigidly in separate classes.

As you read, consider the following questions:

1. Why does Ms. Sayers object to the tendency to class men and women separately?
2. Does Ms. Sayers believe there are any differences between the sexes? Discuss.
3. What advice does Ms. Sayers offer feminists?

Dorothy L. Sayers, *Are Women Human?* Grand Rapids, Michigan: Wm. B. Eerdmans Publishing Company, 1971. Reprinted by permission of Watkins-Loomis Agency.

The question of "sex-equality" is, like all questions affecting human relationships, delicate and complicated. It cannot be settled by loud slogans or hard-and-fast assertions like "a woman is as good as a man"—or "woman's place is in the home"—or "women ought not to take men's jobs." The minute one makes such assertions, one finds one has to qualify them. "A woman is as good as a man" is as meaningless as to say, "a Kaffir is as good as a Frenchman" or "a poet is as good as an engineer" or "an elephant is as good as a racehorse"—it means nothing whatever until you add: "at doing what?" In a religious sense, no doubt, the Kaffir is as valuable in the eyes of God as a Frenchman—but the average Kaffir is probably less skilled in literary criticism than the average Frenchman, and the average Frenchman less skilled than the average Kaffir in tracing the spoor of big game. There might be exceptions on either side: it is largely a matter of heredity and education. When we balance the poet against the engineer, we are faced with a fundamental difference of temperament—so that here our question is complicated by the enormous social problem whether poetry or engineering is "better" for the State, or for humanity in general. There may be people who would like a world that was all engineers or all poets—but most of us would like to have a certain number of each; though here again, we should all differ about the desirable proportion of engineering to poetry. The only proviso we should make is that people with dreaming and poetical temperaments should not entangle themselves in engines, and that mechanically-minded people should not issue booklets of bad verse. When we come to the elephant and the racehorse, we come down to bed-rock physical differences—the elephant would make a poor showing in the Derby, and the unbeaten Eclipse himself would be speedily eclipsed by an elephant when it came to hauling logs.

The Limits of Stereotypes

That is so obvious that it hardly seems worth saying. But it is the mark of all movements, however well-intentioned, that their pioneers tend, by much lashing of themselves into excitement, to lose sight of the obvious. In reaction against the age-old slogan, "woman is the weaker vessel," or the still more offensive, "woman is a divine creature," we have, I think, allowed ourselves to drift into asserting that "a woman is as good as a man," without always pausing to think what exactly we mean by that. What, I feel, we ought to mean is something so obvious that it is apt to escape attention altogether, viz: not that every woman is, in virtue of her sex, as strong, clever, artistic, level-headed, industrious and so forth as any man that can be mentioned; but, that a woman is just as much an ordinary human being as a man, with the same individual preferences, and with just as much right to the tastes and preferences of an individual. What is repugnant to every human being is to be reckoned always as a member of a class and not as an individual person. A certain amount of classification is, of course, necessary for practical purposes: there is no harm in saying that women, as a class, have smaller bones than men, wear lighter clothing, have more hair on their heads and less on their faces, go more pertinaciously to church or the cinema, or have more patience with small and noisy babies. In the same way, we may say that stout people of both sexes are commonly better-tempered than thin ones, or that university dons of both sexes are more pedantic in their speech than argicultural labourers, or that communists of both sexes are more ferocious than Fascists—or the other way around. What is unreasonable and irritating is to assume that *all* one's tastes and preferences have to be conditioned by the class to which one belongs. That has been the very common error into which men have frequently fallen about women—and it is the error into which feminist women are, perhaps, a little inclined to fall about themselves.

Men and Women Are Alike

A lot of misunderstanding between men and women comes from our believing the two sexes are inherently polarized. Actually, they're closer to an androgynous human mean. Men are cursed with the same conflicts we experience—and should not be envied and therefore reviled. The men I know, like the women I know, find it hard to choose between modern life's contraries: the safe routine and the adventurous possibility, the vocation and the avocation, the thrill of affairs and the comforts of marriage, the time they spend alone and the time they spend with others, the satisfaction in being free of children and the urge to have kids. If you talk to a man who is worried about his life, he sounds exactly like the worried woman—as if he's being torn along the same seams as she.

Margaret Edwards, *Working Woman*, May 1985.

Take, for example, the very usual reproach that women nowadays always want to "copy what men do." In that reproach there is a great deal of truth and a great deal of sheer, unmitigated and indeed quite wicked nonsense. There are a number of jobs and pleasures which men have in times past cornered for themselves. At one time, for instance, men had a monopoly of classical education. When the pioneers of university training for women demanded that women should be admitted to the universities, the cry went up at once: "Why should women want to know about Aristotle?" The answer is NOT that *all* women would be the better for knowing about Aristotle—still less, as Lord Tennyson seemed to think, that they would be more companionable wives for their husbands if they did not know about Aristotle—but simply: "What women want as a class is irrelevant. *I* want to know about Aristotle. It is true that most women care nothing about him, and a great many male undergraduates turn pale and faint at the thought of him—but I, eccentric individual that I am, do want to know about Aristotle, and I submit that there is nothing in my shape or bodily functions which need prevent my knowing about him."...

Women and Men Have Same Essential Desires

"What," men have asked distractedly from the beginning of time, "what on earth do women want?" I do not know that women, *as* women, want anything in particular, but as human beings they want, my good men, exactly what you want yourselves: interesting occupation, reasonable freedom for their pleasures, and a sufficient emotional outlet. What form the occupation, the pleasures and the emotion may take, depends entirely upon the individual. You know that this is so with yourselves—why will you not believe that it is so with us? The late D.H. Lawrence, who certainly cannot be accused of underrating the importance of sex and talked a good deal of nonsense upon the subject, was yet occasionally visited with shattering glimpses of the obvious. He said in one of his *Assorted Articles*:

> "Man is willing to accept woman as an equal, as a man in skirts,
> as an angel, a devil, a baby-face, a machine, an instrument, a
> bosom, a womb, a pair of legs, a servant, an encyclopaedia, an
> ideal or an obscenity; the one thing he won't accept her as is
> a human being, a real human being of the feminine sex."

"Accepted as a human being!"—yes; not as an inferior class and not, I beg and pray all feminists, as a superior class—not, in fact, as a class at all, except in a useful context. We are much too much inclined in these days to divide people into permanent categories, forgetting that a category only exists for its special purpose and must be forgotten as soon as that purpose is served. There is a fundamental difference between men and women, but it is not the only fundamental difference in the world. There is a sense in which my charwoman and I have more in common than either of us has with, say Mr. [George] Bernard Shaw [the dramatist]; on the other hand, in a discussion about art and literature, Mr. Shaw and I should probably find we had more fundamental interests in common that either of us had with my charwoman. I grant that, even so, he and I should disagree ferociously about the eating of meat—but that is not a difference between the sexes— on that point, the late Mr. G.K. Chesterton [the novelist] would have sided with me against the representative of his own sex. Then there are points of which I, and many of my own generation of both sexes, should find ourselves heartily in agreement; but on which the rising generation of young men and women would find us too incomprehensibly stupid for words. A difference of age is as fundamental as a difference of sex; and so is a difference of nationality. *All* categories, if they are insisted upon beyond the immediate purpose which they serve, breed class antagonism and disruption in the state, and that is why they are dangerous.

Human Flexibility

If we look at history, present and past, and at the position of women all over the world, among savage and civilized peoples, we find that it is possible for society to do almost anything with the relationships between men and women. There are cultures where women are dominating and men responsive, where women manage the finances and men wheedle pocket money out of them and spend their time daydreaming of forgery and alchemy, where women initiate the love affairs and no man would be so foolhardy as to make the first advances, where both men and women enjoy and rear the children; cultures where fathers are indulgent and loving and mothers stern disciplinarians, where girls grow up envying boys and wishing they had been born boys, and cultures where boys grow up envying girls, wishing they had been born girls. Human beings are exceedingly plastic, and the relationship of men and women to each other is a very flexible thing.

Margaret Mead, *Fortune*, December 1946.

The other day, in the "Heart-to-Heart" column of one of our popular newspapers, there appeared a letter from a pathetic gentleman about a little disruption threatening his married state. He wrote:

"I have been married eleven years and think a great deal of the wedding anniversary. I remind my wife a month in advance and plan to make the evening a success. But she does not share my keenness, and if I did not remind her, would let the day go by without a thought of its significance. I thought a wedding anniversary meant a lot to a woman. Can you explain this indifference?"

Poor little married gentleman, nourished upon generalisations—and convinced that if his wife does not fit into the category of "a woman" there must be something wrong! Perhaps she resents being dumped into the same category as all the typical women of the comic stories. If so, she has my sympathy. "A" woman—not an individual person, disliking perhaps to be reminded of the remorseless flowing-by of the years and the advance of old age—but "a" woman, displaying the conventional sentimentalities attributed to her unfortunate and ridiculous sex.

A man once asked me—it is true that it was at the end of a very good dinner, and the compliment conveyed may have been due to that circumstance—how I managed in my books to write such natural conversation between men when they were by themselves. Was I, by any chance, a member of a large, mixed family with a lot of male friends? I replied that, on the contrary, I was an only child and had practically never seen or spoken to any men of my own age till I was about twenty-five. "Well," said the man, "I shouldn't have expected a woman [meaning me] to have been able to make it so convincing." I replied that I had coped with this difficult problem by making my men talk, as far as possible, like ordinary human beings. This aspect of the matter seemed to surprise the other speaker; he said no more, but took it away to chew it over. One of these days it may quite likely occur to him that women, as well as men, when left to themselves, talk very much like human beings also.

Both Men and Women Are Human

Indeed, it is my experience that both men and women are fundamentally human, and that there is very little mystery about either sex, except the exasperating mysteriousness of human beings in general. And though for certain purposes it may still be necessary, as it undoubtedly was in the immediate past, for women to band themselves together, as women, to secure recognition of their requirements as a sex, I am sure that the time has now come to insist more strongly on each woman's—and indeed each man's—requirements as an individual person. It used to be said that women had no *esprit de corps*; we have proved that we have—do not let us run into the opposite error of insisting that there is an aggressively feminist "point of view" about everything. To oppose one class perpetually to another—young against old, manual labour against brain-worker, rich against poor, woman against man—is to split the foundations of the State; and if the cleavage runs too deep, there remains no remedy but force and dictatorship. If you wish to preserve a free democracy, you must base it—not on classes and categories, for this will land you in the totalitarian State, where no one may act or think except as the member of a category. You must base it upon the individual Tom, Dick and Harry, and the individual Jack and Jill—in fact, upon you and me.

Distinguishing Bias from Reason

The subject of feminism often generates intense emotional responses in people. When dealing with such a highly controversial subject, many will allow their feelings to dominate their powers of reason. Thus, one of the most important critical thinking skills is the ability to distinguish between opinions based upon emotion or bias and conclusions based upon a rational consideration of the facts.

The following statements are taken from the viewpoints in this chapter. Consider each statement carefully. *Mark R for any statement you believe is based on reason or a rational consideration of the facts. Mark B for any statement you believe is based on bias, prejudice, or emotion. Mark I for any statement you think is impossible to judge.* Even when a statement is based on factual observations, many readers find that they disagree with the conclusion the author reaches. Do not base your answers on whether you agree with the statements.

If you are doing this activity as a member of a class or group, compare your answers with those of other class or group members. Be able to explain your answers. You may discover that others will come to different conclusions than you. Listening to the reasons others present for their answers may give you valuable insights in distinguishing between bias and reason.

If you are reading this book alone, ask others if they agree with your answers. You will find this interaction very valuable.

R = a statement based upon reason
B = a statement based upon bias
I = a statement impossible to judge

1. Contemporary feminism has yet to produce a single work that would convince someone who disagrees with feminist ideas.

2. A wandering babboon troop in search of food is organized to keep the pregnant females protectively surrounded by powerful males who guard them from danger.

3. By instructing a child to *act* like a girl or *act* like a boy, the cult of sex differences says "Conform," "Pretend," "Act"; it does not say "Be your best self."

4. The "masculine" characteristics in our culture are antisocial and dangerous while much of what we know as feminine behavior promotes society's well-being.

5. When we say that a woman is as good as a man, we ought to mean the obvious: that a woman is just as much an ordinary human being as a man, with just as much right to individual tastes and preferences.

6. It is unreasonable in the extreme that the nature-nurture, heredity-environment controversy must be addressed today as a serious issue.

7. Gender is one of the earliest concepts children understand since the anatomical, biological, and physical sex differences are among the most visually obvious human characteristics.

8. Women have found their indentities in the care suggested in their bodies and have taken it for granted that the outer world belongs to men.

9. If each individual child has potential for both masculine and feminine behavior and if a society emphasizes "unisex," the child will not learn to respond sexually to the opposite sex.

10. A number of investigators have found that the female brain responds more powerfully to almost any stimulus than does the male brain, which explains the common-sense observation that women are more "sensitive" than men, and more prone to stress.

11. The structure and functioning of the brain are influenced by environment, meaning that genetic and hormonal influences are inextricable from environmental influences.

12. The independence and ego-strength necessary for achievement in certain analytical fields are completely absent from the cultural experience of nearly every girl child.

202

Bibliography

The following list of books, periodicals, and pamphlets deals with the subject matter of this chapter.

Bruno Bettelheim — "Growing Up Female," *Harper's Magazine*, October 1962.

Cynthia Fuchs Epstein — "Ideal Images and Real Roles: The Perpetuation of Gender Inequality," *Dissent*, Fall 1984.

Marilyn French — *Beyond Power: On Women, Men, and Morals.* New York: Summit Books, 1985.

George Gilder — *Sexual Suicide.* New York: Quadrangle Books, 1973.

Herb Goldberg — *The Hazards of Being Male.* New York: Signet, 1977.

Stephen Goldberg — *The Inevitability of Patriarchy.* New York: William Morrow and Company, Inc., 1973.

Florence Howe — "Sexual Stereotypes Start Early," *Saturday Review*, October 16, 1971.

Margaret Mead — *Male and Female: A Study of Sexes in a Changing World.* New York: William Morrow and Company, Inc., 1949.

John Money and Patricia Tucker — *Sexual Signatures: On Being a Man or a Woman.* Boston: Little, Brown and Company, 1975.

Ashley Montagu — *On the Natural Superiority of Women.* New York: Macmillan Publishing Company, 1968.

James C. Neely — *Gender: The Myth of Equality.* New York: Simon and Schuster, 1981.

Peggy Reeves Sanday — *Female Power and Male Dominance.* New York: Cambridge University Press, 1981.

Nancy Makepeace Tanner — *On Becoming Human.* New York: Cambridge University Press, 1981.

Naomi Weisstein — "Tired of Arguing about Biological Inferiority?" *Ms. Magazine*, November 1982.

Barbara Welter — "The Cult of True Womanhood," *American Quarterly*, Summer 1966.

How Does Feminism Affect Society?

Introduction

When Betty Friedan wrote her pivotal book *The Feminine Mystique* in 1963, she questioned the basis of the middle class American woman's existence. Having a husband, children, and a home is not enough for women, she wrote; in fact, some parts of childrearing and most housework requires the intellectual capacity of an 8-year-old. To avoid the boredom, frustration, and waste of talent inherent in this lifestyle, she urged women to pursue a more challenging existence outside the confines of their suburban ghettoes.

Ms. Friedan's analysis obviously touched questions that had privately troubled many women, for astonishing numbers of them read her book and applied it to their own lives. Not only did women change their lives individually, but they began to organize. The National Organization for Women, the first major contemporary women's organization which campaigned, often militantly, for equality of opportunity and treatment in the spheres of work, politics, and home, was one result. The women's movement, vibrant again after decades of dormancy that began after women won the vote, gained support from a large number of politically radical women, many of whom had been actively involved in the civil rights movements of the early 1960s. These moral radical feminists brought to the new movement political and organizational skills, desire to change society's institutions and basic values, and their own outrage at having been expected to play supporting roles in the movements they had participated in earlier. Many of them had not forgotten the words of Stokely Carmichael, black activist and leader of the Student Non-Violent Coordinating Committee, who said that "the only position for women in SNCC is prone."

Contemporary feminism helped change women's lives. More women entered law and medical school and other occupations traditionally reserved for men; more women were elected to political office; school textbooks were revised to remove offensive sexist language and curricula were changed to include new material about women; advertising that fostered stereotypes of women as mindless drones or sex machines, if not entirely eliminated, was strongly challenged and countered with positive female images. In their personal lives, many women broke old patterns of behavior: working out equal partnerships with their mates; choosing not to marry and instead to devote themselves to causes or careers; deciding to bear and raise children alone.

By the end of the 1970s, feminism began to experience a loss of the unity and single-minded purpose that had enabled it to achieve many important goals: Factions within the feminist movement began to speak in louder voices: white middle-class women had been the most visible participants; now black and poor women began more volubly to assert their own causes. Some feminist leaders, seeming simply to tire of the continuing, exhausting effort to achieve political and social gains, moved on to more personal concerns. A major setback occurred when in 1982, despite the commitment of a generation of feminist leaders to its passage, the Equal Rights Amendment to the US Constitution was not ratified. All of this transpired in a society that was becoming less idealistic and more and more anxious about its contracting economy.

The future direction of feminism is unclear. Political radicals are urging feminists to address economic and other issues that will attract more minority and working-class women to the movement. Moving away from her earlier radical position, Betty Friedan now urges women to protect the gains they have made and to renew their commitment to building families and communities in partnership with men. Other feminists maintain that this kind of compromise will return women to the same position they were in in the 1950s.

The following viewpoints illustrate some of the themes of contemporary feminism, from the anger and anxiety men and women express in facing feminist issues to the larger political and social questions raised.

"We have been brought up to feel [that]...a woman is a failure if she fails to please men."

Feminism Rescues Women from Oppression

Sally Kempton

The following viewpoint, although written in 1970, vividly describes the plight of many contemporary women. Sally Kempton, a writer and feminist, details her own liberation from conventional female training and behavior. Women, she writes, are conditioned to be economically and emotionally dependent on men. They can achieve self-esteem and independence, she professes, only through active feminism: careful examination of women's roles in society and in personal relationships, and determined action to change those roles.

As you read, consider the following questions:

1. What essential advantage does the author believe adolescent boys have over girls?
2. Why did Ms. Kempton hate men?
3. Does the author seem to admire women more than men? Explain.
4. Why does the author believe men fear the hatred of women?
5. What hope for the future, if any, does Ms. Kempton see?

Sally Kempton, "Cutting Loose," *Esquire*, July 1970. Reprinted with permission from *Esquire*. Copyright © 1970 by Esquire Associates.

I think most American adolescents hate and fear the opposite sex: in adolescence it seems that only one's lovers can hurt one, and I think that even young people who are entirely secure in other relations recognize and would, if they could, disarm the power the other sex has for them. But for adolescent boys, sexual success is not the sole measure of worth. It is assumed that they will grow up and work, that their most important tests will come in areas whose criteria are extra-sexual. They can fail with girls without failing entirely, for there remains to them the public life, the male life.

But girls have no such comfort. Sex occupies even the economic center of our lives; it is, we have been brought up to feel, our lives' work. Whatever else she may do, a woman is a failure if she fails to please men. The adolescent girl's situation is by definition dependent: she *must* attract, and therefore, however she may disguise it, she must compromise the sticky edges of her personality, she must arrange herself to conform with other people's ideas of what is valuable in a woman.

I was early trained to that position, trained, in the traditional manner, by my father. Like many men who are uncomfortable with adult women, my father saw his daughter as a potential antidote to his disappointment in her sex. I was someone who could be molded into a woman compatible with his needs, and also, unlike my mother, I was too impressionable to talk back. So I became the vessel into which he fed his opinions about novels and politics and sex; he fed me also his most hopeful self-image....

Staying Close to Daddy

Of course, I had to marry a grown-up, a father figure if you will, and my husband, as it turned out, had to marry a child. That is, he had to have an intelligent woman, but one whose intelligence had been, as it were, castrated by some outside circumstances. My youth served that purpose; my other handicaps had not as yet emerged.

Anyway, our romantic personae lasted about one year. For a year he was kind to me and listened to my problems and put up with the psychosomatic diseases which marriage had induced in me, and for a year I brought joy and spontaneity into his drab grownup existence. Then he began to get tired of being a father and I to resent being a child, and we began to act out what I think is a classic example of contemporary marriage.

As it turned out, I realized with horror, that I had done exactly what middle-class girls are supposed to do. I had worked for a year in the communications industry, and my glamorous job had enabled me to meet a respectable, hardworking man who made a lot of money at *his* glamorous job, and I had settled down (stopped screwing around) and straightened myself out (went into analysis), and all that was missing was babies. I defended myself by assuming that we would be divorced in a year, and sneered a lot at Design Research furniture and the other symbols of middle-class marriage, but still I could not escape feeling that I had fallen not just into a trap but into a cliche. On the other hand, I loved my husband, and I was still a writer, that is to say, a privileged woman with a life of her own. I could afford, as I began to at that time, to read feminist literature without really applying it to my own situation.

'I am too listening: Your life seems meaningless. By the way, what's for dinner?'
Reprinted by permission of Chronicle Features, San Francisco.

My husband, although he is nice to women, is a male supremacist, very much in the style of Norman Mailer. That is, he invests women with more or less mystical powers of control over the inner workings of the world, but thinks that feminine power is strongest when exercised in child rearing and regards contraception as unnatural. When I had my first stirrings of feminist grievance, he pronounced the subject a bore; I used to follow him from room to room, torturing him with my recitals of the sexist atrocities I was beginning to find in my favorite novels, and when I complained that magazines were paying me less than they paid men, he accused me of trying to blame the world for my own crazy passivity. But we were engaged at that time in the usual internal power struggle, and my feminism seemed to both of us more an intellectual exercise than a genuine commitment. It was not until many months later that he began to accuse me of hating men.

In the third year of our marriage, we went to live in Los Angeles because of my husband's work. During the year we spent away from home I found that I could not work, and that he was always working, and we suddenly found ourselves frozen into the textbook attitudes of male-female opposition. We fought continually, and always about the same things. He accused me of making it impossible for him to work, I accused him of keeping me dangling, dependent upon him for all emotional sustenance, he accused me of spending too much money and of keeping the house badly, I accused him of expecting me continually to subordinate my needs to his. The difficulty, I realized over and over again without being able to do much about it, was that I had gotten myself into the classic housewife's position: I was living in a place I didn't want to be, and seeing people I didn't like because that was where my man was, I was living my husband's life and I hated him for it. And the reason this was so was that I was economically dependent on him; having ceased to earn my living I could no longer claim the breadwinner's right to attention for my special needs.

More Unhappy than Ever Before

My husband told me that I was grown-up now, twenty-six years old, there were certain realities which I had to face. He was the head of the household: I had never questioned that. He had to fulfill himself: I had never questioned that. He housed and fed me and paid for my clothes, he respected my opinions and refused all his opportunities to make love to other women, and my part of the bargain should have become clear to me by now. In exchange for those things, I was supposed to keep his house and save his money and understand that if he worked sixteen hours a day for a year it was no more than necessary for his self-fulfillment. Which was all quite true. Except that it was also necessary for his fulfillment that I should be there for those few hours when he had time for me, and not complain about the hours when he did not, and that I should adapt myself to his situation or else end the marriage. It never occurred to him to consider adapting himself to mine, and it never occurred to me. I only know that his situation was bad for me, was alien, was in fact totally paralyzing, that it kept me from working, that it made me more unhappy that I had been in my life.

I knew that I was being selfish. But he was being selfish also, the only difference being that his selfishness was somehow all right, while mine was inexcusable. Selfishness was a privilege I had earned for a while by being a writer, that is, a person who had by male standards a worthwhile place to spend her time. As soon as I stopped functioning as a writer I became to my husband and to everyone else a mere woman, somebody whose time was valueless, somebody who had no excuse for selfish preoccupation with her own wants.

The Liberation of Women

The bargaining between married people generally works unevenly: the wife eventually finds that her life has changed radically, but not her husband's....

The essential factor in the liberation of the married woman is understanding of her condition....Essentially she must recapture her own will and her own goals, and the energy to use them, and in order to effect this some quite "unreasonable" suggestions, or demands, may be necessary.

Germaine Greer, *The Female Eunuch*, 1970.

I used to lie in bed beside my husband after those fights and wish I had the courage to bash in his head with a frying pan. I would do it while he slept, since awake he would overpower me, disarm me. If only I dared, I would mutter to myself through clenched teeth, pushing back the realization that I didn't dare not because I was afraid of seriously hurting him—I would have loved to do that—but because even in the extremity of my anger I was afraid that if I cracked his head with a frying pan he would leave me. God, how absurd it was (god, how funny, I would mutter to myself, how amusing, oh wow, what a joke) that my whole life's effort had been directed toward keeping men from leaving me, toward placating them, submitting to them, demanding love from them in return for living in their style, and it all ended with me lying awake in the dark hating my husband, hating my father, hating all the men I had ever known. Probably I had always hated them. What I couldn't figure out was whether I hated them because I was afraid they would leave me or whether I was afraid they would leave me because I hated them.

Hating Men Who Oppress

Because one cannot for very long support such a rage without beginning to go crazy, I tried to think of the problem in political terms. It seemed to me too easy to say that my hatred for men was a true class hatred, that women hate men because women

211

are an oppressed class hungering for freedom. And yet wherever there exists the display of power there is politics, and in women's relations with men there is continual transfer of power, there is, continually, politics. There are political analogies even to our deepest, our most banal fantasies. Freud maintains that the female terror of the penis is a primary fear, and that the male fear of castration by the vagina is merely a retaliatory fantasy, a guilty fear of punishment. The serf fears the overlord's knout, the overlord, guilty, fears the serf's revenge. Women are natural guerrillas. Scheming, we nestle into the enemy's bed, avoiding open warfare, watching the options, playing the odds....

Men Are Beasts

Men are beasts, we say, joking, parodying the Victorian rag, and then realize to our surprise that we believe it. The male has force almost beyond our overpowering, the force of laws, of science, of literature, the force of mathematics and skyscrapers and the Queensboro Bridge; the penis is only its symbol. We cannot share men's pride in the world they have mastered. If you follow that symbolism to its conclusion, we are ourselves that conquered world.

It is because they know that this is true, know it in their bones if not in their heads, that men fear the hatred of women. For women are the true maintenance class. Society is built upon their acquiescence, and upon their small and necessary labors. Restricted to the supportive role, conditioned to excel only at love, women hold for men the key to social order. It is a Marxist truism that the original exploitation, the enslavement which set the pattern from everything which came later, was the enslavement of women by men. Even the lowest worker rests upon the labor of his wife. Where no other claim to distinction exists, a man defines himself by his difference from the supportive sex; he may be a less than admirable man, but at least he is a man, at least he is not a woman.

And if women have fought, they have fought as guerrillas, in small hand-to-hand skirmishes, in pillow wars upon the marriage bed. When they attack frontally, when they come together in groups to protest their oppression, they raise psychic questions so profound as to be almost inadmissible....

When men imagine a female uprising they imagine a world in which women rule men as men have ruled women: their guilt, which is the guilt of every ruling class, will allow them to see no middle ground. And it is a measure of the unconscious strength of our belief in natural male dominance that all of us, men and women, revolt from the image of women with a whip, that the female sadist is one of our most deep-rooted images of perversion.

And although I believe this male fantasy of feminine equality

212

as a euphemism for feminine dominance to be evidence of the oppressors' neurosis rather than of any supporting fact, it was part of the character of my resentment that I once fancied wresting power from men as though nothing less than total annihilation would satisfy my rage. The true dramatic conclusion of this narrative should be the dissolution of my marriage; there is a part of me which believes that you cannot fight a sexist system while acknowledging your need for love of a man, and perhaps if I had had the courage finally to tear apart my life I could write you about my hard-working independence, about my solitary self-respect, about the new society I hope to build. But in the end my husband and I did not divorce, although it seemed at one time as if we would. Instead I raged against him for many months and joined the Women's Liberation Movement, and thought a great deal about myself, and about whether my problems were truly all women's problems, and decided that some of them were and some of them were not. My sexual rage was the most powerful single emotion in my life, and the feminist analysis has become for me, as I think it will for most women of my generation, as significant an intellectual tool as Marxism was for generations of radicals. But it does not answer every question. To discover that something has been wrong is not necessarily to make it right: I would be lying if I said that my anger had taught me how to live. But my life has changed because of it. I think I am becoming in many small ways a woman who takes no shit. I am no longer submissive, no longer seductive; perhaps it is for that reason that my husband tells me sometimes that I have become hard, and that my hardness is unattractive. I would like it to be otherwise. I think that will take a long time.

"Men are the guilty sex. That is...the message
of feminism."

Feminism Destroys Men

Stephen Koch

First published in 1975, the following viewpoint bluntly details
the frustrations many men feel when confronted with the feminist
revolution. The author, Stephen Koch, is a novelist and critic. In
this viewpoint, he claims that in an effort to boost female self-
esteem, feminists have taken away man's function in society. There
can be no positive relationship between the sexes, he writes, until
men are allowed a satisfying role.

As you read, consider the following questions:

1. Why does the author say that men are the "guilty sex"? Do
   you think this represents Mr. Koch's own views?
2. According to the author, for what things do feminists want
   men to feel shame?
3. Why does Mr. Koch believe that a satisfactory definition of
   fatherhood is essential to defining the male role? How do
   you think he would like to see fatherhood defined?
4. What does Mr. Koch say is the feminist ideal of male/female
   relationships? Why does he not like this ideal?

Stephen Koch, "The Guilty Sex," Esquire, July 1975. © 1975 by Stephen Koch. Reprinted
by permission of International Creative Management.

Not long ago, during a radio talk show—the kind with people calling in to explain their philosophies of life—a thirtyish on-the-air sage and a listener were exploring (for a change) the cruel conundrum of becoming an ethical being in a society rotten with macho. Groping his way, the commentator ventured, "Well, I think we—we men..." "Men!" The listener blurted the word again, startled, pained. There was a brief silence while the ugly sound sank in. Then they both giggled.

What's Wrong with Men

That shocked verbal blush may seem strange, but is it really? After all, the word "man" has acquired a rather nasty sound. The last five years have divested it of the old heroic ring; certainly it's no longer okay to talk about being one with any flourish of pride. (It is okay to talk about being a "person" or "human being," but that is slightly different.) Yet these two full-grown members of the male sex positively gagged on the word. Inevitably, the conversation had been all about what's wrong with men. As the most powerful general idea of our time, feminism increasingly dominates *any* discussion of sexual identity or what goes on between men and women—and the feminist discussion of men is mainly about what's wrong with men....

Men are the guilty sex. That is not only the message of feminism, it is what the whole obsessional moral language of the Sixties has at last settled down and resolved itself in to saying. That moral language always needed a "them," and men fit the bill. True enough, there is nothing very new about men's role as the guilty sex. Half the items in feminism's catalog of contempt were already strewn around us, many as old as Huckleberry Finn. There is nothing new in the vision of men as brutal, bemuscled weaklings, cloddishly incapable of appreciating the Higher Things; rough creatures tracking up the rug with their coarse, animalistic emotions. During the nineteenth century, men were the guilty sex because they were the sexual sex; in the twentieth, they are the untender, faithless sex that ruts without love. They are the dishonest sex, destructively competitive, stupidly in continual need of massage for their fatuous pouting male egos. Animals. Children. Longer than anyone can remember, ideas like this have been mixed with many a mother's milk. But the feminists...refined the old-fashioned angry contempt into a modern politicized rhetoric, with some crucial additions. Above all, men are also *unnecessary:* Whatever value a member of the guilty sex might have for a woman, it should, must, not be social, emotional, or economic dependence.

Add other details: Big talkers though they are, men can't take the heat—"men are *terrified* of a sexually liberated or competitive woman. Their poor egos, you know." Add: In personal relations, men are frightened cripples, incapable of a "committed relationship," the current code word for marriage. When not guilty in their false, but oppressive, strength, they are guilty in their unreliable, infantile weakness. Add: Even "good" men are infected with the masculine disease, with little hope of cure. Their "conditioning" is too deep. Add: Since by nature or training men are less sensitive than women, they are also less intelligent. At best, their intelligence is less good, less true, less beautiful. Add: In every way that matters, women are stronger than men, they have fewer "ego problems." Roll over Beethoven. Anything you can do, I can do better. Snakes and snails and puppy-dog tails....

Meanwhile, though feminism keeps on clinging fiercely to the old-fashioned moralism about the evils of the hungry, nasty (male) ego, it very intelligently has no interest whatever in transcending, surrendering, or obliterating the female ego. Hardly. Psychologically, the whole operation resembles a vast, systematic rescue mission for the battered and ignored female ego, with results rather like a new, chic boosterism, more and more orchestrated with good old-fashioned American success stories. Central to this perhaps necessary boosterism has been feminism's reinvention of the word "woman," so that it no longer means the adult female but "Woman," that is, an essentially heroic moral condition....''Woman'' means all at once nourishing suffering, purifying rage, firm determination, outraged victimization, clarity of vision, self-reliance, self-knowledge, richness of passion, action, power. The classical heroic virtues, in short. This heroism is now sexually exclusive: Men have no part in it, they do not participate in these virtues. But men are necessary to the heroic epic of feminism. The vision of Woman cannot survive a day without the vision of the guilty sex, and if the guilty sex had not existed, feminism would have had to invent it.

All this is half symptom, half strategy. Feminism's rescue mission has been significantly successful, and in such a heartening and exciting way that one feels like not noticing that it is built on a certain amount of rhetorical dishonesty. Among many other things, it has indeed shown many women the way out of inspired infantilism and bewildered self-hatred....

Meanwhile the men...confront what they have always confronted: that this culture offers less and less to make any mode of "being a man" acceptable, promising, gratifying, endurable. What's more, they are stuck with a problem: the unshakable belief that the only *nourishing* freedom belongs to the victim, that freedom *means* the victim's process of self-liberation. And if the precious, all-prized right to view oneself as a victim is withdrawn—as feminism has definitively withdrawn it from men—what then?...

Shaming Men into Silence

A nifty dilemma. The greatest silencer of all is shame. It works much better than fear, much better than doubt. We are currently surrounded by an immense, interminable discussion; American writing now is almost totally dominated by the how-to books of alienated sexual identity. But at the center of this discussion there is a silence—a silence about the *actual* masculine experience. And I suppose it could be argued that silence exists because the whole discussion rests upon a notion of masculine failure and guilt; that without that silencing notion, the discussion would come to an end; certainly the terms would change so dramatically as to become almost unrecognizable. But the discussion is not going to end; there is no real reason why it should. More important, it seems to me, is that the problems of sexual identity men currently confront are older and bigger than feminism, and (no doubt because nothing is harder to discuss) nobody seems really prepared to define them. Take, for example,...George Gilder's [1974 book] *Naked Nomads*....

Gilder quotes Margaret Mead: "The recurrent problem of

civilization is to define the male role." Certainly it is the problem that has recurred right now. Why the male role in particular? Because only men can ever be considered socially unnecessary. Whatever the theoretical or real arrangement, whether it is matriarchy, patriarchy, or the hopeful promise of egalitarian mixed doubles, women are essential to the continuing life of the human race. And men are not.

Losses Inflicted by Feminism

The reason I still oppose feminism more than ten years later is that I love my family more than I long to relive a bachelor freedom. I therefore understand the terrible losses inflicted by feminism on the men and women of America today who try to live by its remorseless egalitarian code, who attempt to twist their lives and bodies into the unisex mold, who tangle in loveless sterility on the procrustean beds of emancipation. It may work for the rich and successful for a while. But it will never work for a society at all. As Sweden contemplates its illegitimacy rate of 40 per cent—and America struggles with the harvest of broken families in the ghetto with an illegitimacy rate near 80 per cent in many cases— can we not acknowledge that men and women are different and that families depend on sex roles, however compromised with change, and *vive la difference*?

George Gilder, *National Review*, November 30, 1984.

That is, most men are not. In a given year, it takes one hundred women to make one hundred babies. In theory, it takes only one man. The other ninety-nine are theoretically unnecessary and could be dispensed with entirely. Therefore men must find some service to the society—the society of women, above all—which will make them essential to the continuing life of the society. If, that is, men are to have meaningful lives, if they are to participate in what Gilder calls "responsible love." Without performing that service, men are threatened with meaninglessness in a way that women can never be. For whom do men perform this service? Women. (And if the role is going to last, acquire content, it had better be a service beyond his cock.) Who finally judges the value of that service? Women. Women are the ones born necessary. Women are the center.

Suppose the man fails? Suppose the woman stops valuing his contribution? Suppose he can't perform it, or finds the available ways of performing it unrewarding, unacceptable? He then becomes one of Gilder's naked nomads, the troop of men without meaningful relations to women. Producing both his personal observations and a group of slightly tricky but still pretty convincing statistics, Gilder argues that unmarried men are, on the whole, the most miserable group of any marital status in this society. The statistics range from violent crime (*ninety percent* of it is committed by unmarried men), alcoholism, chronic depression, mental disease, accidental death, suicide and the disguised suicide of the guy who, after drowning his sorrows, decides to make them fly at ninety miles an hour in that spiffy bachelor's Porsche of his. Unmarried women are much better off than the unmarried men in all categories: In addition, the two groups earn about the same amount of money until the age of fifty-five, after which women earn more. In true conservative style, Gilder argues that most men develop meaningful lives—i.e. meaningful relations to women and children—only through institutions. And he triumphantly concludes that there is only one such institution capable of turning the trick in an advanced egalitarian democracy: it is monogamous marriage, and an active role as father and provider.

Unsatisfying Male Roles

Do I agree with all this? I don't know. I don't know. Gilder's ideas about proper sex roles and the necessity of marriage have the weakness of all reactionary arguments, no matter how intelligent: They address a reality that no longer exists. The notion that men and women here and now are in any way ready, willing or able to relate to one another the way they did in 1915 or 1925 really strikes me as laughable. It really deserves some kind of prize, takes the cake. Right now, does the role of father and provider remain truly gratifying and essential, successfully defining how men participate in "responsible love"? No doubt, for a lot of people. But there are a lot of others for whom that idea provokes little more than an angry or despairing groan. Last but not least, you don't need to be [radical feminist] Ti-Grace Atkinson to suspect that a social system arbitrarily forcing women into social, emotional, and economic dependence on men is something less than the most splendid imaginable way of proving how marvelously valuable men are.

Yet Gilder in other ways is dead right. The question of sexual role is above all a matter of how one relates to the opposite sex and to children. That means *the* issue in defining the male role is *the definition of fatherhood.* And since fatherhood requires a definition that motherhood does not, one *must* produce a definition for a specifically male role. It is a simple fact that fatherhood and motherhood are different. It is a simple fact that in the entire history of humanity, not one man has ever given birth alone, nine months after the mother slipped fifty bucks into an envelope and took off to the Coast. It is a simple fact that no man has *ever* given birth to a child without being able to remember the name of that ship—its mother—that passed in the night. Plenty of children have been born without their fathers around. But not a single one ever came into the world without its mother. So what does fatherhood *mean?...*Just why, precisely, is the man around *at all?* Why is he wanted *at all?* Why is he kept around for those nine months? And then for that new lifetime? Above all, why does *he* want to stay around?

"Equality" in "Committed Relationships"

This is no abstract anthropological fantasy. Just ask the fatherless and/or father-hating children of the suburbs (or the ghetto); ask the men picking up junior for their weekly three hours of pain and humiliation at the movies and the zoo. Ask the feminists, or the members of the guilty sex who see less and less even slightly compelling, desirable, or promising in our famous "committed relationship" and its inevitable guilty end. Of course women do, should, and will want to function in the world of income-producing work, just as men do, should, and will. That is not, at heart, a sexual question: It has been for reasons that are plainly archaic, and that everyone knows are archaic. The central issue is this: The male role is in crisis above all because this society is less and less able to produce a necessary, satisfactory or satisfying definition of fatherhood. That fact, at least as much as the collapsing fantasy of male superiority (who ever believed it anyway?) is responsible for our big shake-up in masculine identity.

Children mean there *are* sex roles. The feminist rhetoric, attractive as it is, about "equal human beings" without sex roles therefore actually translates as follows: The female role, as always, will be to bear children. The male role will be to remain with the woman during pregnancy, the woman acknowledging him as the father, whereupon he proceeds to raise the child with her on exactly equal terms, just as they do other work on equal terms. In short, feminism's vision of "equal human beings" blandly assumes the steady continuation of happy, fulfilled, satisfying marriage, in which there is a male role after all: it is to be a *totally accommodating husband.* This, by the way, is why...the dominant feminist literature on the subject ...is all about how women heroically overcome all their old crippling inhibitions and limitations (and those of their men) the better to fulfill perfect marriages. Sexually, the "equal human beings" discussion is a disguised glorification of marriage, and it assumes that marriage is the way men and women should relate to one another.

But from where I sit, that looks less like the solution than the problem. It's a problem damn little likely to be solved by the reigning rhetoric of Women and the guilty sex. As to our rhetorical "equal human beings" and their super marriages, one can only lift a dubious eyebrow, tip one's hat to the lucky winners, and marvel at the amazing simplicity of it all.

"[Feminism] has effectively robbed us of one thing upon which the happiness of most women rests—men."

Feminism Isolates Women

Mona Charen

Mona Charen was a third-year law student at George Washington University when she published this essay. In it she describes several of her most talented, successful feminist friends and how miserable their independence has made them. Ms. Charen's viewpoint details the anxiety and loneliness many women report facing because of feminist choices they have made.

As you read, consider the following questions:

1. How, according to Ms. Charen, does feminism damage relations between the sexes, particularly where marriage and monogamy are concerned?
2. What strategies does the author see many of her friends using to cope with their loneliness? Are these working?
3. Is the author entirely critical of feminism or does she see some advantages in it?
4. Do you think the author portrays the situation correctly?

Mona Charen, "The Feminist Mistake," *National Review*, March 23, 1984. © 1984 National Review, Inc., 150 East 35th Street, New York, NY 10016. Reprinted with permission.

We have arrived at the point where relations between the sexes are vexed, not just because they misunderstand each other, but because the weaker (I say it defiantly) misunderstands itself. Moreover, because of the...adherence to the feminist mistake, women are making both themselves and men (who had a devil of a time understanding women before all this) miserable.

For support, I cite my female friends. They range in age from 24 to 35. All are bright, attractive and privileged. Heiresses of the movement, they are...lawyers, journalists, professors, and producers. The number whose emotional lives are wholesome and fulfilling could be counted on a pitchfork.

My girlfriends' woes are not unusual. I say this because whole forests have given their lives so that the complaints of upper-middle class young women could be enumerated, analyzed, deplored, and sulked about. But in those reams of articles, hours of media specials, and numberless academic symposia lurks a planted presumption: namely, that the nostrum to cure what ails modern woman is more of the poison that first made her ill. Smite that stereotype! Debunk that role model! Man (as it were) the barricades!

The women's movement has not been an unredeemed disaster. But let's take a closer look at the price of victory.

In dispensing its spoils, women's lib has given my generation high incomes, our own cigarette, the option of single parenthood, rape crisis centers, personal lines of credit, free love, and female gynecologists. In return, it has effectively robbed us of one thing upon which the happiness of most women rests—men.

My friends don't read Harlequin romances. Their tastes run more to Jane Austen's Mr. Knightly and Rudolf Nureyev. But the difference is one of sophistication only. In the feminine imagination, all the romantic male figures exude authority. But at this point the feminist intrudes on the reverie and wags a finger at the pounding heart. There'll be none of that! The New American Woman must seek independence, self-actualization, and personal growth. And what is it now permissible to seek in a man? Presumably, only applause.

Lisa

Lisa knows, at some level, that the modern woman is expected to be self-sufficient (loosely translated from feminese—happy without men). Indeed, about every other week she sends me a literate and well-reasoned letter arguing just that. Dependence, she asserts, just isn't practical in our era. There's always untimely death, divorce, fire, flood, and famine to consider. Fair enough. The trouble is, Lisa's epiphanies on the virtues of the single life seem to dovetail with the fortunes of her love life. On alternate weeks, when all is well with Harold, her letters are all church bells and craft fairs.

There is of course nothing new about wounded women hotly vowing to enter convents on Monday and registering silver patterns on Thursday. What the women's movement has done, however, is to pile additional layers of confusion onto a subject that was scarcely clear-cut to begin with. Lisa knows she is wretched after a quarrel with Harold on the dread subject of "commitment." What she doesn't know is whether her demands, and indeed even her feelings, are legitimate. *She* justifies his inconstancy to me. "His career is so terribly important to him. He can't feel tied down right now." Thus is the still small voice in feminism doing its mischief. For how can Lisa, exhorted from every secular pulpit to make her own career and personal growth the *summum bonum*, ask a man to do anything less?

ROTHCO
ORIGINAL

"The independent women in you has emerged—you've got an ulcer!"

© Buresch/Rothco

I'll go further and assert...that for three thousand years Western civilization has consisted of a magnificent conspiracy to tie men down—to hamstring their clamorous hormones and confine their attentions to only one woman. Men always resisted domestication, recognizing (correctly) that the arrangement suited women's needs and desires far more than their own. Unless feminism can come up with a way to make men have babies, monogamy and marriage will continue to serve primarily the interests of women—though men can be taught to like it. For men, marriage is an acquired taste...like caviar.

President Reagan was probably alluding to something of this sort when he remarked, during an address to a meeting of women's groups, that "...if it wasn't for women, we men would still be walking around in skin suits and carrying clubs." The ladies booed, for heaven's sake! The feminist mistake now evidently dictates that women cannot take credit for advancing Western culture. I have actually heard feminists wax argumentative about the statistic that men commit more violent crime than women. "But domestic violence often goes unreported." You see, grandchildren, in their eagerness to obliterate *la différence*, feminists wound up slandering their own sex.

Elizabeth

Elizabeth is a lively, insightful young woman of 26 who lies about herself routinely. We met in the late Seventies at Barnard, where extravagant feminism was so entrenched that even handicapped students had difficulty getting a door opened for them. Our friendship was catalyzed by furtive, mutual confessions of apostasy. In hushed tones we admitted to each other that marrying "the right guy" and raising a family were our most cherished ambitions—indeed, for Elizabeth, those were the only things that held the promise of happiness. Her interests range from deficit spending to subatomic particles, but she never doubted that only a fulfilled family life could make her happy. She sighed over the feminist types, at war with their own best instincts, and felt serene and superior.

As graduation loomed, Elizabeth began to lie—a little to others, mostly to herself. What else could a cheerfully unliberated woman do at such a crossroad? It was easy, after all, while safely behind the gates at 116th Street and Broadway, to forecast a contented, unliberated postgraduate existence. But the drums were beating. Soon we'd be led, single-file, to the scaffold and severed from the university. The right guy was conspicuously absent. Pending his arrival, a career goal would have to be invented and then chirpily pursued. She'd always been interested in banking, Elizabeth would explain. Barnard nodded its approval. Banking gobbled her up, and for all the world she began to look and sound the consummate career woman, i.e., tartly efficient, vaguely harassed, and terribly current.

Outside the office, Liz's true ambition remained unsatisfied. She ricocheted among lovers and suitors like a rapidly deflating balloon. The irony is that she is not an unstable person. It just happens that the one message of the women's movement she accepted uncritically was the notion that "Victorian" hang-ups about sex were best discarded. She clings to this view despite the equally strong conviction that sexual intimacy leaves women more vulnerable than it does men. So while Elizabeth has tumbled freely into bed whenever her own inclination or the entreaties of the young man made it seem appropriate, she is regulary tearful and disconsolate if he fails to call the following day. She feels betrayed and ill-used. But on what grounds? The wisdom of women's lib teaches that the sexual "double standard" was invented to convenience men. The liberated man and the liberated woman, outside the strictures of a "relationship," are now free to couple when ready—and no tiresome touches of courtliness like the morning-after phone call are required. On the contrary, considering that the unspoken premise of their lovemaking was precisely that it was *not* lovemaking at all but simply mutual, carnal gratification, a phone call would be presumptuous. It would suggest that she was motivated not by wholesome, selfish lust, but by a desire to please him.

Men Need Sex Differences

As reluctant as feminists might be to admit it, there is compelling evidence that men need (much more than do women, who seem to require less reassurance of their gender identity) a clearly defined difference between the sexes. Every human culture, until the late 20th century, has provided such a difference, creating an elaborate and often arbitrary contract between men's and women's activities, dress and behavior.

Annie Gottlieb, *Reader's Digest*, January 1984.

So the search for Mr. Right by the reluctantly liberated woman continues to exact its price in emotional scar tissue. And Mr. Right is perfect in all respects save one: He's terribly tardy....

Sonia

The most conspicuously gifted and brilliant of my friends teaches at a prestigious university. The master of several languages, she is an experienced horsewoman, singer, philosopher, and polemicist. Sonia's magnificent wit always verges on the outrageous—which tinges each of our encounters with a certain delightful suspense. Each time I phone her, though, I am filled with suspense much more closely resembling foreboding, because she is also capable of screeching, nose-dive depressions. It is probable, considering her flamboyance and eccentricity, that Sonia would be restless and dissatisfied in any era. But the feminist mistake has allowed her to fall more easily into the kind of error to which she was, in any case, prone.

By temperament excitable and melodramatic, her unfettered life is a virtual blueprint of the feminist ideal: her own apartment, celebrity houseguests, not one but two careers. On these facts, she could pass even the most fastidious feminist white-glove test. But this accomplishment gives her no satisfaction. She regards feminism and all its works with contempt. She lives alone at 35 because she too is waiting for the elusive Mr. Right. Indeed, I sometimes think Sonia's intellectual glitter and razzle-dazzle are the equivalents of the coquette's wiggle or the flirt's mischievous smile—it's all done to appeal to men. That's not quite fair, but knowing Sonia's impish sense of humor, I think she might respond, "Why of course. Why else should a sensible girl read Schopenhauer in the original?"

I don't know if there is a right man for Sonia, or if any man could make her happy. But she does talk more and more of children as the years chug rudely along. When her hideous depressions do strike, they are born of a terrible sense of aloneness. For the most part, this is the result of her own high expectations, but it's also in part the harvest of feminism. Women's lib helped to create a world where it is unseemly to encourage, and positively obscene to pressure, a woman into marriage and motherhood. And no doubt in Heaven the angels are rejoicing at the decision of some shrews to remain childless. But some worthy women (like most men) require a little prodding to let childhood go and settle down to the responsibilities of adulthood. (This is not to disparage singleness across-the-board. In the maiden aunt who devotes herself to parents, it can be noble; in the distracted research scientist, just as well; and in the irredeemably selfish, a blessing.)...

If the single life were less glamorized, Sonia would very likely be married and fruitful by now. She might not be happy, but somehow I know my fingers wouldn't tremble as I dialed her phone number. Those desperate tailspin depressions just wouldn't be possible. She'd be far too busy complaining about how unhappy she was.

Naomi

I do have one friend who is completely comfortable with the timid new world as it is. Perhaps not coincidentally, she is also the most achieving, credential-mad dynamo of my acquaintance (male or female). Naomi did her undergraduate work at Princeton, accumulating honors and awards not passively but with a singlemindedness that would make Captain Ahab look like a Left

226

Bank dilettante. From there she charged into journalism, the glamour field of the Eighties, and captured more trophies. But when, 18 months out of college, her career was advancing only rapidly enough to satisfy an ordinarily ambitious person, she assayed the prestige landscape, spied what would most expeditiously catapult her onto the *New York Times* editorial page, and applied to law school. Harvard.

Naomi is not indifferent to men. Her approach can best be described as "scientific socializing." She is rarely without a steady boyfriend. When one is lacking, she assays the social landscape, fixes her sights on some bright, ambitious fellow, and pursues him doggedly until he surrenders. "You are a very unrealistic person," she once chided me, "you're waiting for someone who'll make you weak in the knees." Naomi's knees are made of tungsten. Perhaps, when she eventually proposes to her future husband, she'll get down on one of them.

Now I have known Naomi for 16 years, so I'm in a position to reveal a secret or two about her. She would not deny, I think, that she was raised in every material respect as a first-born son. She was supposed to be Norman. Not so many years ago, if a disappointed couple had found themselves the parents of a "baby woman" instead of a boy, an unhappy and insecure young lady was almost certain to result. Today you get an editor of the *Harvard Law Review* with knees of steel. There's one other secret I can reveal about Naomi—she reads romance novels.

Suffering the Backlash Against Feminism

It's not just blinding careerism on the part of women that has so aggravated relations between the sexes. It's the incessant carping that accompanies it. Feminists are forever discovering subtle new forms of sexism and then beating men about the head and shoulders with it. It is left to the rest of us to suffer the inevitable backlash this provokes among men....

If the feminists were truly engaged in an effort to reform the nation's manners and morals, I'd grab a banner and join the parade. But their true goal, to neuter our culture, is betrayed by the leveling language upon which they insist. Why should I pretend that women go about ogling and propositioning men when I know it isn't true, for the sake of some artificial parallelism? Women have enough flaws characteristic of their own sex without raiding the provinces of male perfidy.

Worse yet, feminism has contributed some subtle sexism of its own to the decaying discourse. In their headlong rush to complete "equality," feminists have stigmatized "ladylike" behavior as latter-day Uncle Tomism. In consequence, one of the traditional pleasures of female companionship—a certain delicacy of expression and sentiment—is giving way to coarseness and vulgarity.

227

Gentleness is prized today only in men; in women it is regarded as reactionary.

Perhaps my grandchildren will look back on our era as socially aberrant ("Did they really want boys and girls to be the same, Grandma?"). Perhaps not. One things is certain. It's up to the women....Women transmit culture. If feminist competitiveness loses, feminine contentment will win.

"Everybody pays a price for the choices she or he makes...[Waking up alone] is a cost many women are paying now...because there are so many advantages to having the freedom to pursue our own options."

Feminism Enriches Women

Amanda Spake

Amanda Spake writes frequently for and is a contributing editor to *Ms. Magazine*. In the following viewpoint, she comments on the loneliness, often attributed to the effects of feminism, some women without male partners feel. She writes that the feminist movement has made women's options so much broader and richer than they were even twenty years ago that women are finding new means of fulfillment.

As you read, consider the following questions:

1. Who, according to Ms. Spake, are "the Desperate Straights"? From her descriptions through the viewpoint, do you think the term is appropriate?
2. Ms. Spake says that times have changed and so must people's expectations. What kinds of adjustments does she say women must make?
3. What role does friendship play in the author's life? Do you agree with her assessment of the vital importance of friends?

Amanda Spake, "The Choices That Brought Me Here," *Ms.*, November 1984. Reprinted with the author's permission.

Recently, I went to an all-female dinner party in Washington ...where my ear tuned to a conversation about a different sort of modern female dilemma.

"But do you really *want* to get married?" one woman asked a friend of mine.

"I wouldn't mind," my friend responded sarcastically. "But I'm about to give up. I don't think there's a man left out there for me." This woman is a successful television reporter for a prime-time news show. She is attractive, well educated, and highly paid, respected in her field, 35 years old, and she has that same bitter tinge in her voice I've heard so often among a certain group of women. My group, to be specific.

"Somehow," my friend continued, "I never thought I'd be one of those women my mother always felt so sorry for—thirty-five and desperate."

This particular dinner party was not unlike a number of others I've been to in other places and with other women. This dinner, like others before it, was at the home of another "successful" woman. At 41, the hostess considers herself lucky to have been married once and to have had three daughters from that marriage. "My kids have been my mainstay," she interjected. This woman, too, has a career she loves (she runs a foundation), a renovated, inner-city town house, a good income, a terrific figure...and no steady man in her life, nor has she had one for some time. "All the exercise classes in the world can't make up for the fact that I seem to have become too powerful for any man," she lamented. "I like my life, my friends, my family. But I wish my personal life allowed me a relationship."

Paying the Price of Change

The majority of the women at this particular dinner, indeed, many of the women my age I meet nowadays, are very much like the hostess and the television reporter. They are not married, not living with men, not lesbian, and not particularly happy about their personal lives. They find they are spending too many years without intimate companionship...alone. Their lives reflect what has, in my view, become the hallmark of relations between the sexes these days—a crushing ambivalence. It is an ambivalence about sex and intimacy with one another, ambivalence about whether or not the trade-offs now required of *both* men and women in relationships are, after all, worth the price and pain they extract.

In this period of sexual uncertainty, though, one group is paying a high price for these social changes: women of the feminist generation, the baby boomers, that great glut of talented, beautiful women whom I call—in my more cynical moments—the Desperate Straights.

I can call them that, because I am one of them.

230

Who are the Desperate Straights? They are successful, achievement-oriented women, born in the 1940s and early 1950s. Most of us came to adulthood in the 1960s and discovered the key to a "meaningful life" was not necessarily marriage. As one woman put it, "When I was growing up, having a husband and family was absolutely irrefutable, *assumed* for all women. The 'extra' that *we* would try for, was to have a career."

We baby boomers were unique in that we were the first generation of American women to accept, on a mass scale, the awful truth that the traditional female roles we had been raised to emulate, wife and mother, would not be enough to sustain our lives—emotionally or economically. So we have developed a new set of nontraditional female values—ambition, competitiveness, assertiveness, and the will to win—values that fit neatly into our struggle for "meaningful work." I call it feminist determinism. (Our values *had* to change as we entered the male marketplace permanently—unlike our mothers who were fired when the men came back from World War II.)

Toward a Better Human Order

Common enterprises are the channels of redemption. In the words of [Antoine de] Saint-Exupery: "Love does not consist in gazing at each other but in looking together in the same direction." We must pay proper homage to the extravagant visions of the early [feminist] reformers. They dreamed of a new kind of human relationship and helped to make it come partway true. They freed man from the curse of his domination over woman, for however tender and sentimental that domination may have been it did in effect deny woman her full humanity. Nor will the future yield to fantasies of perfect sexual adjustment; man's (and certainly woman's) needs and dreams go beyond such private pleasures. They yearn toward a better human order, a finer race, as the feminists would say. What is needed most is a recovered faith and the stamina to take up the burden that the misunderstood and ridiculed feminists laid down.

Page Smith, *Daughters of the Promised Land*, 1970.

As it turns out, women's new marketplace values are antithetical to building the solid, interpersonal relationships between women and men we took for granted. Men, society, and often women themselves, still expect women to embody primarily "feminine" values—cooperation, nurturance, and impulse to yield. These are the same values traditionally used by women to attract, create, and sustain long-term relationships with men our own age. Men, that is, whose own interpersonal values—and their resulting expectations about women—changed very little.

As our group enters their forties, reports are that there will be more than two unattached women for every unattached man, even considering the skyrocketing divorce rate. Moreover, as Drs. Philip Blumstein and Pepper Schwartz report in their book, *American Couples*, "success at work" seems to statistically diminish a woman's chances of successful marriage. They cite the fact that in 1977, women between the ages of 35 and 44 with post-graduate degrees and personal incomes above $20,000 had four times the divorce rate of women with lower achievement.

Not "Having It All"

This may be the result of the battle between love and work that rages for most career-oriented women in couples. Work-oriented men are traditionally faulted (and excused) for not putting the necessary amount of time and emotional energy into their marriages or relationships. The burden of couple-tending usually falls to women. And as the sociologists are quick to point out, "Work-centered heterosexual women are clearly at a disadvantage...."

It's a disadvantage we single women are sometimes panicked about, too. The panic is often mistakenly labeled a despair over "not having it all," or more frequently, a fear that we will not bear children, since children are always perceived by society as women's only weapon against years without companionship after the men die off (or leave for younger women).

But I don't believe the feelings of panic and desperation many women are experiencing are simply the result of anxiety over the ticking of the Biological Clock. Granted, my research for this article has shown me that women with children are more satisfied with their personal lives than women without them. Children *do* provide an outlet for intimacy. But what seems to cut across the Biological Clock question is a sense of disappointment that life appears to offer less chance for male companionship and sexuality at a time when we want, increasingly, to share our hard-won success with another person. The competition for power and confusion over roles—at work and in bed—are causing single women increasingly to wonder: "Is there any chance for intimacy with men any more?"

It's a question that emerges from conflicts created by the schism between women's new realities and men's (and women's) old expectations. Ultimately, settling these conflicts demands acceptance of risk and choice itself, the need to find comfort and excitement in the lives we've made, even if those are not exactly the ones we believed we'd have.

The Value of Friends

One of the real positives in our lives, in fact, one factor that separated us Desperate Straights from the women of our mothers' generation, is the quality of our friendships—with other women primarily, but also with men. These friendships span many sexual love affairs, marriages, and "meaningful relationships." Yet, they may end up being the relationships in *our* lives that offer us love and meaning most consistently.

It has struck me more than once that the way I describe my friendships—I can't live without them—is the way my mother described her marriage. Does that mean we have chosen friendships over relationships? I hope they are not mutually exclusive. Indeed, many women believe friendships like these are mandatory to sustaining male/female sexual relationships.

"Friends are crucial to my life," one woman said, who recently abandoned her Desperate Straight status. "Not as a surrogate for John, but to keep my relationship with John on track...I don't have to depend on him for my total emotional needs. My friends—with my relationship—form the core of my life."

When the core of our lives is disturbed, even when it is comprised of "just friends," there is a pain that feels like a lover lost. I have seldom been so lonely as when my friend Barbara moved from San Francisco to Washington D.C., because she had established an important relationship with a man and wanted to live and work near him. There was a hole in my emotional life that I never successfully filled in the three years after she left.

Feminism Has Transformed Women's Lives

Like the wave of feminism in the nineteenth century, the [women's] movement has transformed the lives and aspirations of the majority of women in ways unmeasurable by statistics and in areas unreachable by the law. These achievements include the raising of women's intellectual, economic and political expectations, an increased intolerance of wife beating, rape and other violence against women, and a redefinition of women's sexuality.

Linda Gordon and Marla Erlien, *The Nation*, November 28, 1981.

Now that Barbara and I are in the same city again, we talk on the phone every night. We describe the day's events, unload the heavy emotional baggage and make light of it just as surely as my mother and father did when my father returned from the mysterious "downtown." And at the end of the evening's conversation, Barbara usually says, "I love you," and I am grateful. Everyone needs to hear that they are loved.

Intimacy and Commitment

Then, there is Arthur. Arthur and I have been friends since I met him on a street corner in Westwood, near UCLA, in 1967. He was a 21-year-old journalism student from Illinois, passing through California. Arthur immediately asked me to go to San

233

Diego with him the next day, a fact I believed in this period of easy sex that meant he was looking for a lover. I now know this is a common error made by the many women in whom Arthur raises romantic hopes, only to dash them later when they find out he is gay.

Over the last 17 years, Arthur and I haved moved separately back and forth across the country from East Coast to West Coast at least five times, yet somehow, we almost always find ourselves living 15 minutes away from each other. We enjoy being close enough to speak daily on the telephone and to go out together a least once a week. Whether it's fate or design is a mystery I no longer ponder.

Arthur and I probably know as much about each other's history, character flaws, and cantankerous corners as most married couples, and we are a lot more tolerant of them, too. We have seen each other through the emotional storms of countless love affairs (on his part) and two almost-marriages (on mine). We have never been lovers and never will be.

What is this relationship? Is this friendship? Love? Why is there so much concern, support, and commitment—qualities clearly lacking in many of our sexual affairs? Commitment, that's the key. And what I think this relationship represents is exactly the sort of life-sustaining friendship we Desperate Straights learned to develop to provide the warmth, commitment, and stability our fast-track sex lives, or the myth of them, lacked.

My friendships with Barbara and Arthur mean something else, too. They show me that women are learning to acknowledge that some basic needs, which once seemed linked only to sexual relationships, can, in fact, be satisfied by friends instead of lovers.

The Positive Value of Choices

I've come to believe that the way to get around the myths and expectations is to change the focus of my thinking from what I don't have in my life, to what I do: my independence, loving friends, work that gives me meaning and purpose. This requires a new acceptance of my life's choices, an acceptance that I *made* choices and that there is a distinctly positive value in choosing. The road not taken was, perhaps, a dead end after all.

I have to remember that a long time ago I set as my ultimate goal making a mark on the world, being known and remembered—by friends, yes, but not only by friends. I hoped to be remembered for a respected body of work. As a result, my first priority has been not a family, not a marriage, but a writing and political career. I chose this goal, but it chose me, as well. When I'm being honest, I have to admit I do not remember a time when I did not recognize—and feel glad—that this was the path I was on.

Sometimes my choices make me feel very "other," especially

when I am around other women who more closely fulfill the roles expected of them by their families and society. At those times I tell myself this: the fact that lots of *women* have not chosen my kind of life before, has more to do with the systematic stifling of female creativity and ambition, than it does with the long-term happiness of the people involved.

Liberation from Within

The psychological need to avoid independence—the "wish to be saved"—seemed to me an important issue, quite probably the most important issue facing women today. We were brought up to depend on a man and to feel naked and frightened without one. We were taught to believe that as women we cannot stand alone, that we are too fragile, too delicate, needful of protection. So that now, in these enlightened days, when our intellects tell us to stand on our own two feet, unresolved emotional issues drag us down. At the same time that we yearn to be fetterless and free, we also yearn to be taken care of....

We have only one real shot at "liberation," and that is to emancipate ourselves from within.

Colette Downing, *The Cinderella Complex*, 1981.

I go to bed at night with a cat and books and newspapers and I wake up in the morning with a face full of cat hair and papers all over the bed, only sometimes saying, "Why am I alone?" Everybody pays a price for the choices she or he makes. For me, the price is a temporary but disturbing longing for a kind of male/female intimacy I can't always find, sexual connection with another person whom I have learned, over time, to know and love. This is a cost many women are paying now, a price we have learned to bear because there are so many advantages to having the freedom to pursue our own options.

Valuing the pursuit of options is, to me, the key to accepting the lives we've made. Whether those options are new careers, more education, or different friends and lovers, there is a freedom inherent in the road we Desperate Straights have traveled, a freedom virtually unknown to the generations of women before us.

"If we can eliminate the false polarities and appreciate the limits and true potential of women's power, we will be able to join with men ...in the new human politics that must emerge."

Feminists Can Now Work Toward Broader Goals

Betty Friedan

Betty Friedan, writer, teacher, parent, and feminist leader, is the author of *The Feminine Mystique*, the book credited with inspiring the contemporary women's movement. Her most recent book, *The Second Stage*, states that feminism has moved beyond the militancy of the 1960s and 1970s. Feminists, she believes, have wrought enough significant changes that women are on a nearly equal level with men. Now, states Ms. Friedan, men and women can work together for an improved mutual future. Ms. Friedan believes that the old "sexual politics" (viewing each sex as a political class in competition with one another) can be replaced by a more flexible, cooperative "human politics." The following viewpoint, excerpted from *The Second Stage*, reflects this view.

As you read, consider the following questions:

1. Why does Ms. Friedan believe that the time for "sex-role polarization" has ended?
2. What are some of the positive things the author says that feminism has accomplished?
3. What kind of relationship does Ms. Friedan visualize for men and women today?

Betty Friedan, *The Second Stage*. New York: Summit Books, 1981. Copyright © 1981 by Betty Friedan. Reprinted by permission of Summit Books, a division of Simon & Schuster, Inc.

Though the women's movement has changed all our lives and surpassed our dreams in its magnitude, and our daughters take their own personhood and equality for granted, they—and we—are finding that it's not so easy to *live*, with or without men and children, solely on the basis of that first feminist agenda. I think, in fact, that the women's movement has come just about as far as it can in terms of women alone. The very choices, options, aspirations, opportunities that we have won for women—no matter how far from real equality—and the small degree of new power women now enjoy, or hunger for, openly, honestly, as never before, are converging on and into new economic and emotional urgencies. Battles lost or won are being fought in terms that are somehow inadequate, irrelevant to this new personal, and political, reality. I believe it's over, that first stage: the women's movement. And yet the larger revolution, evolution, liberation that the women's movement set off, has barely begun. How do we move on? What are the terms of the second stage?

First Stage Goals

In the first stage, our aim was full participation, power and voice in the mainstream, inside the party, the political process, the professions, the business world. Do women change, inevitably discard the radiant, enviable, idealized feminist dream, once they get inside and begin to share that power, and do they then operate on the same terms as men? Can women, will women even try to, change the terms?

What are the limits and the true potential of women's power? I believe that the women's movement, in the political sense, is both less and more powerful than we realize. I believe that the personal is both more and less political than our own rhetoric ever implied. I believe that we have to break through our own *feminist* mystique now to come to terms with the new reality of our personal and political experience, and to move into the second stage....

The Second Stage

The second stage cannot be seen in terms of women alone, our separate personhood or equality with men.

The second stage involves coming to new terms with the family—new terms with love and with work.

The second stage may not even be a women's movement. Men may be at the cutting edge of the second stage.

The second stage has to transcend the battle for equal power in institutions. The second stage will restructure institutions and transform the nature of power itself.

The second stage may even now be evolving, out of or even aside from what we have thought of as our battle....

The women's movement didn't start with heroics, or even with the political rhetoric of revolution. For me, as for most others, it

237

started with facing the concrete, mundane personal truth of my own life and hearing the personal truth of other women—the "problem that had no name" because it didn't quite fit the image of the happy suburban housewife we were all living in those days—that image of woman completely fulfilled in her role as husband's wife, children's mother, server of physical needs of husband, children, home. That image, which I called the "feminine mystique," bombarded us from all sides in the fifteen or twenty years after World War II, denying the very existence in women of the need to be and move in society and be recognized as a person, an individual in her own right.

Learning to Be Ourselves

We broke through the image. So for nearly twenty years now, the words written about and by and for women have been about women's need to be, first of all, themselves...to find themselves, fulfill themselves, their own personhood...to free themselves from submission as servants of the family and take control of their own bodies, their own lives...to find their own identity as separate from men, marriage and childrearing—and to demand equal opportunity with men, power of their own in corporate office, Senate chamber, spaceship, ballfield, battlefield, at whatever price. Organizing the women's movement, we broke through the barriers that kept women from moving, working, earning and speaking in their own voice in the mainstream of society. For nearly twenty years we have been pressing our grievances against men in office and home, school and field, in marriage, housework, even sex.

Reconciliation Between the Sexes

The eleventh megatrend is a shift from sex roles to synergy. It reflects a reconciliation between the sexes at a deep level, a greater harmony between qualities we used to consider either masculine or feminine. It could well mean the end of the battle of the sexes....

Although women are gaining access to power individually, the very nature of power will change as their numbers mount. A synergy of male and female leadership qualities will emerge, a new combination that is to everyone's advantage.

John Naisbett, *Esquire*, May 1983.

I remain committed to these unfinished battles. We had to do what we did, to come out of the shadow of the feminine mystique, and into our personhood, as women. We had to fight for our equal opportunity to participate in the larger work and decisions of society and the equality in the family that such participation entails and requires. This was the essence of the women's movement—the first stage. It happened, not because I or any other feminist witch somehow seduced otherwise happy housewives by our words, but because of evolutionary necessity. Women could no longer live out an eighty-year life span as childbearers, wives and mothers alone. For function, identity, status in society, and their own economic support, women—for the first time in history freed from passive, necessary submission to their role as breeders of the race—were forced by the longer span of their lives to take their own place, as individuals in society....

New Questions to Ask

There is no going back. The women's movement was necessary. But the liberation that began with the women's movement isn't finished. The equality we fought for isn't livable, isn't workable, isn't comfortable in the terms that structured our battle. The first stage, the women's movement, was fought within, and against, and defined by that old structure of unequal, polarized male and female sex roles. But to continue reacting against that structure is still to be defined and limited by its terms. What's needed now is to transcend those terms, transform the structure itself. Maybe the women's movement, as such, can't do that. The experts of psychology, sociology, economics, biology, even the new feminist experts, are still engaged in the old battles, of women versus men. The new questions that need to be asked—and with them, the new structures for the new struggle—can only come from pooling our experience: the agonies and ecstasies of our own transition as women, our daughters' new possibilities, and problems, and the confusion of the men. We have to break out of feminist rhetoric, go beyond the assumptions of the first stage of the women's movement and test life again—with personal truth—to turn this new corner, just as we had to break through the feminine mystique twenty years ago to begin our modern movement toward equality.

Saying no to the feminine mystique and organizing to confront sex discrimination was only the first stage. We have somehow to transcend the polarities of the first stage, and even the rage of our own "no," to get on to the second stage: the restructuring of our institutions on a basis of real equality for women and men, so we can live a new "yes" to life and love, and can *choose* to have children. The dynamics involved here are both economic and sexual. The energies whereby we live and love, and work and eat, which have been so subverted by power in the past, can truly be liberated in the service of life for all of us—or diverted in fruitless impotent reaction....

"Is it ended, then?" the daughters ask. No, it never ends; and, yes, this part is over. They want to be able to take it for granted; they don't even want to think about it any more; they've got new problems, they tell me. And yet they can't take it for granted; they still have to pay their dues. And it is very important indeed that they start thinking about the movement in new terms.

The vicious circle has been broken. It has to be reversed, and the healing energies have to be liberated by those who begin in a different place from where we leave off. It is very important indeed that the daughters and the sons hold to the dream of equality in the years ahead. Of course, they have new problems. They can live with those real problems if they don't succumb to false fears and turn back into that vicious circle. The daughters will go further than we could envision. They will be new kinds of women, different from their mothers, as I was different from mine. And in some ways, they will not be different. They will find themselves sometimes being surprisingly strong, and still acting weak; gutsy and adventurous, and also soft and vulnerable. They can trust their feelings and their strengths. They already have strengths we lacked, and feelings they are not afraid of (partly because of us) as well as opportunities and supports from society itself now, role models and affirmation from other women, and different expectations from the men in their lives.

New Wisdom and Caring

What is wrong with the old feminist? Since I am one, I am inclined to reply charitably. The old feminist represents a part of myself that I have put away. The reflexive, hostile put-down of men and the persistent whine of the victim have no place in the second act of the women's movement. Instead, let there be wisdom, softness, caring and strength by the good women who will volunteer their time to knock on doors, to get out the vote, to help our candidates win.

Frances Lear, *The Nation*, December 12, 1981.

The daughters don't have to be afraid to let that confidence, that strength, that joy shine through. They can say "no" to super-woman standards—in their work or their homes—because they already feel good enough about themselves as women to trust themselves. Sure, they will have problems, putting it all together, but they won't have as many problems and guilts as we did. Yes, they have more choices—and those very choices may seem like a burden. But they already know that they are strong enough to risk pain, loneliness, rejection: to risk not being perfect—and to risk mistakes. Well, they've had to, learning to be a doctor, lawyer, business person, to do their work. Risking pain, and not always being in control, trusting their own feelings, they still risk falling in love—if that's what they still call it.

240

In the second stage, perhaps, the daughters will stop looking for supermen. They've begun to understand that their own super-woman drive and assertion of absolute independence is a mask for that residue of soft need to remain dependent. They have begun to realize that a little dependence is nothing to be afraid of, and that they won't drown in it—they wouldn't have to drive themselves so hard if they let themselves have those feelings once in a while. And they have also begun to see that those young men are just as afraid as they are—maybe more afraid, if they're still expected to be supermen. The sons are just beginning to be able to express those feelings the daughters now know are their life's blood....

If we cannot, at this moment, solve the new problems we can no longer deny, we will at least pass on the right questions to our daughters and sons. These second-stage questions reflect the most urgent problems now facing this nation. Improbable as it may seem, we could bridge the old conservative-liberal chasm, if we realize the true potential of that elusive new male-female, second-stage mode....

The second stage is not going to be marked by magic orthodox "solutions" emanating from one central source—massive public programs from the Government, or simplistic ideological dogmas handed down by commissars of the Right or Left or priests of any church. The second stage is going to be defined by a fluidity, flexibility and pragmatism demanding more individual responsibility and voluntary pooling of community resources than has been demanded of American democracy for many years—though it is the essence of American tradition. It is what we demand of ourselves in the women's movement.

Human Politics, Human Liberation

If we can eliminate the false polarities and appreciate the limits and true potential of women's power, we will be able to join with men—follow or lead—in the new human politics that must emerge beyond reaction. And this new *human* liberation will enable us to take back the day *and* the night, and use the precious, limited resources of our earth and the limitless resources of our human capital to erect new kinds of homes for all our dreams, affirm new and old family bonds that can evolve and nourish us through all the changes of our lives, and use the time that is our life to enrich our human possibility, spelling our own names, at last, as women and men.

"The first task of a renewed feminist offensive is to reaffirm without evasion or apology the moral legitimacy of women's liberation."

Feminists Must Continue to Work for Women's Rights

Ellen Willis

Ellen Willis, a staff writer for *The Village Voice* and author of a book of essays *Beginning to See the Light*, is one of the many feminists who responded negatively to Betty Friedan's *The Second Stage* (see previous viewpoint). In the following viewpoint, Ms. Willis states that Ms. Friedan is wrong in believing that the struggle for women's liberation is over. Although many feminists have become complacent, she says, it is vital that they reevaluate what has and has not been accomplished by the women's movement. It is just as vital to remarshall feminist forces and continue to fight for women's equality.

As you read, consider the following questions:

1. In what ways does Ms. Willis say that Betty Friedan was inaccurate in her assessment of feminist history?
2. At one point Ms. Willis states that "the objective result of every feminist reform...is to undermine traditional family values." In what sense does she see this as a positive goal?
3. What does Ms. Willis believe should be feminism's task?

Ellen Willis, "Betty Friedan's *Second Stage*: A Step Backward," *The Nation*, November 14, 1981. Reprinted with permission, *The Nation* magazine, Nation Associates, Inc. © 1981.

I agree with Betty Friedan that feminism is at a critical point in its history. The momentum of the movement has drastically slowed, and if it is to survive, let alone progress, it must regroup and begin a new offensive. The success of that offensive will depend on our ability to combat not only the direct political challenge of the right but also the wave of cultural conservatism now engulfing people on every part of the political spectrum. Unfortunately, Friedan's book is less a prescription for the feminist dilemma than a symptom of it....

Friedan's version of feminist history bears no resemblance to my experience of it. Her basic thesis is that feminism's "first stage" concentrated solely on equal participation in the public world of business and politics and ignored women's need for a fulfilling personal life. In the "second stage," therefore, we must turn our attention to the family. Friedan's organization, the National Organization for Women, did start with this limited view of feminism. But radical feminists explicitly rejected the liberal integrationist model. We emphasized the connection between women's exclusion from full participation in the public world and their subordination in the so-called private sphere of familial and sexual relations. We insisted on the importance of such issues as women's sexual freedom and satisfaction, equality and mutuality in personal relations with men, and equal sharing of housework and child care.

Need for Freedom of Alternative Families

It is absurd, then, for Friedan to call the family the "new frontier" of feminism. The family is and always has been a central concern of feminism. Friedan is really saying that feminists should embrace the current trend toward mindless sentimentality about the family and abandon our abrasive habit of analyzing and criticizing it. She sees no need to discuss how the conventional family oppresses women; she suggests that we simply extend the concept of family to cover whatever nontraditional arrangements we have in mind. The reality, however, is that before we can make alternative forms of "family" practical for large numbers of women, we must first establish our freedom to reject existing family relations—to separate sex from procreation and both from marriage, to be single, childless or lesbian—without suffering legal or social penalties. And it is exactly this set of demands that Friedan devotes much of her book to condemning as love-denying, individualistic, hedonistic, offensive to right-thinking Americans and injurious to respectable feminist goals....

Clearly, Friedan's idea of how to preserve feminism in the face of an accelerating backlash is to adopt a strategy of retrenchment and appeasement. We are not to challenge the right's "pro-family" propaganda by forcefully asserting women's moral right to freedom (including sexual freedom) and equality. Rather we should

243

disavow any basic disagreement with traditional values and justify feminist reforms on pragmatic grounds, stressing their benefit
to the family: child care is necessary because in an inflationary
economy most families need two incomes; abortion is necessary
to safeguard women's health for future childbearing, and so on.
I think such a strategy is doomed to failure. In fact, it has already
failed. For several years now the movement's liberal mainstream
has doggedly pursued a policy of conciliation and pragmatism; the
dismal results for the E.R.A. and abortion rights are plain to see.

It is a bad mistake to imagine that the women's movement can
concede the right's moral assumptions and retain any credibility

"IT'S FOR A SICK MAN WHO STILL THINKS A WOMAN'S
PLACE IS IN THE HOME."

for its political agenda. Feminism is not just an issue or a group of issues; it is the cutting edge of a revolution in cultural and moral values. In place of a traditional patriarchal morality based on sexual repression, submission to authority and self-abnegation, the feminist moral vision proposes to extend to women—and to the entire realm of familial and sexual life—the democratic principles of self-determination, equality and the right to the pursuit of happiness. In place of a coercive, hierarchical family structure, feminists envision forms of community shared by free and equal participants.

Fear and Vulnerability

It is hardly surprising that this profoundly radical project has provoked a right-wing reaction. Perhaps less obvious, however, is the pervasive influence of that reaction on the thinking of people who do not identify politically with the right, including liberals, leftists and even feminists themselves. A deteriorating economy, international upheaval, the social tensions that inevitably erupt whenever old rules break down, and the frightening uncertainties of change itself have made people fearful. And with fear comes nostalgia for the past and vulnerability to the right's guilt-mongering moralism. As a result, the right has come to control the terms of the debate on social issues (just as it does on economic issues), so that even its political opponents feel obliged to pay tribute to its definitions of moral rectitude.

But feminists can never win on these terms. The objective result of every feminist reform, from legal abortion to the E.R.A. to child-care programs, is to undermine traditional family values and increase women's personal and sexual freedom. Feminists who adopt their enemies' moral framework (or simply ignore it and talk about "practical problems") convey a self-negating double message. When right-to-lifers define abortion as murder, and their opponents respond with euphemisms about "choice," "reproductive rights" and the need for medical services—or with defensive assurances that "we think abortion is terrible, but..."—the public may be forgiven for concluding that feminists are unwilling to assert women's moral right to autonomy and sexual love, and therefore their moral right to kill an unwanted fetus. And if we are unwilling to defend our principles wholeheartedly, why should anyone else support us? The more feminists assume that they cannot afford to take a stand because the atmosphere is too conservative, the more that assumption becomes a self-fulfilling prophecy.

Reaffirm Legitimacy of Liberation

In short, the first task of a renewed feminist offensive is to reaffirm without evasion or apology the moral legitimacy of women's liberation. It is time to remind people about human suffering that led women to rebel against traditional values in the first place;

to remind women, in particular, that it is neither immoral nor self-indulgent nor narcissistic to resist oppression.

Another priority, in my view, is challenging cultural feminism, an ideology second only to liberal pragmatism in its stifling grip on feminist thought. The logic of feminism as a political movement leads to ending sexual role divisions and rejecting the idea of opposing masculine and feminine natures. Cultural feminists, on the other hand, redefine women's liberation as escape from the influence of corrupt "male" values and the reassertion of superior "female" values. Cultural feminist assumptions underlie the equation of feminism with lesbianism or with an alternative women's culture or simply with female bonding. Such assumptions have also become popular in the peace and ecology movements, where women are often seen as "natural" pacifists whose nurturing function gives them a special responsibility to save the world. They form the basis of the antipornography movement, with its neo-Victorian view of male and female sexuality.

Goals for Feminism

Genuine, radical feminism addresses...the need for the deghettoization of women's work, for equal pay for equivalent work, for incomes and pensions for full-time homemakers, for supportive social services—and all the other measures that could free women from an uneasy dependence on individual males. But genuine, radical feminism is culturally invisible, almost an underground phenomenon. And what *is* visible—the lifestyle feminism of the rising young managerial or professional woman—offers no comfort: If you can't make it in a man's world, tough luck; if you can't take the heat, better stay in the kitchen.

Barbara Ehrenreich, *Radical America*, Spring 1981.

While cultural feminism has always been one tendency in the women's movement, in recent years it has become increasingly prominent and more aggressive in attempting to establish itself as *the* feminist orthodoxy. It has been a drag on the movement in two ways. First, it provides no intellectual basis for a concrete antisexist politics. If anything, it does the opposite, channeling female energy into counter-cultural projects, fantasies of restoring an alleged golden age of matriarchy, or moral crusades against male vice. It also reinforces oppressive cultural stereotypes, especially the assumption that men have a monopoly on aggression and active genital sexuality (cultural feminists often equate the two), while women are nonviolent, nurturing and more interested in affection than in sex.

Since cultural feminists confuse loyalty to feminism with

adherence to their conception of female values—which tends to coincide with traditional criteria of femininity—their logic has impelled them to fierce, moralistic attacks on women whose attitudes are deemed too aggressive, openly sexual or otherwise "male-identified." At a time when the right is putting increasing pressure on women to conform to traditionally feminine, sexually repressive norms, this parallel trend within the women's movement has deeply disturbing implications. It has already stirred enough concern among feminists to prompt a passionate debate on sexuality—the healthiest development in the movement in a long while.

Bullying with Guilt

Finally, since the antifeminist backlash is part of a larger assault on democratic gains in every area of political and economic life, the future of feminism depends in part on the future of the left in general. The future of the left, in turn, depends a great deal on whether feminists can influence its direction. The conventional wisdom on the left is that economics and international affairs are its central concerns, while questions of sexual politics are peripheral at best. There is also a strong strain of left cultural conservatism, based on arguments similar to Friedan's. Both positions ignore the crucial role of a repressive sexual politics in making people feel guilty about aspiring to freedom and happiness, and thus more inclined to bow to corporate and governmental authority. The same moral arguments used to bully people into accepting sexual inequality and repression—that we must stop being selfish, demanding, hedonistic and undisciplined—have been used quite successfully to win support for (or at least paralyze opposition to) conservative economic and urban policies. Conversely, a strong and militant opposition to "pro-family" politics could spearhead a more general left resistance. It is in feminists' interests to make this argument as strongly as possible. Maybe this time (male) progressives will be desperate enough to listen.

"Privileged feminists have largely been unable to speak to, with, and for diverse groups of women, because they either do not understand fully the inter-relatedness of sex, race and class oppression or refuse to take this inter-relatedness seriously."

Feminism Ignores Race and Class Oppression

Bell Hooks

Bell Hooks is the pseudonym of Gloria Watkins, an assistant professor of Afro-American studies at Yale University. In this viewpoint, taken from her recent book *Feminist Theory: From Margin to Center*, she argues that white feminists have focused too exclusively on problems of gender, which affect mainly upper middle-class women. This narrow focus has made their cause irrelevant to the masses of poor and Black women.

As you read, consider the following questions:

1. Ms. Hooks believes that Betty Friedan's work, the *Feminine Mystique*, strongly affected contemporary feminism. What was the focus of Ms. Friedan's work and why does Hooks believe it is mistaken?
2. How did the author's personal experience growing up in the South affect her approach to feminism?

Bell Hooks, *Feminist Theory: From Margin to Center*. Boston: South End Press, 1984. Reprinted with permission.

Feminism in the United States has never emerged from the women who are most victimized by sexist oppression; women who are daily beaten down, mentally, physically, and spiritually—women who are powerless to change their condition in life. They are a silent majority. A mark of their victimization is that they accept their lot in life without visible question, without organized protest, without collective anger or rage. Betty Friedan's *The Feminine Mystique* is still heralded as having paved the way for the contemporary feminist movement—it was written as if these women did not exist. Friedan's famous phrase, "the problem that has no name," often quoted to describe the condition of women in this society, actually referred to the plight of a select group of college-educated, middle and upper class, married white women—housewives bored with leisure, with the home, with children, with buying products, who wanted more out of life. Friedan concludes her first chapter by stating: "We can no longer ignore that voice within women that says: 'I want something more than my husband and my children and my house.'" That "more" she defined as careers. She did not discuss who would be called in to take care of the children and maintain the home if more women like herself were freed from their house labor and given equal access with white men to the professions. She did not speak of the needs of women without men, without children, without homes. She ignored the existence of all non-white women and poor white women. She did not tell readers whether it was more fulfilling to be a maid, a babysitter, a factory worker, a clerk, or a prostitute, than to be a leisure class housewife.

Sexism and the Leisure Class

She made her plight and the plight of white women like herself synonymous with a condition affecting all American women. In so doing, she deflected attention away from her classism, her racism, her sexist attitudes towards the masses of American women. In the context of her book, Friedan makes clear that women she saw as victimized by sexism were college-educated, white women who were compelled by sexist conditioning to remain in the home. She contends:

> It is urgent to understand how the very conditions of being a housewife can create a sense of emptiness, non-existence, nothingness in women. There are aspects of the housewife role that make it almost impossible for a woman of adult intelligence to retain a sense of human identity, the firm core of self or "I" without which a human being, man or woman, is not truly alive. For women of ability, in America today, I am convinced that there is something about the housewife state itself that is dangerous.

Specific problems and dilemmas of leisure class white housewives were real concerns that merited consideration and change but they were not the pressing political concerns of masses of women.

Masses of women were concerned about economic survival, ethnic and racial discrimination, etc. When Friedan wrote *The Feminine Mystique*, more than one third of all women were in the work force. Although many women longed to be housewives, only women with leisure time and money could actually shape their identities on the model of the feminine mystique. They were women who, in Friedan's words, were "told by the most advanced thinkers of our time to go back and live their lives as if they were Noras, restricted to the doll's house by Victorian prejudices."

Relating to Women's Lives

Women need to know (and are increasingly prevented from finding out) that feminism is *not* about dressing for success, or becoming a corporate executive, or gaining elective office; it is *not* being able to share a two career marriage and take skiing vacations and spend huge amounts of time with your husband and two lovely children because you have a domestic worker who makes all this possible for you, but who hasn't the time or money to do it herself; it is *not* opening a Women's Bank, or spending a weekend in an expensive workshop that guarantees to teach you how to become assertive (but not aggressive); it is most emphatically *not* about becoming a police detective or CIA agent or marine corps general.

But if these distorted images of feminism have more reality than ours do, it is partly our own fault. We [feminists] have not worked as hard as we should have at providing clear and meaningful alternative analyses which relate to people's lives, and at providing active, accessible groups in which to work.

Carol Ehrlich, in *Women and Revolution*, 1981.

From her early writing, it appears that Friedan never wondered whether or not the plight of college-educated, white housewives was an adequate reference point by which to gauge the impact of sexism or sexist oppression on the lives of women in American society. Nor did she move beyond her own life experience to acquire an expanded perspective on the lives of women in the United States. I say this now to discredit her work. It remains a useful discussion of the impact of sexist discrimination on a select group of women. Examined from a different perspective, it can also be seen as a case study of narcissism, insensitivity, sentimentality, and self-indulgence which reaches its peak when Friedan, in a chapter titled "Progressive Dehumanization," makes a comparison between the psychological effects of isolation on white housewives and the impact of confinement on the self-concept of prisoners in Nazi concentration camps.

Friedan was a principal shaper of contemporary feminist thought. Significantly, the one-dimensional perspective on women's reality presented in her book became a marked feature of the contemporary feminist movement. Like Friedan before them, white women who dominate feminist discourse today rarely question whether or not their perspective on women's reality is true to the lived experiences of women as a collective group. Nor are they aware of the extent to which their perspectives reflect race and class biases, although there has been a greater awareness of biases in recent years. Racism abounds in the writings of white feminists, reinforcing white supremacy and negating the possibility that women will bond politically across ethnic and racial boundaries. Past feminist refusal to draw attention to and attack racial hierarchies suppressed the link between race and class. Yet class structure in American society has been shaped by the racial politic of white supremacy; it is only by analyzing racism and its function in capitalist society that a thorough understanding of class relationships can emerge. Class struggle is inextricably bound to the struggle to end racism....

Male Dominance and Tyranny

My awareness of feminist struggle was stimulated by social circumstances. Growing up in a Southern, black, father-dominated, working class household, I experienced (as did my mother, my sisters, and my brother) varying degrees of patriarchal tyranny and it made me angry—it made us all angry. Anger led me to question the politics of male dominance and enabled me to resist sexist socialization. Frequently, white feminists act as if black women did not know sexist oppression existed until they voiced feminist sentiment. They believe they are providing black women with "the" analysis and "the" program for liberation. They do not understand, cannot even imagine, that black women, as well as other groups of women who live daily in oppressive situations, often acquire an awareness of patriarchal politics from their lived experience, just as they develop strategies of resistance (even though they may not resist on a sustained or organized basis).

These black women observed white feminist focus on male tyranny and women's oppressions as if it were a "new" revelation and felt such a focus had little impact on their lives. To them it was just another indication of the privileged living conditions of middle and upper class white women that they would need a theory to inform them that they were "oppressed." The implication being that people who are truly oppressed know it even though they may not be engaged in organized resistance or are unable to articulate in written form the nature of their oppression. These black women saw nothing liberatory in party line analyses of women's oppression. Neither the fact that black women have not organized collectively in huge numbers around the issues of "feminism" (many of us do not know or use the term) nor the fact that we have not had access to the machinery of power that would allow us to share our analyses or theories about gender with the American public negate its presence in our lives or place us in a position of dependency in relationship to those white and non-white feminists who address a larger audience....

Privileged Feminists

Privileged feminists have largely been unable to speak to, with, and for diverse groups of women because they either do not understand fully the inter-relatedness of sex, race, and class oppression or refuse to take this inter-relatedness seriously. Feminist analyses of woman's lot tend to focus exclusively on gender and do not provide a solid foundation on which to construct feminist theory. They reflect the dominant tendency in Western patriarchal minds to mystify woman's reality by insisting that gender is the sole determinant of woman's fate. Certainly it has been easier for women who do not experience race or class oppression to focus exclusively on gender. Although socialist feminists focus on class and/or gender, they tend to dismiss race or they make a point of acknowledging that race is important and then proceed to offer an analysis in which race is not considered.

Mistakenly Narrow View of White Feminism

Many white women have the mistaken notion that there is only one women's community and that its needs and goals are a reflection of white society. This premise is not only narrow, it is incorrect....Many white women ignore the fact that as Third World women we have to struggle against racism as well as sexism....True, we struggle against sexism in our various Third World movements, but we also struggle against racism in the women's movement. We do not see masses of white women coming forward to eliminate the racism in this society. To...turn our backs on the problems of racism in this society would be akin to suicide.

Zulema, in *Top Ranking*, 1980.

As a group, black women are in an unusual position in this society, for not only are we collectively at the bottom of the occupational ladder, but our overall social status is lower than that of any other group. Occupying such a position, we bear the brunt of sexist, racist, and classist oppression. At the same time, we are the group that has not been socialized to assume the role of exploiter/oppressor in that we are allowed no institutionalized "other" that we can exploit or oppress. (Children do not represent an institutionalized other even though they may be oppressed by parents.) White women and black men have it both ways. They can act as oppressor or be oppressed. Black men may be victimized by racism, but sexism allows them to act as exploiters and oppressors of women. White women may be victimized by sexism, but racism enables them to act as exploiters and oppressors of black people. Both groups have led liberation movements that favor their interests and support the continued oppression of other groups. Black male sexism has undermined struggles to eradicate racism just as white female racism undermines feminist struggle. As long as these two groups or any group defines liberation as gaining social equality with ruling class white men, they have a vested interest in the continued exploitation and oppression of others.

Different World View

Black women with no institutionalized "other" that we may discriminate against, exploit, or oppress often have a lived experience that directly challenges the prevailing classist, sexist, racist social structure and its concomitant ideology. This lived experience may shape our consciousness in such a way that our world view differs from those who have a degree of privilege (however relative within the existing system). It is essential for continued feminist struggle that black women recognize the special vantage point our marginality gives us and make use of this perspective to criticize the dominant racist, classist, sexist hegemony as well as to envision and create a counter-hegemony. I am suggesting that we have a central role to play in the making of feminist theory and a contribution to offer that is unique and valuable. The formation of a liberatory feminist theory and praxis is a collective responsibility, one that must be shared. Though I criticize aspects of feminist movement as we have known it so far, a critique which is sometimes harsh and unrelenting, I do so not in an attempt to diminish feminist struggle but to enrich, to share in the work of making a liberatory ideology and a liberatory movement.

Evaluating Sources of Information

A critical thinker must always question sources of information. Historians, for example, usually distinguish between *primary sources (eyewitness accounts)* and *secondary sources (writing or statements based on primary or eyewitness accounts or on other secondary sources)*. A diary kept by a leader of the women's suffrage movement is an example of a primary account. An article by a journalist about the suffrage movement based on that diary is a secondary source.

In order to read and think critically, one must be able to recognize primary sources. However, this is not enough. Eyewitness accounts do not always provide accurate descriptions. Historians may find ten different eyewitness accounts of an event and all the accounts might interpret the event differently. The historians must then decide which of these accounts provide the most objective and accurate interpretations.

Test your skill in evaluating sources of information by completing the following exercise. Pretend that your teacher tells you to write a research report about the women's movement today. You decide to include an equal number of primary and secondary sources. Listed below are a number of sources which may be useful in your research. Carefully evaluate each of them. Then, *place a P next to those descriptions you believe are primary sources.* Second, *rank the primary sources* assigning the number (1) to what appears to be the most objective and accurate primary source, the number (2) to the next most objective, and so on until the ranking is finished. *Repeat the entire procedure, this time placing an S next to those descriptions you feel would serve as secondary sources and then ranking them.*

If you are doing this activity as a member of a class or group, discuss and compare your evaluation with other members of the group. If you are reading this book alone, you may want to ask others if they agree with your evaluation. You will probably discover that others will come to different conclusions than you. Listening to their reasons may give you valuable insights in evaluating sources of information.

$$P = primary$$
$$S = secondary$$

1. a copy of a speech by Emma Goldman about the necessity of feminist reform

2. viewpoint one from this chapter

3. a book titled *Women and Progress: The Feminist Movement Since 1910*

4. a speech given at the most recent annual meeting of NOW (the National Organization for Women)

5. a newspaper article about the annual meeting of NOW

6. a chapter called "The Roots of Feminism" in a book titled *World Feminism*

7. a televised debate between a feminist activist and a leader of the Moral Majority on the morality of today's feminist movement

8. an editorial by an Indianapolis homemaker urging women to give up the "murderous frenzy" of corporate life and return to the home

9. a magazine article about Geraldine Ferraro, the first woman Vice-Presidential candidate

10. an article by a gynecologist saying that the women's movement has helped improve women's health

11. a short story by a feminist author about a woman who accidentally maims her husband because she is enraged at his inability to understand her

12. a biography of Elizabeth Cady Stanton

13. the book *Our Bodies, Our Selves*, written by a group of feminist women to enlighten women about their own physical, emotional, and spiritual health

14. a book review of *Our Bodies, Our Selves*

15. an article by a psychologist outlining the harm the feminist movement has done to women's psychological health

16. a play about two contemporary sisters and their differing responses to feminism

17. an article about current feminist activities in New York City

18. a book on great feminist leaders of the 20th century

Bibliography

The following list of books, periodicals, and pamphlets deals with the subject matter of this chapter.

Jo Freeman	"The Origins of the Woman's Liberation Movement," *American Journal of Sociology*, January 1973.
Betty Friedan	*The Feminine Mystique.* New York: W. W. Norton Company, 1963.
Herb Goldberg	*The New Male-Female Relationship.* New York: William Morrow and Company, 1983.
Bell Hooks	*Ain't I a Woman: Black Women and Feminism.* Boston: South End Press, 1981.
Elizabeth Janeway	*Man's World, Woman's Place: A Study in Social Mythology.* New York: William Morrow and Company, 1971.
Gloria Joseph and Jill Lewis	*Common Differences: Conflicts in Black & White Feminist Perspectives.* Boston: South End Press, 1986.
Anne Koedt and others, eds.	*Radical Feminism.* New York: Quadrangle Books, 1973.
Aileen Kraditor, ed.	*Up from the Pedestal: Selected Writings in the History of American Feminism.* New York: Quandrangle Books, 1968.
Elinor Lenz and Barbara Meyerhoff	*The Feminization of America.* New York: Tarcher, 1985.
Robin Morgan, ed.	*Sisterhood Is Powerful: An Anthology of Writing from the Women's Liberation Movement.* New York: Vintage Books, 1970.
Toni Morrison	"What the Black Woman Thinks about Woman's Lib," *New York Times Magazine*, August 22, 1971.
Sheila Ruth Tobias, ed.	*Issues in Feminism: A First Course in Women's Studies.* Boston: Houghton Mifflin Company, 1980.
Gayle Graham Yates	*What Women Want: The Ideas of the Movement.* Cambridge, MA: Harvard University Press, 1975.

General Bibliography

Lois Banner	*Women in Modern America*. New York: Harcourt Brace Jovanovich, 1974.
Susan Brownmiller	*Against Our Will: Men, Women, and Rape*. New York: Simon and Schuster, 1975.
Susan Brownmiller	*Femininity*. New York: Linene/Simon and Schuster, 1983.
William H. Chafe	*The American Woman: Her Changing Social, Economic, and Political Roles, 1920-1970.* New York: Oxford University Press, 1972.
William H. Chafe	*Women and Equality: Changing Patterns in American Culture*. New York: Oxford University Press, 1977.
Phyllis Chesler	*Women and Madness*. Garden City, NY: Doubleday, 1972.
Nancy F. Cott	*Root of Bitterness: Documents of the Social History of American Women*. New York: E.P. Dutton and Company, Inc., 1972.
Carol Gilligan	*In a Different Voice*. Cambridge, MA: Harvard University Press, 1982.
Vivian Gornick and Barbara K. Moran, eds.	*Woman in Sexist Society*. New York: Basic Books, 1971.
Carolyn G. Heilbrun	*Reinventing Womanhood*. New York: W. W. Norton and Company, 1979.
Jaqueline Jones	*Labor of Love, Labor of Sorrow: Black Women, Work, and the Family from Slavery to the Present*. New York: Basic Books, 1985.
Robert Jay Lifton, ed.	*The Woman in America*. Boston: Houghton Mifflin, 1967.
Wendy McElroy, ed.	*Freedom, Feminism, and the State*. Washington, DC: The Cato Institute, 1982.
Margaret Mead and Frances B. Kaplan, eds.	*American Women: The Report of the President's Commission on the Status of Women*. New York: Scribner's, 1965.
Henry L. Mencken	*In Defense of Women*. New York: Alfred Knopf, 1926.
David M. Potter	"American Women and the American Character," in *History and American Society: Essays of David Potter*, ed. by Don E. Fehrenbacher. New York: Oxford University Press, 1973.

Index

Abbott, Lyman, 40
Adams, Clifford R., 145
Addams, Jane, 45, 56
American Revolutionary War, 38
American Social Hygiene Association, 54
Anthony, Susan B., 32
Atkins, Zoe, 146
Atkinson, Ti-Grace, 219

Beard, Charles A., 38
Beard, Mary R., 52, 53
Blakely, Mary Kay, 100
Bleier, Ruth, 175
Bluebird Theory, 101-102
Blumstein, Philip, 232
Bock, R. Darrell, 171
Brooklyn Woman Suffrage Association, 30
Bryce, James, 43
Bush, George, 97, 102, 103

careers
    for women, 79, 124
Charen, Mona, 221
Cleveland, Grover, 24
Cronan, Sheila, 142
Cyrus, Della D., 88

Darwin, Charles, 27
    theory of evolution, 178
de Beauvoir, Simone, 160, 193
Decter, Midge, 134
divorce rate, 79, 120
Doane, William Croswell, 22, 44
Dowling, Colette 132, 235
Dubno, Peter, 94

economics
    and women, 74-77, 79, 87, 88
    of working women, 66-70
Edwards, Margaret, 197
Ehrenreich, Barbara, 246
Ehrlich, Carol, 250
Emerson, Ralph Waldo, 84
equal pay for equal work, 35, 36
Equal Rights Amendment (ERA), 244, 245
Erikson, Erik H., 155, 163-167

Erlien, Marla, 233

Feinste: Dianne, 104
feminism
    and alternative families, 243
    and fatherhood, 218, 219, 220
    and marriage, 221-228, 229-235
    as a doctrine, 169
    as racist and classist, 248-253
    as a revolution, 245
    changes in, 236-241
    does not isolate women, 229-235
    effects of
        destroys men, 214-220
        frees women, 207-213
        isolates women, 221-228
            con, 229-235
        on men, 238
        on women, 221-228, 229-235
    first stage, 237, 239, 243, 244
        as over, 237-241
    goals of, 243-247
    images of, 250
    is dishonest, 217
    myths about men, 215, 216, 217
    second stage, 237-241
    stifled by traditional family, 243-245
    see also women's movement
feminists
    as privileged, 249-253
Ferraro, Geraldine, 96, 97, 102, 103
Figes, Eva, 121
Flower, Elliot, 67
French Revolution
    and suffrage, 19, 22, 41
Freud, Sigmund, 94, 163
Friedan, Betty, 236, 243, 249, 250

Gelman, David, 190
gender identity, 183, 184
    learning of, 190-194
Gilder, George, 82, 184, 217,

218, 219
Gilman Charlotte Perkins, 71, 74, 75
Goldberg, Lucienne, 125
Goldberg, Steven, 157, 172, 173
Goldman, Emma, 119
Gordon, Linda, 233
Gottlieb, Annie, 225
Gould, Robert, 93, 101, 102, 105
government
    and the family, 19
    purposes of, 18
Greer, Germaine, 128, 211
gynecocracy, 19, 20

Harris, Sydney, 102
Hooks, Bell, 248
housewives
    and feminism, 249
    are not slaves, 125
    as slaves, 86-92, 143-148
    receive few benefits, 87, 88, 89

industrial revolution, 66, 79

Kempton, Sally, 207
Koch, Stephen, 214
Kolakowski, Donald, 171
Kuhn, Irene Corbally, 84

Lathrop, Julia, 49
Lear, Frances, 290
Lee, Vernon, 71
Lessing, Doris, 138
Levin, Michael, 168
Lewontin, Richard, 190
Lunt, Christine, 97

Maccoby, Eleanor, 165
marriage
    and courtship, 137, 138
    and feminism, 221-228
    and love, 144, 145
        at odds, 120
    and romance, 114, 117
    and working women, 66, 68, 70, 72-75, 81, 82, 103
    as a contract, 125, 126, 130, 143, 144, 146
    as a failure, 120-122
    as an economic arrangement,

120
    as security, 124-127, 135, 140
    as slavery, 86-92, 129, 130, 142-148
    as women's work, 113-118
    degrades women, 120-122
    does not provide security, 128-133, 143, 145, 146
    effects
        on men and women, 139, 140
    fails because of women, 116-117
    fulfills women, 123-127, 134-141
    legal responsibilities of, 144, 145
    rationale for, 138, 139
Marton, Kati, 102
McClelland, David C., 166
Mead, Margaret, 199, 217-218
men
    and aggression, 171, 173, 179
    and feminism, 214-220
    as individuals, 195-200
    don't like women, 94, 95
    fear marriage, 138
    should express emotions, 103
men and women
    friendships, 232, 233, 234
    have same desires, 198, 199
Meyer, Agnes E., 78
Meyer, Annie Nathan, 53
Mill, John Stuart, 32
Miller, Harriet, 101
Miller, Kate, 181
Millett, Kate, 162
misogyny, 106
Money, John, 171
Moore, Eva, 38
motherhood, 121
    as a career, 124

Naisbett, John, 238
National American Woman Suffrage Association, 36, 47
National Organization for Women (NOW), 243
Neff, Miriam, 136

Owen, Robert L., 34

259

Paget, Violet, 71
Parkman, Francis, 18, 27, 29, 30
Pogrebin, Letty Cottin, 188

Ramey, Estelle, 170
Reagan, Ronald, 224
Robinson, Margaret C., 51
Rogers, Agnes, 113
Rogers, Anna A., 83
Roosevelt, Theodore, 44
Rossi, Alice, 173

Sakol, Jeannie, 125
Sarachild, Kathy, 143
Sayers, Dorothy, 195
Schlafly, Phyllis, 123, 186
Schroeder, Pat, 104
Schwartz, Pepper, 232
Schwimmer, Lawrence D., 95
sex differences
    "anatomy is destiny", 160
        as partially correct, 166
    and sexual attraction, 185,
        186
    are essential for society, 182-
        187, 218, 219
    are innate, 168-174
        as questionable, 175-181
        Sociobiological theory, 176-
        181
    are learned, 162-167
    are unimportant, 195-200
    biological, 158, 159, 169-174
        in the brain, 159, 171-172,
        176
    crossing boundaries, 159-160,
        185
    in primates, 157-158
    psychological
        as innate, 155-161, 163
    teaching of
        dangers of, 188-194, 211
sex role stereotype, 192, 193
    creates anger, 209-211
sex roles, 174
    as learned, 94-96, 136-137,
        159, 165, 166, 181, 208-213
    dangers of, 188-194
Slater, Philip, 103
Smith, Page, 231
Solis-Cohen, Myer, 127
Spake, Amanda, 229

Stanton, Elizabeth Cady, 26
Stein, Sara Bonnett, 182
Stern, Edith M., 86
suffrage
    alternatives to, 52-58
    as a burden, 44
    as a natural right, 33
    as necessary for society,
        26-33, 45-49
    as unnecessary, 18-25, 43,
        44
    benefits everyone, 37
    dangers of, 52-58
    destroys women's influence,
        53, 54
    does not affect women's
        wages, 42, 43
    elevates women's status, 38,
        39
    is not a natural right, 41
    results of,
        in Chicago, 56, 57
        in Colorado, 37, 38
        in San Francisco, 54-56
        in Wyoming, 31, 32
    women are unfit for, 40-44
    see also voting
Swift, Dean, 117

Tarbell, Ida M., 115
The Feminists, 143
Thompson, Flora McDonald, 65
Tiger, Lionel, 163

United States Supreme Court, 41

voting
    and economic equality, 34-39,
        42
    could provoke war, 25
    women
        as naive, 23
        as politically unprepared,
        21,22
        as taxpayers, 24, 33
        should, 26-33
        should not, 18-25
        unnecessary, 24

war
    and men, 170, 171
Watkins, Gloria, 248

Weissstein, Naomi, 164, 177
Wiley, Harvey, 52
Willis, Ellen, 242
Wilson, E.O., 176
Witelson, S.F. 159
women
  and aggression, 165, 170-171
  and discrimination, 147
  and education, 79
  and government, 29
    history of, 19, 20
  and instincts, 20, 21, 126
  and men
    similarities in, 27
  and political responsibility, 21
    22, 23
  and traditional careers, 79,
    124
  as emotional, 20-23
  as equal to men, 27-33, 36
  as housewives, 86-92
  as powerful influence, 24, 25
  as responsible for society's
    morals, 79-85, 114
  as responsible voters, 31, 32,
    33
  as subordinate to men, 72, 73,
    91, 96, 125, 126
  as wage earners, 35, 42-43
  changing the public attitude
    toward, 29
  duties of, 44
  effects of feminism on, 221-
    228
  have contributed little to soc-
    iety, 114
  have no natural limitations,
    27
  in business, 66-70, 72, 84
    and sexual relationships,
      98
    as harmful, 67, 68, 69, 83,
      84
    as workaholics, 103
    discrimination of, 94
    displace men, 68
    neglect families, 69-70, 82,
      83
    should act like men, 96-99
    should look like men, 97,
      98
    should not act like men,

    102-106
    should not look like men,
      103-105
  involvement in government,
    48, 49
  need economic equality, 35
  need to marry, 135-141, 221-
    228
    unimportant 128-133, 147
  only as wives and mothers,
    74, 79-85, 86-91, 113-118
  rehearse for marriage, 136,
    137, 138
  relationships to fathers, 136
  should not
    be aggressive, 83, 84, 85,
      97
    be restricted to the home,
      71-77, 86-92
      con, 72, 81, 82
    vote, 18-25
      con, 26-33
    work outside the home,
      65-70, 79-85, 113-118
  see also feminism
women and men
  as individuals, 195-200
  friendships, 232, 233, 234
  have same desires, 198, 199
women's movement
  and marriage, 143
  as necessary, 237-239
  changes in, 236-241
  effect on
    men, 94, 238
    women, 94, 115, 116, 237
  fallacies of, 126, 214-220, 221-
    228
  first stage
    as over, 243-245
      con, 237-241
  resulting from men's actions,
    116
Wylie, Philip, 170

Zulema, 252